The Concordia Pulpit *for* 1984

CONTRIBUTORS

Hubert Beck
College Station, TX

George H. Beiderwieden Jr.
Decatur, IL

David S. Belasic
Cuyahoga Falls, OH

Eugene R. Bertermann
Orange, CA

Samuel Boda
Granite City, IL

George W. Bornemann
Detroit, MI

Donald L. Deffner
Moraga, CA

Edwin Dubberke
St. Louis, MO

Ronald G. Folle
Luverne, MN

John D. Fritz
Houston, TX

Oscar A. Gerken
Eustis, FL

Joel D. Heck
Valley Park, MO

W. Theophil Janzow
Seward, NE

Richard G. Kapfer
Ames, IA

Arthur O. Kaul
Tell City, IN

Frederick W. Kemper
Stevensville, MD

Frederick G. Klein
Charlotte, NC

Erwin J. Kolb
St. Louis, MO

T. Richard Marcis Sr.
Farmington Hills, MI

Norman P. Metzler
Eugene, OR

Curtis R. Moermund
Wilton, IA

Lyle D. Muller
Lombard, IL

Rudolph F. Norden
St. Louis, MO

Kenneth Rogahn
St. Louis, MO

Donald Rousu
Edmonton, AB

Rex D. Spicer
Fenton, IA

Arthur J. Spomer
Broken Arrow, OK

Mark J. Steege
Arlington Heights, IL

Otto W. Toelke
Fairview Park, OH

Dirk van der Linde
Kearney, MO

Dean O. Wenthe
Fort Wayne, IN

The Concordia Pulpit *for* 1984

Publishing House
St. Louis

3558 S. Jefferson Avenue, St. Louis, MO 63118
ISBN 0-570-08451-2
MANUFACTURED IN THE UNITED STATES OF AMERICA

BV4200 The Library of Congress Cataloged This Serial as Follows:
.C65 The Concordia Pulpit.

v. 24 cm. annual.
Began publication in 1930. Cf. Union list of serials.

1. Lutheran Church—Sermons. 2. Sermons, American.
BV4200.C65 251 51-26518 ‡
Library of Congress [1]

CONTENTS

Foreword

Readers and users of THE CONCORDIA PULPIT will notice a change in this volume's table of contents. Instead of an appended section of occasional sermons, the PULPIT, beginning last year, features an introductory essay on how to preach. The second essay in the series is by Norman Metzler: "How to Preach Sanctification."

By this change in the PULPIT we hope to help preachers apply certain criteria to their sermon writing and criticism. In these essays we will review various elements of preaching with the aim of sharpening sermonic preparation and offering practical assistance in applying essential homiletical and exegetical principles.

The need for collections of occasional sermons continues, and it is being met by Concordia in periodic publications of occasional sermons, covering many more occasions than we could accommodate in the pages of the PULPIT.

We believe these old and new elements of THE CONCORDIA PULPIT multiply its benefits and help make for a more effective proclamation of the Gospel of Jesus Christ.

—The Publisher

How to Preach Sanctification

Norman P. Metzler

If proclaiming the law is the easiest task a preacher faces and if correctly proclaiming the Gospel is considerably more difficult, then preaching sanctification must be reckoned as the ultimate test of the craftsman's skill.

1. It is all too easy to preach the Law, because the Law is the most familiar everyday experience for preacher and layman alike. A common truth of psychology is that one tends to criticize in others what one most dislikes in oneself. Since the preacher is intimately acquainted with the reality of sin, he will readily pick up on this dimension of life and expound on it with vigor and conviction. It is relatively easy to develop the "malady" (Richard R. Caemmerer's term for Law in *Preaching for the Church* [St. Louis: Concordia Publishing House, 1959]) inherent in a particular text or theme. Indeed, the danger is that the preacher will spend too much time and energy on the Law, lending a tone of Law to the whole sermon.

It is my conviction that the people to whom we preach are living all week in the real world of Law—the real world of sin, fear, despair, and death—and do not need to hear a heavy dose of "Law in general" in every sermon. The task of the preacher is to recognize that his parishioners are immersed in a world of Law and to *identify* that reality in relationship to the particular sermon theme. When, for example, in a sermon on fear, explicating Mark 4:35-41 (Jesus asleep in the boat during the storm), the preacher observes:

> But it's not as if the experience of the disciples is so distant from our lives. For in one way or another we all know that fear of the dangers and threats in life. Indeed, like Luther and Kierkegaard, we also experience in our own ways that existential angst, that fundamental anxiety over life itself, with all its unknowns, its questions, its ambiguities, its threats.

he is not simply referring to modern psychology or philosophy in order to reinforce his point. He is proclaiming the *Law;* he is articulating the sinful reality of the world, which needs so badly a word of Good News, a word of assurance and comfort, of confidence and trust. To unfold life in the world today in relationship to a specific sermon theme, therefore, is to proclaim the Law in a meaningful, issue-related fashion that people can grasp and apply to their own lives.

2. It is not so easy to preach the Gospel. Because the proclamation of the Law comes so easily and because the Gospel is less of a "natural" reality in our lives, the proclamation of the Gospel as Gospel—clearly distinct from the Law—is a demanding task. Despite our Lutheran emphasis upon justification by grace alone through faith and the centrality of this insight for all of Christianity, we often have a hard time proclaiming the pure and simple Good News so that it clearly comes across as the sweet, consoling love of God in Christ.

Rather we tend to couch the Gospel message in terms that demand right belief or correct behavior, or the proper choice or appropriate institutional practice. When the preacher proclaims:

> Thank God for His preserving the good news of our salvation through Christ Jesus our Lord in all its truth and purity in the teachings of our [fill in the denomination or synod] church. May we ever hold fast and adhere closely to these teachings, so that we might proclaim to all the world the true message of the Gospel as it stands in the Scripture, unclouded by all the interpretations foisted upon it by so many false teachers in the churches around us today.

he may be trying to affirm the Gospel, but his preoccupation with right belief and institutional superiority muddies the water and casts a sense of Law around the pure, sweet Gospel affirmation of our salvation through Christ. After all, saving faith is trust in the gracious promise of the Gospel, not the act of holding a body of teaching.

Furthermore, we can get so worked up driving home the Law that our strident and angry tone continues to pervade our delivery of the Gospel message as well, thereby confusing the parishioner in the pew. How often have we not heard evangelistic preachers pounding the pulpit for emphasis as they bellow out:

> But JEEESUS will snatch your soul from the very *jaws* of eternal damnation, HEEEE will rescue you from the clutches of sin. But you must *repent* and *believeve,* brothers and sisters, you got to BELIEEVE that Gospel!!!

This preacher's sermon is not really bad, but his *style* of delivery comes across much more like Law than Gospel.

It is a tremendous challenge to proclaim the true consolation and joy of the Gospel clearly and winsomely, so that this message touches deeply the lives and hearts of people and builds in them a sense of trust and confidence in their loving and saving God, who has revealed Himself in Jesus Christ as the Good News for their lives. And as with the Law, so likewise the Gospel must be related specifically and concretely to the particular theme for the day, and not just become a weekly restatement of the "Gospel in general." It is not enough to continually paraphrase John 3:16 or repeat in every sermon, "Christ died for your sins, and His blood washes you clean and justifies you by His grace." Effective preaching meets the listeners in the reality of their lives; the theme is addressed to them in terms of some particular aspect of their daily living. On loneliness, for example, preaching from 1 Kings 19 (Elijah's experience of aloneness):

> God's love accepts us in our loneliness and despair; Christ befriends us when it seems we have no friend in the whole world. He reassures us that He knows very well our lonely, despairing feelings—"My God, My God, why have You forsaken Me?"—and yet is Himself the presence of God with us, to comfort us and give us hope. In Christ, we are never totally alone, no matter how lonely we may feel.

The art of effectively proclaiming the Gospel—relevantly interweaving the Gospel into life's experiences—is an art practiced and developed only with much toil and trouble, much anguish and soul-searching. And it is a struggle that must never cease.

3. Clearly the most demanding aspect of preaching, however, is the effective proclamation of sanctification. Here the preacher is beset, not only with the twin pitfalls of trying to preach Law and Gospel effectively, but also with the difficulties inherent in attempting to relate these two clearly and appropriately to their concrete expression in Christian lifestyle and behavior. Preaching sanctification is really where the rubber hits the road. It is the practical application of the Gospel to Christian life. Here most of all the preacher's sensitivity to life as his people are experiencing it, his awareness of and solidarity with the full scope of the "real world out there" are summoned to their utmost, drawing out of him the very finest in proclamation. The Law may roll easily off the tongue; the Gospel may be preached in pious generalities; but if sanctification is not proclaimed in an honest, cogent manner, which brings both Law and Gospel to bear on the lives of the listeners so that it makes sense and makes a difference, there is nothing that can mask or redeem a preacher's failure.

It is to this most difficult and challenging task that this essay addresses itself. First we will examine briefly the concept of sanctification; then we will consider the context within which the proclamation of sanctification takes place. Next we will turn our attention to various perspectives on the content of preaching sanctification. Finally we will discuss a style of proclaiming sanctification that befits the content. Our intent is to focus on the preaching of sanctification in such a way that you might be spurred to reexamine your own style of preaching and perhaps gain some helpful insights that might make your future preaching of sanctification more effective.

I. The Concept of Sanctification

Properly speaking, sanctification designates "the internal spiritual transformation of the believer or the holiness of life which follows upon justification." (See Franz Pieper, *Christian Dogmatics,* vol. 3 [St. Louis: Concordia Publishing House, 1953], p. 4 ff.) It is basically synonymous with "renewal," and it is also closely allied with "good works," since the concrete form sanctification assumes is rooted in good actions internally and externally. It is the fruit of faith, the outgrowth and result of justifying faith (James 2:14-26). Our Lutheran theology makes the distinction between justification—the divine action outside the person by which God by His pure grace objectively declares the individual righteous, and the person subjectively grasps hold of this justification by God (Eph. 2:8-9)—and sanctification—the divine action inside the person, by which the individual is inwardly transformed and becomes more personally and subjectively righteous and holy (1 Thess. 4:1-3). It is the grace of God that is actually making the individual gracious.

Now just this definition of sanctification itself is no simple matter for Lutherans to affirm, even though this definition comes directly from Luther and the Lutheran Confessions. The Lutheran emphasis upon justification must be understood against the backdrop of the practices of the Roman Catholic Church at the time of the Reformation. At least in practice, if not in theology, the necessity of good works was so strongly stressed that Luther's reassertion of justification by grace alone, grasped by faith alone, and measured against Scripture alone, amounted to a Copernican revolution in theology. Luther and the Reformers reveled in the sweet light of God's grace and made justification by grace through faith the touchstone of their theological position. Of course Luther knew and made clear that although we are justified by faith alone apart from works, faith is in fact never alone and apart from works. There is an inseparable connection between justification and sanctification; where there is justification, there is also always sanctification. It was therefore on the basis of good churchly theology, and not just for the sake of political considerations, that the Roman Catholic theologians, in the discussions following the initial presentation of the Augsburg Confession, could accept and affirm *all* of the first 21 articles of that confession, including article 4—the classic statement of our Lutheran position concerning justification. At the same time it was no accident, nor concession to any pressure, that Luther continually reasserted the *necessity* of good works—not, to be sure, necessary to obtain or retain salvation, but necessarily the fruit of saving faith (AC VI). Despite his intense dislike for the Book of James, Luther endorsed the intimate relationship between faith and works explicated in that portion of Scripture (Luther, SL v 16, 224 f).

Nevertheless, by virtue of the very fact that the Lutheran Reformers stressed justification over against the Roman Catholic tendency toward works righteousness and defined themselves in terms of that contrast, it lay all too close at hand for Lutherans to distort the Christian faith in the opposite direction from the Roman Catholic distortion that they protested. They tended to stress justification to the detriment of the proper emphasis on sanctification and on the indissoluble bond between the two. Most Lutherans have not gone to the extreme of Nicholas of Amsdorf, who held that good works are actually detrimental and injurious to salvation, but we are broadly guilty of propagating what Dietrich Bonhoeffer called "cheap grace." (See *The Cost of Discipleship* [New York: Macmillan Publishing Company, Inc.], 1959) Our Lutheran paranoia over sounding too legalistic, too Roman or Calvinistic or Armenian, runs us into the risk of separating justification from sanctification, simply proclaiming adherence to belief in the grace of God without constantly presenting that grace as "costly grace," grace which takes hold of one's life and transforms it, claims it for Christ's service. We easily tend toward antinomianism (opposition to all laws and rules), while at the same time, as noted earlier, often making right belief in justification, or right practice and structure, into a new legalism, thereby confusing Law and Gospel.

Now because our Lutheran position does assert the reality of sanctification, Lutheran preaching does have the likelihood of saying more to the hearer about the ongoing life of faith and sanctification than does much evangelistic preaching, geared as it is every week to conversion and altar calls. This latter approach, in attempting to maintain the "simple Gospel message," constantly reasserts sin and salvation, damnation and conversion week after week, with no consistent attention to how that life of grace is to be lived out beyond conversion, repentance, and rededication. Nevertheless, our Lutheran congenital fear of works righteousness of any sort, whether in Roman Catholic or Protestant dress, has sustained a tension between justification and sanctification, with voices pleading for the extremes in both directions, antinomianism's "cheap grace" and George Major's semi-Pelagianism (good works are necessary for salvation).

In a very real sense sanctification goes *beyond* Law and Gospel, sin and grace. Sanctification is another whole question, another whole dimension. It presupposes Law and Gospel and their proper distinction. It must surely grow out of the Gospel as the fruit of faith. But once it has been established that we are in fact justified by God's grace apart from the deeds of the Law; once we have determined that our eternal salvation is given us as a free gift—then immediately Law and Gospel are subsumed in a new way in the discussion of sanctification, and the whole concern for relating too closely to either Law or Gospel immediately breaks down. Both Law and Gospel now become factors in the new dimension of living out the life of faith, the life of growth in holiness. The Law no longer can save us, but it becomes a rule and guide for living discipleship (Deut. 12:8, 28, 32; Ps. 19:7-9). The Gospel is no longer an excuse for living an easy Christianity. Rather it becomes the motivation and stimulation for a new life in Christ. In a sermon this might take shape thus:

> The love of God that we've experienced personally in Christ, that tremendous price that He has placed on our lives in proclaiming us worthy of salvation, cannot help but move us to respect the worth, the dignity, and position of every other person. The commandment to honor our parents, to love and respect them, gives us the clue as to how we are to deal with all people, how we are to show them the respect and worth we believe *is* theirs already in Christ.

Luke 17:3 embraces the rebuking Law and the forgiving Gospel, but the "must" of verse 4 is the language of sanctification. The Gospel, not the Law, is clearly the motivating force for compelling the follower of Christ to practice the sanctified life of unlimited forgiveness.

The distinctions between Law and Gospel and between justification and sanctification are and must be made for conceptual, doctrinal, pedagogical purposes. When it comes to homiletics, however, these scholastic distinctions must be superceded by effective proclamation of the whole message, especially the message of sanctification. The proclamation of the Good News cannot be divorced from explaining and advocating the practical effects or results of that Good News on the lives of people. This is what sanctification is all about.

II. The Context of Sanctification

So much, then for the concept of sanctification itself as it pertains to preaching. I wish now to consider the context within which the preaching of sanctification occurs. For if the preaching of sanctification is the proclamation of the actual effects of the working of grace upon the individual and within the church, then it is important for us to keep in mind the context of that proclamation.

a. The preaching of sanctification occurs within the fellowship of the *baptized* and can only be appropriate within this context. The preaching of repentance and conversion is fitting for an audience of unbelievers, who are being called to an initial fellowship with Christ, called to be washed in the waters of regeneration. But preaching sanctification in that context is senseless, for the unbelievers as yet have not entered the whole new framework of the Christian perspective. They do not yet live by the motivation of the Gospel.

The proclamation of sanctification *does* make sense in the fellowship of the baptized, those who have accepted the Good News for their lives and are now Gospel-oriented persons. Of course repentance is necessary throughout the life of faith. Yet Christian preaching among the baptized can and must presuppose that the hearers are committed to following Christ, and are needing to grow in their awareness of what that implies for their everyday lives. These baptized believers are destined for the kingdom of God; they are working now on how to live out that Kingdom-life more effectively. Yes, they need to keep on hearing the Law; they continue to need the sweet message of the Gospel as well. But now these are closely woven together in their meaning and relationship for the ongoing life of sanctification, of growth in good works befitting faith (Eph. 2:8-10).

There is certainly a sense in which every sermon is evangelistic. It proclaims the Law and the Gospel so that an unbeliever hearing it would be confronted with the call to repentance and be invited to respond in faith. But the indissoluble bond between justification and sanctification requires that sanctification be preached to those who are baptized, who have already responded in faith and now seek to serve Him. In the congregation, then, the proper preaching of sanctification will include the Gospel declaration as it pertains to the theme of the day, as the Good News for the hearer's lives, which alone can enable them to will and to do good works.

b. The preaching of sanctification occurs within the whole context of the liturgy. Lutherans have generally not succumbed to the Protestant overemphasis on preaching at the expense of the whole experience of the liturgy. This means that we in our preaching can and should count on and reckon with the total message and impact of the worship experience: songs, prayers, lessons, anthems, children's sermonettes, Eucharist, everything. These various elements of worship complement, support, reinforce, and expand the sermon. The preacher does not have to worry about getting everything into the sermon every week, covering all the bases every time. He needs to plan and prepare the whole liturgy in such a way that it revolves around the theme for the day and that it communicates that theme in a number of ways. This frees him to proclaim sanctification in a clear, concise, and focused fashion, trusting the liturgical experience to provide the worshiper with the broader affirmations of the faith.

c. The preaching of sanctification presupposes the *gift of the Holy Spirit.* Lutherans trust that through Baptism all Christians are given the gift of the Spirit of Christ, so that by the Spirit's working, they are actually capable of becoming even more holy. The Spirit that convinces the believer of the Good News of God in Christ is the same Spirit that works to bring that believer's life in tune with Christ more and more. We are not alone in our efforts to do good works, evidencing the fruits of faith. The Spirit of God is with us, empowering us to live more completely in love. We can depend on that Spirit working in the hearts and lives of our listeners as we unfold for them the challenge to holiness which the Gospel entails for their lives.

d. The preaching of sanctification reckons with the fact that the hearers are baptized and Spirit-filled, but it also sees they are human: weak, fragile, prone to legalism, lazy, susceptible to the suggestion of easy grace. Just as it is important to remember that we are preaching to the communion of saints, so it is also important to recall that we are continually announcing the forgiveness of sins, recognizing that we are sinners as well as saints—and both at once. This awareness of the reality of human weakness is crucial for speaking a word that can make a significant difference in our listeners lives.

It is most helpful to remember these various aspects of the context within which we proclaim sanctification, as we move now into an examination of different perspectives on the actual content of preaching sanctification.

III. The Content of Sanctification

Preaching sanctification is where it all comes together for the preacher: theology, psychology, spirituality, practical experience, prophetic courage, pastoral sensitivity—every resource and trick in the book is absolutely necessary to communicate the challenge of the Christian life in such a way that it gets through and makes sense, effecting real changes in lives. This is the point where the preacher, after summoning up all of these resources and giving it his best effort, faces the enormity of the task and his gross inadequacy in meeting it, and so is thrust back again upon the humbling realization that it is only by the Holy Spirit's working that his lowly efforts can have any impact at all.

For this task is nothing less than unfolding the actual practical meaning of the Gospel, drawing out for saintly sinners the shape and texture of the fruits of the Spirit in their lives. It is the task of inviting the hearers to look at themselves again and again, constantly reevaluating how they are living out that faith in Christ. It means appealing to them to take up their cross anew and serve Christ more sacrificially, inviting them to be transformed by the renewing of their attitudes and dispositions, taken over more fully by the loving will of Jesus Christ (Rom. 12:2).

Proclaiming sanctification involves holding up before the people of God the vision of His coming Kingdom, the vision of that Kingdom's wholeness and love, its peace and justice, its mercy and joy, in such a way that that future hope beckons them to live anew right now. As that Kingdom was the passion of Christ's life, the center and goal of His preaching and teaching, His miracles and self-sacrifice, so that Kingdom and its righteousness is for Christians today likewise the goal and motive of their lives of faith and action (Matt. 6:33). The life of Christ as he lived toward that Kingdom is the model for how we are to live out the love of God's kingdom in our lives.

This kingdom perspective on Christian sanctification influences the preaching of sanctification in two ways. On the one hand it gives to our preaching a leading edge of hope and joy, for the vision of the coming kingdom as the gift of God is a joyful and hopeful vision, calling us beyond the realities of the past and present into the newness of the mercies of God's future. It gives a leading edge of promise to the Christian life, filling every present moment with significance because of its relationship to our eternal destiny. Thus in a sermon on compassion, based on Mark 5:35-43 (the raising of Jairus' daughter), the preacher might well conclude:

> I pray for all that God's Spirit will fill us more and more, to get beyond our very small and limited human view of things, to see how God's great compassion in Christ can give us new strength and vision to reach out in acts of mercy and love in our daily lives. May we not be blinded by our all-too-human "but that's impossible!" and be open to the transforming power of God which can even raise the dead—and will indeed ultimately raise us all to that perfect love and compassion of the heavenly kingdom.

In our preaching, as in life itself, the lowly cup of water given to the thirsty person becomes a sign, an anticipation of that kingdom to come in which all thirst will be satisfied. To give drink to the thirsty is to serve God Himself, pointing toward that new age when all creation and all people will serve Him perfectly.

On the other hand the Kingdom perspective on sanctification helps us to keep in view the provisionality, the incompleteness, the brokenness of all our best present efforts—lest we become haughty about the significance of our actions. Only as they point beyond themselves to Christ and His kingdom do our sin-tainted good works have any real meaning and value. This keeps us mindful that the life of sanctification must be viewed realistically as well as hopefully. We must constantly remain aware that our hearers still walk by faith and not by sight, continually doing the evil they would not do, and failing the good that they would do (2 Cor. 5:7; Rom. 7:19). When, for example, the preacher sets forth a "theology of glory" on the basis of 1 Cor. 15:54-57, as in the following:

> . . . Yes, you and I were indeed sinners, condemned to eternal damnation because of our sins. But now, having been washed in the blood of the Lamb, we are totally new creatures, victorious over sin, death, and the devil. Our lives are completely turned around, we are Christ's holy nation. We now walk in the light, we are the reflections and beacons of that light. There is no way we can slip back now to our former ways; we must constantly manifest the joy of the Gospel, since we are His new people. We have left our sinful ways completely behind and are now walking the completely new path of righteousness.

he is failing to make clear to his hearers the imperfection and ambiguity that is part of all present Christian life and effort, compared with the perfect fulfillment and complete victory in God's coming Kingdom. More appropriate and honest to life would be:

> Yes, in Christ we already possess the victory over sin and death. Our faith is sure, our confidence secure. But let us not deceive ourselves; Paul is speaking of that imperishable and immortal reality which we still await, still hope for in faith and trust. We must still reckon with living in the present mortal framework, full of sin and death, of grief and despair. We still "see through a glass darkly," as Paul puts it. Our old nature still struggles against our new.

The effective preacher of sanctification takes up the hearers with him, embraces them in all their human weakness and sin, all their lethargy and boredom, and lovingly but firmly nudges them toward that hopeful vision of the Kingdom. The preacher conjures up from the ruins and frustrations and impotence of today new dreams and visions of how they can really believe their baptism, leave their past behind, forgiven and forgotten, and start fresh with a more holy, dedicated, loving lifestyle.

One dimension of this life of sanctification is the growth of greater trust and confidence in God, the inner spiritual life. This is the aspect of sanctification of which Soren Kierkegaard wrote in *Purity of Heart Is to Will One Thing*—namely to will the good, which is the will of God. Every Christian needs to grow in the inner life of love for God and self, bringing one's thought, will, and desire more fully into line with God's loving will. The nurture of this inner spiritual life, while experiencing something of a renaissance in recent years with the renewed popularity of Christian asceticism and contemplation, as embodied in such figures as Mother Theresa and Thomas Merton, is still difficult to bring to the attention of most of our parishioners. Their attention is distracted and distorted by the superabundance of material goods and goals, while the tempo of contemporary society pushes people along too fast for them to stop and reflect on anything of significance in their inner lives, particularly anything as profound as their relationship to God and their eternal destiny. It demands the utmost and more of the preacher's skill to disturb his comfortable, distracted listeners, to prod them into looking again at their motives and priorities, their attitudes and desires, and challenge them to believe that they actually *can* renew and redirect their inner spiritual patterns by the power of God's Spirit.

> "Ye shall be holy. Take time to be holy. Ha! I can hardly take time to enjoy my own backyard, never mind 'take time to be holy,' whatever that means!" And I can appreciate very much this frustration you may feel in our go-go world. It seems almost impossible to get clear of life's hassles and get in touch with your spiritual life. Indeed, on our own it *is* impossible. But we are not alone. The transforming power of Christ's Spirit in our lives can deepen us in our faith, increase our awareness of living our lives in tune with God's loving will.

Thus might the preacher address himself to this very real issue of seeking inner holiness in the midst of an unholy world.

The other important dimension of the life of sanctification is growth in reaching out to others in love and care. The Good News of God's saving love in Christ not only touches and transforms our inner thoughts and feelings and attitudes, it necessarily also affects our outward behavior toward others as well. It is the awesome responsibility of the preacher to raise up and scrutinize the various aspects of our Christian life and behavior, lovingly appealing to the listeners to join him in this scrutiny and to reevaluate their outward Christian lives. Formidable barriers stand between proclaimer and listener in this dimension of sanctification. Our society encourages self-interest, self-satisfaction, and selfishness in general. It promotes and tantalizes the ease and affluence of the individual, raising the materialistic expectations ever higher, so that Christians can easily become totally absorbed in improving their physical and material lot in life, achieving their potential in career, hobby, or sport. In the process they can be effectively distracted from any serious consideration of the human relationships and needs all around.

The preacher of sanctification is given the responsibility of breaking through these barriers by identifying the world's realities that so absorb the listeners, getting so closely in touch with these realities that he is able to jog the hearers out of their self-centeredness and invite them to find new avenues for offering their lives in sacrificial service for others. A sermon on Eph. 5:21 ff., concerning how husbands and wives are to relate to one another in Christ, may well spell it out thus:

> Everyone has a certain desire to be boss, to be in charge, to call the shots, control the situation. Even the most timid, passive individual can think (if not say), "I want it done *my* way!" Therefore, it's easy for husbands to accept and relish the emphasis usually placed in this passage upon the wife submitting to him, letting him be in charge. But the very first words of the text say clearly, "Be subject to *one another* out of reverence for Christ"! That is, if we've been

> touched by the love of Christ, we are to subject ourselves to one another and not lord it over the other person in a bossy fashion. We are called to put ourselves at the disposal of the other, to *serve* the other person, just as Christ served the church, giving His life for it.

And this call to greater holiness cannot stop with the consideration of interpersonal relationships, individual needs, and personal lifestyles. The prophetic preacher is duty-bound to also draw out the implications of sanctification for social structures and communities, organizations, nations, and corporate entities. So much of our modern world has to do with these larger corporate realities and their impact upon the lives of many people that the conscientious preacher of sanctification will have to unpack with much care and trepidation this Pandora's box of social issues. Daring to speak a prophetic word to his people from James 2:14, the preacher must risk challenging the hearers to consider:

> how often we are saying in effect to our starving world "go in peace. Be warmed, be filled," and yet do not take action to feed them. James says clearly that such a faith is a dead faith—for a living faith in Christ, who nourishes us spiritually and physically, cannot help but show itself in some efforts to address the issue of world hunger. True, the problem is immense, the issues complex; I'm not denying that. This does not, however, excuse us from doing some work of mercy and love for the hungry—gathering food, contributing it to Lutheran World Relief, writing letters to congressmen urging more aid for world hunger needs, raising the hungry to God in prayer often—whatever is possible for you individually, or for us as a congregation. The hungry cry out, and the love of Christ in us must respond to that cry. We need to tune our ears and hearts to hear and see Christ Himself calling to us in these hungry masses.

The preacher must undertake this with the full realization of the limitedness and tenuousness of our human perceptions, lest he abuse the sacred trust of prophetic proclamation by misguided and unloving crusades and attacks. We all see "through a glass darkly" and therefore need to guard against simplistic, self-righteous diatribes masquerading as prophetic concern. Yet prophesy he must, with the urgency of the Gospel message and all its social/structural/systemic implications.

Every time the preacher steps up to the pulpit to speak the Word of the Lord concerning the life of sanctification, he will be struck once again with the need to be more and more deeply immersed in the life of the real world of his hearers and the issues of that larger world around him. Nothing can substitute for this immediate awareness of and sensitivity to that world in which our people struggle to make sense of the 9-to-5 life of faith. This is a burden that the preacher of sanctification must always bear for the sake of more effective proclamation that will truly touch the lives of his people and inspire them to newness of life.

In all of these calls to the sanctified life, it is important to remind ourselves that the motive is and always will be the Gospel. The "must" of "necessity" of sanctification is *not* the condemning "thou shalt" of the Law; it is a legalistic perversion of sanctification when the preacher berates his listeners:

> How can we call ourselves Christians and turn in such a poor record of contributions to our congregation so far this year? If we have the love of Jesus Christ in our hearts, we've just *got* to improve our financial track record, we've *got* to have a tithe from all of our members. Jesus didn't die for your sins so that you could simply let your church budget collapse; He expects you to give generously, dig deeply, support the church operation—or you're simply missing the mark.

There is no doubt that the need is urgent, but that doesn't justify turning sanctification into legalism. This infusion of Law into the preaching of sanctification points up the need to be clear that the "necessity" of sanctification is a joyful, freeing necessity arising purely from the Gospel, not a degrading demand that only serves to thrust the hearers back into the Law, into their own weakness and guilt.

IV. The Style of Proclamation

With all the theological acumen, psychological insight, rhetorical skill, and pastoral empathy in the world, the preacher of sanctification will still be ineffective unless he can also deliver the message in an inviting and compelling style. The preacher is motivated by the Gospel and lives by that hopeful vision of God's coming kingdom. He is appealing to his listeners in a positive way to take up more fully their new life in the Spirit of Christ. He is inviting the hearers to engage in a self-analysis which can lead to greater holiness.

Unfortunately many preachers betray this praiseworthy *content* of their message of sanctification by their *style* of preaching. Their pompous, boisterous, accusing words and gestures look more like they are beating their listeners into submission than beckoning them to come and follow Christ. Their tone of voice and nonverbal communication is speaking so loudly that their message of sanctification cannot be rightly heard.

The story is told of the little boy who attended worship with his father and sat through a very loud and boisterous sermon. After the service the boy commented to his father, "Gee, Dad, that pastor sure seemed to be angry at everyone today! What was he scolding us about?" To which the father replied, "He wasn't scolding us, son. He was preaching to us about love!"

Our preaching of sanctification must not only be free from legalism in its content, it must also be clearly Gospel-oriented in its style of delivery. The parishioners need to know that the pastor is on their side, that he really cares for them and knows the condition of their lives. And this has to be communicated in a caring, sympathetic style so that they see clearly that they are being warmly and lovingly, if firmly, nudged and encouraged to grow in holiness. They need to know they are not being bludgeoned by harsh-sounding words and authoritarian gestures. The holiness to which the preacher calls them must be evident in the holiness, love and care of his style. Just as sanctification is inextricably bound up doctrinally with the Gospel and justification, so the call to a renewed commitment to serve Christ with one's life must exhibit the same joy, warmth, and sincerity as the style used to proclaim the Gospel. The raised voice, the pounding fist, the pointing finger, the scowls and menacing gestures—all of these produce a contradiction between what is being proclaimed and how it is being communicated and received.

The effective preacher of sanctification works to bring his style into line with the content being proclaimed. He should actually evaluate the whole service in order to discover to what extent nonverbal communication is or is not consistent with what is being said.

Conclusion

I have no illusions about my own capacity to produce tremendous changes in the preaching of sanctification by those who read this essay. If nothing else I hope that these thoughts and brief examples have caused the reader to at least think through his own sermon style and content. My further hope and prayer is that he may be spurred to put a higher priority on the effective proclamation of sanctification, so that the transformation and renewal of the everyday lives—which is the bottom line for all preaching—may become increasingly apparent and revolutionizing among us.

"Where there is no sanctification, there is also no faith." And where sanctification is not proclaimed winsomely, lovingly, and effectively, there is also no Gospel truly proclaimed. May the challenge of preaching sanctification more effectively become a passion for all preachers!

Sermons on the Gospel Lessons
Series A
Three-Year Lectionary

News That's New!

FIRST SUNDAY IN ADVENT
MATTHEW 24:37-44

Dean O. Wenthe

"Have you not heard the latest?" Most of us hope we have. We want to know what's happening both locally and globally.

Perhaps many of us look at the morning newspaper and a rich cup of coffee as a reentry kit to begin the routine of our daily lives after a night's sleep. If the paper isn't there, I begin the day feeling shortchanged. Things have happened, but without the printed page I remain ignorant—not to mention the empty feeling that comes from missing the latest antics of Snoopy in the cartoons.

But if we reflect for a moment, why are we so concerned to have heard the latest? Haven't we, after all, heard it all before? The tragedies and triumphs, the horrors and heroes, the dreams and disappointments, the loves and the losses—all these ingredients in the human drama have been served up to us before.

Imagine for a moment that none of us had received the newspaper this morning, none had heard or seen a newscast. Couldn't we fill in the great majority of the events? The names we wouldn't have, nor the places, nor the precise time, but the events would be known to us. We've heard them all before and will hear them all again with monotonous consistency.

This very point is made by Solomon, who had seen all of man's ambitions and tried a goodly number of them, when he writes:

> What has been will be again,
> what has been done will be done again;
> there is nothing new under the sun.
> Is there anything of which one can say,
> "Look! This is something new"?
> It was here already, long ago.
> (Ecclesiastes 1:9-10)

The Promise of the New

Will there be anything new in the news today or tomorrow? The answer is "No!" Mankind's exploits are limited. What we propose to do, "has been already in the ages before us."

But God is not limited! He has some news for you this morning that is really new! The actions and announcements of God break out of the confines of our arena.

Jesus says this new thing will be the "coming of the Son of man." And He contrasts this news with the hum-drum monotony that human history displays.

> As were the days of Noah, so will be the coming of the Son of Man. For as in those days before the flood they were eating and drinking, marrying and giving in marriage, until the day when Noah entered the ark, and they did not know until the flood came and swept them all away, so will be the coming of the Son of man (Matthew 24:37-39 RSV).

Noah's days were characterized by the same routine as ours—eating, drinking, marrying. Man's options are limited, but the mistake that Noah's generation made and that we are all tempted to make is to conclude that God's options are also limited.

One man, Noah, and his family knew that God's options were *open.* They believed that God could do a new thing—something that had never happened before and would never happen again. And so when the flood was upon them, only Noah had the news of its coming.

Jesus gives us a similar announcement that a new thing will be happening.

> Watch therefore, for you do not know on what day your Lord is coming. But know this, that if the householder had known in what part of the night the thief was coming, he would have watched and would not have let his house be broken into. Therefore you also must be ready; for the Son of man is coming at an hour you do not expect (Matthew 24:42-44 RSV).

These words should stir our hearts. Think of the results if our generation would hear and read them with the devotion that it directs to the newspapers and newscasts. Many a Bible is left closed in the corner while the newspaper is opened wide on the table or lap. How inappropriate!

We've read about eating and drinking and marrying thousands of times. We've seen the sighing, crying and dying night after night. There's nothing new or refreshing about such news. It's depressing, and sometimes it overwhelms us with an awareness that things aren't right with mankind.

But in our Bibles we read about stupendous events that directly affect each one of us. These events are not like far-off wars and distant battles; they happen right in our backyards and living rooms.

Are we watching and ready for them? Advent invites us to renew our vigil. We stand and wait for a new day of the Lord, because we have already seen the explosion of man's limitations in His first coming.

Jeremiah promised what we have already seen and participated in:

> Behold, the days are coming, says the Lord, when I will make a new covenant with the house of Israel and the house of Judah, not like the covenant which I made with their fathers when I took them by the hand to bring them out of the land of Egypt, my covenant which they broke, though I was their husband, says the Lord. But this is the covenant which I will make with the house of Israel after those days, says the Lord: I will put my law within them, and I will write it upon their hearts; and I will be their God, and they shall be my people. And no longer shall each man teach his neighbor and each his brother, saying, 'Know the Lord,' for they shall all know me, from the least of them to the greatest, says the Lord; for I will forgive their iniquity, and I will remember their sin no more (Jer. 31:31-34 RSV).

We believe God can do new things, because with Noah and with Jeremiah we have experienced his forgiveness.

The Failure of the Old

Paul knew how limited man's life is without the Gospel.

> For since, in the wisdom of God, the world did not know God through wisdom, it pleased God through the folly of what we preach to save those who believe (1 Cor. 1:21 RSV).

The story that's really old, one that we all know all too well, is man's effort to dress up his life. Our life is like the newspapers, isn't it? We try to be good, but we fail. And so we do it all over—perhaps with the illusion that the real reason we didn't make it was someone else—our spouse, our fair-weather friends, our coworkers. We deceive ourselves with the thought that if we were only given a chance, if the world and others would just leave us alone, we'd make it. Even God would approve of us and seek our company.

How boring! How old it sounds, doesn't it? You and I have been this way many times before, and we've all ended at the same place—failure. You can't make it! I can't make it!

The Promise Fulfilled

But Christ has made it! He has done something never done before—obeyed the perfect will of God. He has done what man would not even have thought of—taken upon Himself the sins of the world. He lives, whereas all we could do was die. He continues to do new things as He daily comforts us with the promise that all these new things are ours. He has loved each of us from eternity and poured out that love in our baptism. He serves that love in the Lord's Supper and announces it in the Gospel.

Now this is worth getting excited about! It's worth telling others about! It's news that is truly *new!*

On this First Sunday in Advent we watch for new things. We

look forward to the coming of the Son of Man, because we have seen His first coming at Bethlehem.

We bring our worn-out excuses and our tiresome stories of failure and ask for fresh and full mercy in Christ. The way that Jesus went—from the right hand of God to the manger of Bethlehem—had never been traveled before. The road to Jerusalem and Calvary and back to the throne of God was occupied by the solitary figure of Christ. But that journey has delivered us from the most boring place of all—a world restricted and compressed by man's feeble effort.

Great Christian writers like Dante have captured this insight in their portrayal of hell. Hell is an excruciatingly boring place. Everything is false and phony and flat, a fitting place for the "father of lies." It is like that because God is not there.

By contrast, the coming of the Son of Man is attended by new heavens and a new earth. We will be set free in Christ from the limitations that the fall of Adam imposed on us. There will be an eternal freshness and freedom and fulfillment, precisely because God will dwell in our midst.

The prophets and apostles describe the return of Christ with words that convey something more wonderful than our minds can imagine. Christ's coming will mean a great banquet, the festive atmostphere of a marriage, mansions prepared for each of us who are in Christ.

Perhaps we should dwell on these images in the midst of a world like ours. For instance, at the center of many American dreams is that perfect home—a lovely place appointed with just the furniture and conveniences that we've always wanted, located in an idyllic setting with the ideal climate. Imagine how and where you would construct your dream home. Make is as luxurious and perfect as you can.

Now know that this ideal abode is a shack compared to what you will enjoy in the mansion that has been tailor-made for you by the Savior. He has gone to prepare a place for us so that where He is, we may be also. That place will surpass anything we might mentally or literally construct on earth. His return will establish us as the eternal residents of a city not made with hands, nor subject to decay.

Prepare for the New

Now, that is news! And Jesus invites us to watch and be ready for its coming, even as we prepare to observe how wonderful beyond all thought was His first coming.

Mary and Joseph were surprised. Simeon and Zechariah were astonished by the remarkable nature of God's new covenant. God had actually become flesh and tented among the shabby huts of the Palestinian hills.

Prepare yourself for the same miracle as we journey toward Bethlehem! Watch for that new advent which Jesus holds before us!

This morning Christ said, "Your sins be forgiven." He said it to Noah, to Jeremiah, to Mary. One day we will hear it with similar directness on the day of the coming of the Son of Man.

Our impatience, our inclination to get things backward—to regard the Gospel as boring and the human story as exciting—our love for any old story as long as it's about ourselves have all been blown away. The Gospel has exploded these old things and exposed them for what they are—lies of Satan.

We have heard a new song and so we sing it. The psalmist captured the news that is new:

> O sing to the Lord a new song; sing to the Lord, all the earth! Sing to the Lord, bless his name; tell of his salvation from day to day. Declare his glory among the nations, his marvelous works among all the peoples! For great is the Lord, and greatly to be praised; he is to be feared above all gods. For all the gods of the peoples are idols; but the Lord made the heavens. Honor and majesty are before him; strength and beauty are in his sanctuary. Ascribe to the Lord, O families of the peoples, ascribe to the Lord glory and strength! (Ps. 96:1-7 RSV).

Singing a new song—that's what our lives are all about. That's what the church is all about. In our worship, in our prayers, in our life together there is the melody of the new song. Everyone who sings with the psalmist looks forward to the day of the Son of Man.

The noises and clatter of this world's stories are boringly dull to us. Their tunes are all the same and those who sing them can expect only more of the same—and then, death.

We sing and watch and wait for a day of life when our Savior will join our voices to all the saints who have sung His song.

News that's new! You've heard it! You've seen it! Go share it! Go sing it! In the name of the Son of Man.

"State Of The Art" Advent

SECOND SUNDAY IN ADVENT
MATTHEW 3:1-12

Dean O. Wenthe

Do you have a "state of the art" stereo or digital watch? If you do, others will no doubt be a bit envious. "State of the art" has come to mean the most advanced example of a device that modern technology has been able to produce.

Consider, for example, the modern photocopier. Instead of laboriously copying by hand an important article from a magazine or a book, in seconds we can now duplicate the information we are after. These machines get ever smaller, faster and more efficient. After using one, a person wonders how mankind ever managed before.

The "state of the art" in photocopiers is a real blessing. Wouldn't it be cruel for an executive to require those outmoded steps of typing and duplicating, when the secretary could more economically benefit from the "state of the art"?

What, we might ask, is the "state of the art" in religious matters? If there has been advances in religion, would it be just as cruel for someone to require outmoded and laborious practices in this area of life as in any other?

One of the first items which various religions have sought to drop is "repentance." The practice of admitting guilt, asking forgiveness and acting differently has a long history of human hostility. In a word, man hates the thought of it.

Deliverance, Salvation, Fulfillment, Freedom, Faith—these ideas are not offensive to most. But "repentance" evokes a medieval torture chamber in the minds of many. It sounds almost masochistic.

John the Baptist knew all this, as had the prophets who preceded him, and still he preaches, "Repent, for the kingdom of heaven is at hand" (v. 2). In a direct address he tells the Pharisees and Sadducees, "Bear fruit that befits repentance" (v. 8). He describes his ministry as one in which "I baptize you with water for repentance" (v. 11). Preparation for Jesus' coming, in John's view, is essentially repentance.

Matthew describes the beginning of Jesus' own proclamation with these words: ". . . Jesus began to preach, saying, "Repent, for the kingdom of heaven is at hand" (Matt. 4:17 RSV).

Repentance—what is it? How do we do it? Is it really necessary?

Repentance As Effort

Most frequently, the marks of repentance are imagined to be outward—the grimace of a person in pain, the gauntness resulting from fasting, the gritty self-flagellation that the world knows so well.

If that is what John had preached, if that is what Jesus had asked of his listeners, they would have accepted it. The "state of the art" religion in New Testament times was exactly this. People multiplied fasts and put on quite a display.

But that is not what John or Jesus wanted, for in His "Sermon on the Mount" our Lord warned:

> Beware of practicing your piety before men in order to be seen by them; for then you will have no reward from your Father who is in heaven. Thus, when you give alms, sound no trumpet before you, as the hypocrites do in the synagogues and in the streets, that they may be praised by men (Matt. 6:1-2 RSV).

No, the repentance which John sought and which we offer to God in Advent is that of the first beatitude: "Blessed are the poor in spirit, for theirs is the kingdom of heaven" (Matt. 5:3 RSV).

Repentance of the outward kind is common. People will run to the desert or to a university to hear what is required of them. They will go to any length and make every effort to achieve salvation. If money and success are being sought, then family, friends and faith will be sacrificed. If pleasure is worshipped, then health is often shattered in the alleys of drugs and promiscuity.

We could catalogue the various religions which compete for man's heart, and without exception they cost. Human life is spent, as surely as money is spent, day after day and week after week on the religions of our day.

Repentance in its most fundamental form means "a turning"—*away* from one thing and *towards* another. And people, unlike machines, have made no significant advances in this basic process. Today they are turning towards gods which have been the objects of worship countless times before. They turn so swiftly that they become dizzy. First here, then there, each tries to find a place to spend his life and invest his loyalty.

But what about John's words, "Repent, for the kingdom of heaven is at hand"? Are they like our other options? Can we turn to them or away from them like other "religious" invitations?

The answer is an emphatic "No!" Repentance for the Christian means the exact opposite of repentance in every other religious alternative.

Repentance As Reception

For the Christian *repentance is reception.* We do not lift ourselves by means of our lives or our piety and prayers. Rather, God receives us into His kingdom. The kingdom of God or, as Matthew's Gospel puts it, the kingdom of heaven comes to us.

You are members of this kingdom through your baptism. You are perfect and upright members who can stand tall before God because Christ's atoning death has given you that position. You are important in the kingdom. Jesus has personally delivered you from that other kingdom, where Satan demands pain and anguish and all those things normally associated with repentance.

The "state of the art" in every other religious system is slavery. There one must strive, struggle and stretch for a repentance that is going to reach the goal. And it is all, quite simply, for nothing. Satan never delivers the goods. Not once has man advanced an inch before God by any of these forms of repentance.

John says that repentance means reception. God comes and gives us all. Absolutely everything is already ours in the kingdom of God. We have no miserly king, but a loving and extravagant Heavenly Father who sends us the Kingdom in the gift of His Son.

In this second week of Advent we turn to God, not to win His approval, but to receive His Son. This turning in repentance finds its focus and definition, not in the catalogue of our sins, but in Him who bore our sins for us. Christian repentance is the "state of the art" for our Advent preparation and for our lives.

Our repentance is an affirmation of God's mercy first, and a denial of our sins second. We refuse to reverse the order and slip back into slavery. We refuse to say that our sins will be conquered or paid for, *before* we meet God.

God has already met us! He has faced our sins—those rebellions which made it impossible for us to be citizens of His kingdom. He met them on Calvary's cross. And in Christ he obliterated them.

Repentance As Renewal

Now God faces us as John announces the reality of the kingdom of God that we receive. With thankful hearts we conduct our life of preparation for Christ's birth, confessing the fact that the Kingdom is established now and forever.

John warns against a religious repentance which produces unsatisfactory results:

> Bear fruit that befits repentance, and do not presume to say to yourselves, "We have Abraham as our father"; for I tell you, God is able from these stones to raise up children to Abraham. Even now the axe is laid to the root of the trees; every tree therefore that does not bear good fruit is cut down and thrown into the fire (Matt. 3:8-10 RSV).

He describes Jesus' work: "His winnowing fork is in his hand, and he will clear his threshing floor and gather his wheat into the granary, but the chaff he will burn with unquenchable fire" (v. 12). No production can occur until one is in the kingdom. There the trees abound with fruit, and the fields flourish with grain.

You and I are those trees and fields. If we purchased an expensive apple tree, and despite our careful tending it never produced apples, doubts would arise in our minds as to whether, in fact, it was an apple tree at all. So with us kingdom trees. We naturally, inevitably rejoice in the Gospel, relish our weekly worship and receive the Holy Spirit's power to produce fruit, for, as St. Paul puts it, "the fruit of the Spirit is love, joy, peace, patience, kindness, goodness, faithfulness, gentleness, self-control" (Gal. 5:22-23 RSV). The *unnatural* thing for us, as baptized Christians, is to do the deeds of the flesh which the apostle also specifies in detail—"immorality, impurity, sensuality, idolatry, sorcery, enmities, strife, jealousy, outbursts of anger, disputes, dissentions, factions, envyings, drunkenness . . . ." (Gal. 5:19-21 NASB).

So when we commit these deeds—and is there one which we haven't?—we sorrow. We repent because we have acted like briar bushes instead of kingdom trees. We turn to the Author and Finisher of our faith—Jesus Christ—for forgiveness and for assurance that we are His. In our families, among our friends, Christ plants peace and patience through us, His fruitful trees.

Our Advent is a turning toward the King, the Prince of Peace, who comes to Bethlehem's manger. It's a turning away from our feeble efforts to overcome sin.

Our King takes us from those failures and clothes us with the robes of His righteousness. As we savor the colors of such garments and marvel over His boundless love, the Holy Spirit empowers us to fight the good fight of faith. We're now aliens to that other kingdom, snatched away from its tyrant by the mighty arm of our God.

Repentance is reception of Christ's kingdom. It is celebration of our citizenship. This kind of repentance goes deep. It touches the very heart of our being and bursts forth into all our life.

This repentance is not outmoded or antiquated; it's the "state of the art"! Nothing will ever replace it, for it is a part of that eternal kingdom which came in Christ.

He who lives and reigns, now and forever, has guaranteed it with His death and resurrection.

The Proper Message For Advent Preparation

THIRD SUNDAY IN ADVENT
MATTHEW 11:2-11

Eugene R. Bertermann

The Advent weeks properly provide a time of preparation for the "coming" of our Lord and Savior Jesus Christ. They afford a precious opportunity to meditate on His coming into our hearts *through His Word,* His second coming in glory and majesty *on the great Day of Judgment,* and His coming *into the flesh* long centuries ago, "when the fullness of the time was come."

Can anyone doubt that this period of Advent preparation is extremely necessary and important? These Advent weeks have dawned upon some of the most critical days in all of human history. The signs and tokens foreshadowing the second coming of our Lord and Savior Jesus Christ are being fulfilled in our day as never before in all of human history (See Luke 21:25-36).

The pre-Christmas season has always been a time of preparation. Christian congregations conduct special Advent services. Regular Sunday worship reflects the coming of the Lord. The spirit of preparation for the coming holiday reflects itself also amid the general public. Stores and shops are filled with Christmas merchandise. Billboards proclaim Christmas greetings and activities. Newspapers are filled with advertisements offering Christmas gifts. Radio and television are filled with special Christmas programs. Regrettably, many of these reflect a spirit of commercialization, rather than of proclaiming the Christ of Christmas.

The text for the Third Sunday in Advent sets forth

The Proper Message For Advent Preparation

as it points us to the greatest of all Advent preachers, Saint John the Baptist. Let us learn from this mighty Old Testament prophet how properly to prepare for Advent!

I. Let Us Look to Christ As Our Coming Savior!

The text takes us near the close of John's remarkable ministry. His fearless indictment of sin and His stalwart witness to Christ as the Messiah led to his imprisonment in the Fortress Machaerus near the Dead Sea. The evangelist Saint Matthew reports that "John was cast into prison" (4:12 KJV). He later adds, "For Herod had laid hold on John, and bound him, and put him in prison for Herodias' sake, his brother Philip's wife" (14:3 KJV). Later, on Herod's birthday, "the daughter of Herodias danced before them, and pleased Herod." At her request Herod "sent, and beheaded John in the prison. And his head was brought in a charger, and given to the damsel; and she brought it to her mother" (14:10-11 KJV).

John the Baptist, fearless wilderness prophet, is one of the most remarkable figures on the pages of the Bible. His ministry had already been prophesied in the Old Testament. Writing 700 years previously, the prophet Isaiah predicted, "The voice of him that crieth in the wilderness, Prepare ye the way of the Lord, make straight in the desert a highway for our God. Every valley shall be exalted, and every mountain and hill shall be made low, and the crooked shall be made straight, and the rough places plain, And the glory of the Lord shall be revealed, and all flesh shall see it together; for the mouth of the Lord hath spoken it" (Is. 40:3-5 KJV). And Malachi, the last of the Old Testament prophets, writing 400 years before the event, declared, "Behold, I will send my messenger, and he shall prepare my way before me, and the Lord, whom ye seek, shall suddenly come to His temple, even the messenger of the covenant, whom ye delight in; behold He shall come, saith the Lord of hosts" (Mal. 3:1 KJV).

Therefore, when we look for the proper message for Advent preparation, we immediately look to the proclamation of John the Baptist, the Savior's forerunner.

John had performed his duties faithfully. He proclaimed the message of repentance and faith without fear or favor. He dared to tell King Herod that he was an adulterer because he was living with Herodias, his brother's wife, who had disowned her previous husband to become a queen. For his fearless testimony, John was cast into prison, never to be free again.

Even in prison, however, he continued his ministry. He had a few faithful disciples who served him there. He was filled with a burning desire to witness to the truth that Jesus was the promised Messiah, foretold in Old Testament prophecy. Now he saw another way of convincing them. He sent two of his disciples to Jesus with this question: "Art Thou He that should come, or do we look for another?"

That is proper Advent preparation, pointing men to Christ. Today we cannot go to Christ personally, as did John's disciples, but we can find Him in His Word. Our Savior declares, "If ye continue in My Word, then are ye My disciples indeed; and ye shall know the truth, and the truth shall make you free" (John 8:31-32 KJV).

What answer did John's disciples receive? Saint Luke tells us that when the disciples came, Jesus was in the act of healing the maimed, the blind, and the deaf. Our Savior replied, "Go and show John again those things which ye do hear and see: The blind receive their sight, and the lame walk, the lepers are cleansed, and the deaf hear, the dead are raised up, and the poor have the Gospel preached to them" (Matt. 11:4a-5 RSV).

These aspects of our Savior's ministry had been predicted in ancient prophecy. Isaiah foretold, ". . . the eyes of the blind shall be opened, and the ears of the deaf shall be unstopped. Then shall the lame man leap as an hart, and the tongue of the dumb sing . . ." (Is. 35:5-6 KJV). And again Isaiah foretold, "The Spirit of the Lord God is upon me, because the Lord hath anointed me to preach good tidings unto the meek; He hath sent me to bind up the broken-hearted, to proclaim liberty to the captives, and the opening of the prison to them that are bound; to proclaim the acceptable year of the Lord, and the day of vengeance of our God; to comfort all that mourn; to appoint unto them that mourn in Zion, to give unto them beauty for ashes, the oil of joy for mourning, the garment of praise for the spirit of heaviness . . ." (Isaiah 61:1-3 KJV).

Proper Advent preparation therefore directs us, first of all, to look to the Lord Jesus Christ, who, during the days of His earthly ministry went about "preaching the Gospel of the kingdom, and healing all manner of sickness and all manner of disease among the people" (Matt. 4:23 KJV).

Let us therefore look to Christ this Advent season as we prepare our hearts for the anniversary of the Savior's nativity! Look to the cross for love, for life, for light! Look to Jesus, the Son of the eternal God and the Son of the lowly Virgin, for full, free, and finished salvation! Look to Christ for strength in every sorrow, courage in every crisis! Look to His cross for eternal compassion! Look to the Crucified, to Him alone, to Him always for eternal life!

Significantly, our Savior added, "Blessed is he, whosoever shall not be offended in Me." The disciples of John the Baptist may have found Jesus too plain and simple. Today, too, we may be "offended" when we witness the infant Babe of Bethlehem in the humility and lowliness of the manger. May God grant that we shall "not be offended" in the infant Babe of Bethlehem!

II. Let Us Look to Christ's Word of Sin and Grace!

As the disciples of John the Baptist returned to the wilderness preacher, we may assume that they were indeed convinced that Jesus was the Messiah, the fulfillment of Old Testament prophecy.

Jesus then took occasion to describe the truly towering stature of His forerunner. We note first of all that He described John as proclaiming God's truth *firmly and courageously.* He was not a "reed shaken with the wind." He had spoken alike to the poorest beggar, to the proudest Pharisee, and finally to King Herod himself. His message appealed, "Repent ye, for the kingdom of heaven is at hand" (Matt. 3:2 KJV). And at this point the evangelist continues, "For this is He that was spoken of by the prophet Esaias, saying, The voice of one crying in the wilderness, Prepare ye the way of the Lord, make His paths straight" (Matt. 3:3 KJV).

The clarion call of this hour also asks for stalwart witnesses to God's grace who will indict sin in high places and low, but who will also continue, "The kingdom of heaven is at hand."

Our Savior also described John the Baptist as standing up for the truth *self-sacrificingly*. He continued, "But what went ye out for to see? A man clothed in soft raiment? Behold, they that wear soft clothing are in kings' houses." He did not seek riches or gain for himself. He "had his raiment of camel's hair, and a leather girdle about his loins; and his meat was locusts and wild honey" (Matt. 3:4 KJV).

When we work for the King of kings, outward appearances are negligible. God searches the heart. His standards of loyalty to the truth are still the same: the proclamation of repentance and faith. It was to John's ministry of proclamation that Jesus pointed by giving him the title "prophet." In what way, we ask, was John "a prophet" and "more than a prophet"?

First of all, our Savior explains, "For this is he, of whom it is written, Behold I send My messenger before Thy face, which will prepare Thy way before Thee" (Matt. 11:10 KJV). None of the prophets had been foretold by God except John the Baptist. Our Savior thus declared that John's ministry of preparing the Savior's way into the hearts of men was direct fulfillment of such passages as Mal. 3:1.

Again, John was "a prophet" and "more than a prophet," because he alone could witness *directly* to the Savior. All of the other prophets could only say: "The Messiah is coming; believe and wait!" But John could say: "Jesus is here. 'Behold the Lamb of God, which taketh away the sin of the world.'"

Thereupon the Savior, whose way John was preparing into the hearts of men, paid him His highest tribute: "Verily I say unto you, among them that are born of women there hath not risen a greater than John the Baptist" (Matt. 11:11 KJV). Can any witness to Christ ever receive a higher tribute? Yet our Savior concludes His tribute to the powerful wilderness figure with an even more striking declaration: "Notwithstanding he that is least in the kingdom of heaven is greater than he." As high as had been His tribute to John, there is an even greater glory for us in our present day.

Today we have the much fuller record of our Savior's suffering, death, and resurrection set forth on the pages of the New Testament. Ours is the "more sure Word of prophecy; whereunto ye do well that ye take heed, as unto a light that shineth in a dark place, until the day dawn, and the day star arise in your hearts" (2 Peter 1:19 KJV).

As we look into this "more sure Word of prophecy," we find the Biblical message of sin and grace, of human guilt and divine forgiveness. God's Word proclaims this truth that "all have sinned, and come short of the glory of God." Even our supposed righteousness, the best that we have and are, in God's sight are but "filthy rags."

Praise God, however, that the message of Advent assures us that Christ is coming "to save His people from their sins"! When "the fullness of the time was come," He came into our world of sin and sorrow to suffer and die as the Redeemer of all mankind. Today we can declare that the Savior's work is finished, that the Father's anger is appeased. Now we are free from sin, completely and totally.

May God grant that we will stand firm in our testimony, directing men to Jesus Christ, the Messiah, and proclaiming His Word of sin and grace fearlessly!

Before the birth of John the Baptist, his father, the priest Zechariah, brought this beautiful depiction of the ministry of his coming son in the well known words of the "Benedictus": "And thou, child, shalt be called the prophet of the Highest; for thou shalt go before the face of the Lord to prepare His ways; to give knowledge of salvation unto His people by the remission of their sins, through the tender mercy of our God; whereby the Dayspring from on high hath visited us, to give light to them that sit in darkness and in the shadow of death, to guide our feet into the way of peace" (Luke 1:76-79 KJV).

The world is our field. The time is now. Let us look to Jesus as our Savior; let us believe what John believed: "Jesus, the Christ Child, is the promised Messiah, our Savior from sin and our King."

On Jordan's bank the Baptist's cry
Announces that the Lord is nigh;
Awake and hearken, for he brings
Glad tidings of the King of kings!

Then cleansed be every life from sin;
Make straight the way for God within,
And let us all our hearts prepare
For Christ to come and enter there. (*LW* 14)

The Saving Name of Jesus

FOURTH SUNDAY IN ADVENT
MATTHEW 1:18-25

Eugene R. Bertermann

One name—and only one name—can bring peace to bewildered minds in our modern civilization. It does not designate a military leader, because even titled strategists can fail in an emergency and be deposed under the pressure of heavy charges. This marvelous name does not denote a diplomatic genius, for the plans of statecraft can bog down completely. Nor does it mark a scientific inventor or a famous scholar, since almost every discovery has been misused in the destructive services of sin.

At first glance the name which alone holds hope, the last hope, seems completely out of keeping with our modern ideals and ambitions. It represents earthly poverty, while we crave riches; it emphasizes purity and chastity, but the world pursues lust and licentiousness; it urges humility, while our age applauds pride; it pleads for blessed peace, while nations engage in war. Yet it is eternal, unchanging. In more than a thousand languages it is adored by men who differ in race and color. It is the holy, peerless name given the Babe of Bethlehem soon after His birth. It is—thank God that with our simple lips we can speak it!—the name of names: *Jesus!*

Historians tell us that often when ancient Greek orators found their audiences inattentive or sleeping, they used one word by which interest could be reawakened and enthusiasm sustained. In the midst of important orations they would suddenly stop to cry out, "Marathon!" And the people, recalling their glorious national victory of Marathon, would listen with renewed attention. How much more do we need the name Jesus for our self-indulgent world! Cry out "Jesus!" in the midst of heathen darkness, and idols with their hideous superstitions crumble. Proclaim "Jesus!" throughout our nation, let that Savior be accepted by the masses, and this nation will become morally mighty, spiritually unconquerable! Preach "Jesus!" in decadent churches, and they revive with fresh zeal and power. Put "Jesus!" into the hearts of sin-stricken humanity, the homes of the suffering and sorrowful, the lives of those embattled against God, their fellowmen, and their own selves, and amazing peace will reign supreme!

As on this Fourth Sunday in Advent we stand in the hallowed hush of Christmas before the manger crib of the Christ Child, let us hear more of this name at which, according to the Holy Scripture, "every knee should bow, of things in heaven, and things in earth, and things under the earth" (Phil. 2:10 KJV)—the password through the sentries of death into the gates of heaven,

The Saving Name of Jesus!

which our text explains.

I. How This Name Was Given

There is a glorious history behind this glorious name. It was sent from heaven; a holy angel came to declare, "Thou shalt call

His name Jesus!" Because of its celestial origin, no human title ascribed to Christ can ever be as blessed and powerful. Designations used by the world today—the carpenter's Son, the Great Galilean, the Judean Teacher—are earthly; the real and most appropriate name, Jesus, was given by God Himself and transmitted by a heavenly messenger.

Significantly, the angel brought this announcement to Joseph. We know little about the Savior's foster father, but the few facts the Bible supplies leads us to understand that Joseph was indeed well-chosen for this distinction. He was a devout, God-fearing man. Almost every time he is mentioned in conjunction with our Lord's infancy, angels address him as the responsible head of the Holy Family, one deeply concerned about the divine Child whom Christmas Day had put under his charge. Fathers today should similarly realize that the Lord has ordained them as the heads of their households—not merely the breadwinners, but the spiritual leaders who are to bring up their children "in the nurture and admonition of the Lord."

Let us note well Joseph's implicit obedience to the angel's "Thou shalt call His name Jesus"! In fulfillment, as an obedient echo, we read, "He called His name Jesus." The New Testament records that whenever the foster father received divine direction, he followed unquestioningly. An angel explains the mystery of the virgin birth, and Joseph accepts it. An angel warns him to flee from Herod's murderous vengeance, and unhesitatingly he arises at night and starts the perilous journey into Egypt. God give us fathers today who will courageously follow His guidance! Let all fathers remember that God expects the spirit of Joseph in your home. May God put the strength of Jesus into your heart and keep Him in your home!

According to Saint Luke, the Virgin Mary had also been told that the Christ Child's name was to be *Jesus*. Perhaps this is to show us, even if incidentally, that husband and wife are to share in the family plans. In any event Mary likewise accepted this Gift from heaven and gave a high example of Christian womanhood. Today, too, our country needs mothers who will follow the divine will for their home life.

How directly children are influenced by their parents' spiritual strength or weakness! The homes in our land require the constant contact with God which the Holy Family enjoyed, the obedience to the divine will which Joseph and Mary showed in following the divine direction, "Thou shalt call His name Jesus."

II. Why This Name Was Given

We need hardly explain that the name Jesus is of the utmost importance. All intelligent persons, whether they accept or reject

Christ, should understand that He is the most important Figure in history. Jesus occurs more than 600 times in the New Testament; and while some 200 titles are otherwise given Christ, *Jesus* is the real name of our Lord—His name when His earthly existence began at Bethlehem and when it ended on Calvary, where Pilate wrote as the superscription on the cross, "Jesus of Nazareth." It is His first and last designation in the New Testament, and, whether spoken in English or in any other language, it should be the first and last on every believer's lips.

He is not, however, the only person to be called by this name. The Hebrew form for Jesus was also given to Moses' successor, Joshua, and to many others in Jewish history. There is a lesson in this, too. So completely did Jesus become man, that He took a name common among men. He was like every one of us in everything except sin, and in His complete humanity He knew our weaknesses and sorrows. He understands our temptations, for He was tested as we are. He sympathizes with us in every need; we are never forced to tread any pathway, however hard and apparently cruel, where Jesus has not gone before us.

Yet it is remarkable that after our Lord became known as Jesus, the name fell into disuse among His countrymen, as though it were a title reserved for Him. In truth, He alone can fully live up to its meaning. Our English word "Jesus" is taken from a Hebrew term which really means "The Lord is Salvation." And assuredly He is both our God and the Redeemer of our race. Every time you hear His name, you should also perceive the promise of divine redemption in this glorious word.

Call Him Master, Teacher, or Leader occasionally if you must, but let His real name, the one you repeat and love, ever be and remain "Jesus." There are other masters, teachers, and leaders; but there can be only one Jesus, one Lord and Redeemer.

When the angel announced the name to Joseph, he explained its meaning with the promise, "He shall save His people from their sins." In other words, Jesus is called Salvation because He *is* our salvation. There is no misrepresentation or exaggeration here. Christ is called Salvation because He is, in absolute truth, heaven's only Redemption.

Jesus is the name above all others because the deliverance which it signifies is the highest, deepest, widest love that God Himself could show. Our heavenly Father was not—and in His holiness could not be—satisfied with smiling at our violations of His law, as an indulgent parent amuses himself at a baby's mistake. He could not simply overlook our transgressions, as a kindly teacher closes his eyes to a pupil's hasty error. He could not forget our iniquities, as a Christian wife might overlook a husband's failings. God is so holy, just and perfect that every transgression must be punished. Yet while He hates sin and demands the full penalty for His broken law, He loves His fallen children with such devotion that He sent His Son to become the sinner's Substitute, the universal Ransom.

Have you ever taken time to measure, as far as the mortal mind can, the matchless mercy God showed in sending Christ? What love beyond measure we can find in the name Jesus when we see the Savior, unresisting and uncomplaining, go unswervingly to Calvary for us!

Jesus means *completed* salvation. When our Lord, nailed to the cross, bowed His head in death with the cry, "It is finished," He left nothing undone for our redemption. Our deliverance has been definitely accomplished, now and forever.

Jesus also means *free* salvation. If you had all the money stored in the world's great treasuries, the billions spent daily for war's destruction, you would not have enough to purchase forgiveness for a single sin. The cleansing of our souls is offered freely through Christ's heavenly mercy. "By grace are ye saved through faith" the New Testament summarizes, "and that not of yourselves; it is the gift of God, not of works, lest any man should boast" (Eph. 2:8 KJV). May God's Holy Spirit help you to realize today that simply by faith you can have pardon without money, blessing without payment, access to the throne of Christ's mercy without any human intermediary!

Jesus means *universal* salvation, redemption offered everyone. When Jesus was born "in the fullness of time" after long centuries of expectation, liberty was promised to the whole race. "God so loved the *world,* that He gave His only begotten Son, that *whosoever* believeth in Him should not perish, but have everlasting life" (John 3:16).

Jesus means our *only* salvation. God's Word declares with heaven's authority, "There is none other name under heaven given by men whereby we must be saved" (Acts 4:12). Jesus is the one way from earth to blessed eternity.

Jesus means *comforting* salvation. On the grave of John Newton this inscription has been carved: "John Newton, clerk, once an Infidel, and a Libertine, a servant of slavers in Africa, was, by the rich Mercy of our Lord and Savior Jesus Christ, preserved, restored, pardoned, and appointed to preach the Faith he had long labored to destroy" (W. G. Polack, *The Handbook to The Lutheran Hymnal,* 2nd ed. [St. Louis: Concordia Publishing House, 1942] p. 555). He looked to Jesus and found the comfort that made him write a score of hymns, including, "How Sweet the Name of Jesus Sounds in a Believer's Ear!"

Jesus means *unchanging* salvation. The names of men, even the greatest, are often forgotten. Yet as long as you look to the Savior, you will never forget His name or His mercies. They will be renewed to you every morning in such an impressive way that you will daily grow in grace.

Jesus means *sure* salvation. There's no guesswork about His Gospel. His mercies have been proved in many millions of hearts. His power, in century heaped upon century, too constantly changes the lives of men, too repeatedly gives them calm in the chaos of world strife, to be denied or even questioned. The longer and more intently you behold the Son of God and work with Him and for Him, the more dearly you immerse yourself in His Word, the more clear your conviction grows that He is what His name implies: Salvation, Deliverance, Atonement, Redemption, Pardon for all the world and especially for you.

III. What We Must Do With This Name

What, then, does the name of names mean to us? In taking a spiritual inventory we remember our grievious weaknesses, our smallest mistrusts, our misuse of the Savior's name, our refusal to spread abroad the marvels of His mercy—in short, our many repeated sins. In deep humility we approach the Lord to plead for mercy instead of justice; and, blessed Savior that He is, He assures us that no matter how marred and spotted each of our daily entries are, the handwriting against us is blotted out. His precious name proves the truth that "He shall save His people"—and through faith you, too, are His inseparably and eternally—"from their sins."

We should accept the name Jesus as the pledge of our own salvation, defend it whenever it is attacked, and make it the center of our prayers, believing His promise, "whatsoever ye shall ask in My name, that will I do" (John 14:13). As we approach the anniversary of our Savior's coming into the flesh, let us bow before God and plead with Him to bless our country, speaking our petitions in Jesus' name. Let us acknowledge our own sins and our country's shortcomings.

As we approach the celebration of Christmas, let His name ring throughout the land! Let church leaders acclaim Christ both God and Savior! Let the churches return to the full acceptance of Jesus as the Redeemer who "shall save His people from their sins." Our pulpits should echo and reecho with Jesus' name, which to the believer is balm and healing for the soul.

During these Christmas days, the marvelous creation of Handel, *The Messiah,* will be prominently featured on television, on the radio, and in churches by oratorio societies. In that work the composer pays a spiritual and artistic tribute to Jesus. Handel, however, should be known not only for this musical masterpiece, but also for his trusting faith. When he felt his last hour approaching, he summoned his servant and asked to hear the 91st Psalm. "That was beautiful," Handel whispered when the reading was finished. Then he continued, "Oh, that is food that nourishes! That is refreshment! What a splendid thing it is to be sure of one's faith!"

Through faith in the saving name of Jesus, we, too, can have the assurance that we shall in God's good time enter the heaven of hallowed bliss and glory. There we shall sing far grander praises than even Handel's "Hallelujah Chorus." Until then, with Jesus in our hearts and on our lips, let us sing:

Dear Name! The Rock upon which I build,
My Shield and Hiding-place;
My never-failing Treasury, filled
With boundless stores of grace.

Weak is the effort of my heart
And cold my warmest thought;
But when I see Thee as Thou art,
I'll praise Thee as I ought. (*TLH* 364:3, 6)

Behold How Great a Wonder!

THE NATIVITY OF OUR LORD
CHRISTMAS DAY
LUKE 2:1-20

George H. Beiderwieden Jr.

The economy is bad. Military expenditures are sky-rocketing. There's lots of strife and friction. Does it sound like the 1980s? No, it was A.D. 101. Things don't change much, do they?

And *then* many said sadly, "Look what our world's coming to!" But there were a few—called "CHRISTians"—who kept saying, "Look what's come to our world!"

We're here to think on that!

"Behold How Great a Wonder!"

I. The Wonder That God Came Down

First, *God came down here today.* Note that an angel announced His birth. "The glory of the Lord shone round about them" (v. 9)—some of heaven's light, a window up there left ajar. Born is the Lord. He is called "Christ." That's the predicted One. And that's God. Isaiah proclaimed, "Behold, a virgin shall conceive, and bear a son, and shall call his name Immanuel"—that's "God-with-us"—(Is. 7:14 KJV); and again: "For unto us a child is born, unto us a son is given; . . . and his name shall be called . . . The mighty God . . . ." (Is. 9:6 KJV). Further, the angel host cried, "Glory to God" who did something this day. "Peace on earth"—only God could effect that! "Good will toward men." God had to take the initiative.

Yes, God came down here today. "In the beginning was the Word, and the Word was with God, and the Word was God. The same was in the beginning with God. All things were made by him; and without him was not any thing made that was made. . . . And the Word was made flesh, and dwelt among us, . . ." (John 1:1-3, 14a). "And without controversy great is the mystery of godliness: God was manifest in the flesh" (1 Tim. 3:16a KJV).

Now, ponder what that's saying. The eternal, timeless One enters days and weeks and years. The almighty Creator of all becomes a dependent Babe. The holy Judge steps down off His throne. Surely that establishes this as a day worth marking every year for all time. God came down today! J. B. Phillips isn't exaggerating when he suggests that what renders our earth unique isn't any of the distinctions we often think of. It's rather that *we are the Visited Planet!*

But maybe we ought to try to forget that fact. Why did He come down here? Was it an inspection tour? He sees quite well from where He is. In fact, we're told what He sees from where He sits: "The Lord looked down from heaven upon the children of men, to see if there were any that did understand, and seek God. They are all gone aside, they are all together become filthy; there is none that doeth good, no, not one" (Ps. 14:2-3 KJV). And isn't that just what our conscience would suggest, if we gave it half a chance? The shepherds felt it. "They were sore afraid" (v. 9b).

So maybe we'd better forget Christmas, or crowd out of our consciousness what really happened today. We can do it with Santa Claus, or trees, or buying, or whatever. But we must cancel out the fact. For God, holy God, came down, and we might feel better if He hadn't. We had it coming. And He came to clobber. After all, wasn't Caesar Augustus squeezing extra taxes from the poor. And there was no room for a pregnant woman. And there's plenty more to clobber! What else could He, the holy Judge, do with accused such as you and I?

Ah, we've seen only a small part of the wonder. God came down here this day, and He came to *rescue.* The angel announces, "Unto you is born this day . . . a Savior" (v. 11). How about that! The holy God came to rescue the rebellious humans. Here is given us an x-ray of the heart of God. "I have loved thee with an everlasting love" (Jer. 31:3 KJV). In Eden it should have been Adam and Eve who wept. But God felt sorrow, too. Our Lord expressed it Himself, "Oh, Jerusalem, Jerusalem, . . . how often would I have gathered thy children together, even as a hen gathers her chickens under her wings, and ye would not!" (Matt. 23:37 KJV).

And mark how He who came down here will do this saving. You can know He'll do it in a way that works. We get a cue from His becoming a human baby. He comes to take our place. He'll do it all for us—our Substitute. Oh, boy! How that relieves us from uncertainty! He comes to make the payment. There's a further cue here, if we look carefully enough. The Owner of all has no crib better than the cattle's feeding trough. Paying the price will cost the Maker. None makes room for Him on His first night on earth. "Coming events cast their shadow before!"

There's more here. The angel calls God "Christ." The Scriptures have told us about the Christ. Isaiah predicted, "Surely He hath borne our griefs, and carried our sorrows. . . . He was wounded for our transgressions; He was bruised for our iniquities; the chastisement of our peace was upon Him, and with His stripes we are healed" (Is. 53:4a, 5 KJV). David in Psalm 22 foretold, "They pierced My hands and My feet" (v. 16b). It will cost this God-become-a-baby. He will suffer to save.

What a wonder! Today the Maker came down to the earth He created. And He came not to act in justice, but to shower mercy—to save His finest creature gone bad—to do it all for the humans. What a Wonder! Who would have expected it?

II. The Wonder That He Came to Shepherds

But "there were in the same country shepherds abiding in the field, keeping watch over their flock by night" (v. 8). Is this mere scenery, a bit of minor history? Shouldn't the angel have taken this awesome news to Rome and Caesar Augustus, and then to the Hebrew churchmen and King Herod? After all, it's God who came. He should move in the right circles. There's such a thing as protocol. Some are entitled to respect. And some don't count enough—like shepherds.

Wonder again: "And, lo, the angel of the Lord came upon them, and the glory of the Lord shone round about them" (v. 9b). When He came to rescue the race, the first He wished to hear of it were shepherds. That was pretty far down on the social scale. They weren't wealthy, certainly, nor leaders, nor people consulted for advice. No one respected, admired, or emulated them. They were just there, sitting with one eye open—pretty monotonous—on the lookout for possible wolves.

Why did He pick them? It's not too hard to figure out, is it? He didn't want any to feel excluded. He also came for those who are not big, or respected—who don't have clout. He came for anyone, for the least, for everyone—for me.

Oh, I'm so glad for that, so thankful for those shepherds! They assure me that it doesn't matter that my yesterdays have included some shameful pages. The hymn stanza echoes my past: "Thou knowest all my griefs and fears, Thy grace abused, my misspent years." I have hurt Him; I have hurt people. I have disappointed Him, and served myself. Still He came—even for me.

It doesn't matter that I fail Him still. "The good that I would I do not; and the evil that I would not, that I do" (Rom. 7:19 KJV). I don't pray as I should. My hunger for His Word should have grown more. Yet He came to save me.

Oh, wonder of wonders! He came for me and for all other shepherds. The great God came to earth to save such as us! What a Wonder!

III. The Praise That Follows Wonder

And there's something else that's not a wonder at all. It follows inevitably. "Us? The Lord eternal came down to save *us*? Let's go!" "Let us now go . . . and see this thing . . ." (v. 15). And when they found the stable, they must have fallen down and worshipped Him, as later visitors from the east did. What else would come as naturally? Shepherds still do that, don't we? Isn't it the only fitting life-style—"glorifying and praising" such a God every Friday, each Tuesday, any Wednesday?

"And when they had seen it, they made known abroad the saying which was told them concerning this child" (v. 17). Peace had come to earth—peace for sinners—peace with a holy, just God. And they had been directed to it. And they knew so many other shepherds, the owners of the sheep, their neighbors in town, even relatives, who didn't know what had happened this night. "We cannot but speak the things which we have seen and heard" (Acts 4:20 KJV).

So many have missed what happened today. Some missed it because their childhood home had only the trimmings and omitted the essence. Some missed it because they'd come to associate this day's development with "church," and that had somehow soured with them. Some missed it because some sin in their life has rendered them cynical, hopeless, and despairing—running from any reference to a God. But let's not criticize them, or despise them, or appear in any way condescending. An angel has told us shepherds where peace lay. That's the only difference. "There but for the grace of God . . ." May we leave no stone unturned that as many of these as possible find out what really happened today!

Behold, how great a wonder!

The Bright Side of a Dark Beginning

FIRST SUNDAY AFTER CHRISTMAS
MATTHEW 2:13-15, 19-23

George H. Beiderwieden Jr.

This second chapter brings all St. Matthew tells us of our Lord's childhood. St. Mark and St. John tell us nothing. St. Luke covers different periods.

The Jews of that day attached great importance to children. They had no less than eight different words to mark the stages of development from newborn babe to young man. Obviously, then, what's here is not "according to St. Matthew," the Jew, left to himself. Plainly he spoke or was silent as God the Holy Spirit moved or restrained.

So let's see what God the Spirit has for us at the beginning of a new year on

"The Bright Side of a Dark Beginning"

I. Escape to Egypt

Let's note first the incident. Our Lord is just an infant. The Magi have reported King Herod's intention to come and worship the Christ Child. That night they were given directions to return to the east by another route. And apparently the same night "the angel of the Lord appeareth to Joseph in a dream, saying, Arise, and take the young child and his mother, and flee into Egypt" (v. 13a KJV). Herod is duplicitous. Egypt is about 60 miles away. It's a Roman province. There are many Jews there. And Joseph obediently jumps out of bed, takes Mary and the holy Child, and journeys at night. They walked; or did Mary ride on a donkey holding the child as is often pictured? We're not told.

Here is inserted a strange parenthetical note: "And was there until the death of Herod" (v. 15a). That's reported again later (v. 19a). Why here? Perhaps it was in anticipation. Some have prolonged this stay in Egypt. They have made the Lord learn the magical arts there, scratching into His skin formulas which He would afterward practice in the Holy Land as miracles. Perhaps, therefore, St. Matthew has this double report of the death as if to say: "No, He wasn't in Egypt more than a year or two." Of the death itself Josephus in his *Antiquities* reports it was horrible. Herod's entrails rotted, producing worms, unbearable stench, and convulsions. It was prolonged with useless attempts at cures, producing bloody, murderous thoughts—truly the death of a moral monster!

With Herod dead, an angel appears again to Joseph bidding him return to Israel's land. He leaves it up to Joseph specifically where. It's safe. Probably Joseph preferred to return to Bethlehem. It was near Jerusalem where the temple was, the center of the faith. It seemed only proper to Joseph that the young Messiah grow up in the neighborhood of the Holy City. "But when he heard that Archelaus did reign in Judea in the room of his father Herod, he was afraid to go thither" (v. 22a). When Archelaus found some commiserating survivors of his father's victims, he ordered the calvary to enclose the temple and killed 3,000. The rest fled to the mountains. The Passover was abandoned, lest something worse should ensue. Joseph heard of this upon approaching the area. "Notwithstanding, being warned of God in a dream, he turned aside into the parts of Galilee" (v. 22b). God directed Joseph toward the county of Galilee. Joseph naturally chose Nazareth. It was his former home. Both he and Mary had many friends there.

II. Preview of Suffering

Why is this incident reported by the Spirit? What does it tell us of our Lord? Well, it certainly tells us that God's Savior is rejected. The Jewish king, who should know the Old Testament prophecies well, seeks to kill God's Christ already as an infant. Oh, the perversity of the natural human heart! What folly! We need this sin-payment so desperately, and our pride refuses Him! But He is still God's chosen. You don't take a popularity poll on Him! As He would later say: "Blessed is he, whosoever shall not be offended in me" (Matt. 11:6 KJV). May neither friends, nor relatives, nor business associates throw us! The king was wrong.

There is something else here. He is a suffering Savior! It sets in early. There is no room in the inn. He is laid in the cattle's feeding trough. And now they must run with Him for His life. It's an obvious prediction of His rejection, Gethsemane, the mockery and Calvary. He is a King who wins subjects by suffering. That's not weakness but strength. For we know He volunteered for this suffering. He will hereby take our sin. That costs. Such is His love, His concern for you and me. And that becomes a tremendous magnet. Many will find themselves unable to resist it. They will be joined to Him forever. "And I, if I be lifted up from the earth, will draw all men unto me" (John 12:32 KJV).

And yet for all the heavy opposition, God maintains His salvation plan. That plan was conceived long ago: ". . . that it might be fulfilled which was spoken of the Lord by the prophet, saying,

Out of Egypt have I called my son" (Matt. 3:15b). And again: "that it might be fulfilled which was spoken by the prophets, He shall be called a Nazarene" (v. 23b). Here is God's plan: He is indeed to die—but not yet. What encouragement is implied here! God the Spirit still works today. He stubbornly follows through on that salvation plan. We are blessed to the extent that we are involved!

And there's still more: Joseph is bidden by the angel to flee "into Egypt" (v. 13b). That's interesting, when you stop to think of it, isn't it? The Promised Land is unsafe for God's Son. Egypt, the land of God's people's bondage, receives Him and shelters Him. Doesn't that suggest something sobering? You know, one day a Roman army officer manifested unusual trust in God's Christ. The Lord marveled and exclaimed, "I have not found so great faith, no, not in Israel." And then He added, "Many shall come from the east and the west, and shall sit down with Abraham, and Isaac, and Jacob, in the kingdom of heaven. But the children of the kingdom shall be cast out into outer darkness; there shall be weeping and gnashing of teeth" (Matt. 8:10-12 KJV). Some of us have known the heavenly Father and His blessed Son and the mighty Spirit for a long, long time. Why, we grew up, you might say, "not knowing anything else"! And, if we can be that honest, there is a very real danger that we may take all of it for granted and grow cool. Should I attend Bible class? Well, that's for those who do not know it as well as I. We're safe. "We . . . were never in bondage to any man" (John 8:33 KJV). It's the recently initiated, the new converts to Christianity, who often recognize their need. They remember the darkness of unbelief, and they seize the study opportunity. "Flee into Egypt!" Let's do it, no matter how long we've known Him!

III. The Bright Side for Us

What does this incident in the life of our Lord suggest for the new year? Well, it certainly suggests that life has its ups and downs for His disciples, too. "The servant is not greater than his Lord" (John 13:16a). Surely we do well at the beginning of another year to be realistic. There will be things in our life, also this new year, that we would not choose. He said to us, "In the world ye shall have tribulation" (John 16:33b KJV). And St. Paul insisted, "We must through much tribulation enter into the kingdom of God" (Acts 14:22b KJV). The writer to the Hebrews assures us, "For whom the Lord loveth he chasteneth, and scourgeth every son whom he receiveth" (Heb. 12:6 KJV). But our Father in heaven is always there. He has promised, "All things work together for good to them that love God" (Rom. 8:28a). And with regard to the chastening that characterizes sonship: "Now no chastening for the present seemeth to be joyous, but grievous; nevertheless afterward it yieldeth the peaceable fruit of righteousness unto them which are exercised thereby" (Heb. 12:11 KJV).

And right here in this incident is another assurance we dare never forget—God provides, but in His own way and time. He could have protected the Baby by having Herod die two years earlier. He chose this way. This would make it easier for us to see that He was doing the protecting. We often need things to be very obvious so we get the point. He is doing it in our life! Three times He gives directions. He directs Joseph back to Israel, and then leaves the choice to Joseph. He directs that it's acceptable not to be so near Jerusalem, and Joseph picks Nazareth. That's just fine; now the Christ Child would be known as the Nazarene, and that's just what the prophets had predicted—a cause for reproach. Without trumpet or fanfare, so very quietly yet altogether effectively, He works out His marvelous plan. He takes care of His own. Doesn't that make you feel warm and safe for the new year? It does me!

But back to the thought of "reproach." The Son, God's own dear Son, assumed your sin. Therefore the holy Son is a "Reproach." Forever He shall be so called. The spike marks He keeps in glory. Ah, that's all we need for the New Year, no matter what comes!

May I suggest two ways we allow His assumption of our reproach to make this new year different? I know that some of you read the Scriptures faithfully each and every day. I fear many of us do not. It's a good time to start over. Read every day. "Speak, Lord, for thy servant heareth!" Make it a habit this year.

And then a second change for the better—much more prayer. Our world has so many situations we so easily feel futile about changing. We can pray. God hears and responds. Each of us has personal problems. We fear we can't—sometimes we know we can't—change things. Have you forgotten? God is still there! Make a prayer list, and then work on it every day, day after day.

These will make Him glad—letting Him have His say and speaking to Him every day. We owe it to Him. These four lines say it all:

> I asked Jesus,
> "How much do You love me?"
> He said, "So much,"
> And stretched out His arms and died.

Shadow and Substance

THE EPIPHANY OF OUR LORD
MATTHEW 2:1-12

Frederick W. Kemper

For a year (or was it two?) they followed a bright star. The caravan moved slowly across the desert sea by night, following the beckoning light on the western horizon. When the star disappeared as they neared Jerusalem, they thought God had deserted them. King Herod knew nothing of the mysterious light, but when he heard the news that a star-crossed King of the Jews had been born, his oriental superstition flared. He who murdered any pretender to his throne must know the whereabouts of the Child. He called the Sanhedrin together. They recalled a prophecy about Bethlehem and immediately informed the king. He in turn relayed the information to the travelers but only when he extracted the promise that they would return with the new-born King's whereabouts that he might worship Him, too.

The star reappeared that night, and the journey continued. A few short hours later the star seemed to stop. Indeed, the journey had come to an end, for beneath the star was the Child.

They entered the house, saw the Child, and with kingly majesty knelt before Him, laying out gifts befitting the King of kings. Now their objective obtained, they took their leave. An angel messenger bid them return by the southern route to avoid Jerusalem and its king, for he would surely follow his established pattern and murder the Child.

Thus the Magi move across the pages of sacred history, leaving deep mysteries about their origins, their persons, even their purpose in the journey.

There are clues to the mystery of the Wise Men. The fact that their story is the theme for Epiphany is in itself a clue. This is not their story after all. It is the story of the infant Jesus—King of all kings and Lord of all people—being presented to the world. It is His Epiphany, His manifestation, the announcement of His visit to this planet for the salvation of all people.

Shadow and Substance I: Prophecy

Prophecies are like shadows—two-dimensional, real, but only shadows of things to come. They are scattered through the Old

Testament from the story of the expulsion from Eden to Malachi. As shadows are hard to "read" or to explain, so prophecies in themselves are elusive. Who can know whose shadow is cast upon the wall, friend or enemy, until the person is revealed? Matthew writes in elation. The substance, the shadow person has arrived. Three times in the brief account of the Wise Men, he remembers the troubling shadow and as often rejoices that the mystery of the shadow is solved. Of course, out of Bethlehem One should come who would be the Shepherd of Israel. And when the women of Bethlehem wept for their children at the slaughter of the innocents, he rememberd once more how the women of Rama had wept.

History may be a shadow, too. Matthew remembers how the Pharoah of Egypt wouldn't believe and how he hardened his heart against the God of the Israelites time and time again. He sees history repeated in the hardheartedness of Herod and Jerusalem—so much like Pharoah of old. And as Moses fled from Egypt to escape the possible punishment for his misdeed, this new Moses, this Christ Child, flees the country, too—to Egypt—the one shadow, the other substance.

Shadow and Substance II: The Wise Men

Matthew's account of the Wise Men is itself a shadow. It is his purpose to present the substance as he unfolds the story of the Child grown to adulthood. He sees so many of his peers rejecting God's offer of salvation which He made to them in the Messiah Jesus—and so many Gentiles accepting the offer. At this point Herod and the people of Jerusalem are representatives of the Jews; the Magi are representatives of the Gentile world. God will not be thwarted. If the Jews will not accept the Savior and thus forfeit salvation, the Good News will move on to the Gentile world. The old Israel will be replaced with a new people of God, who have come to faith and commitment in the Christ. It is Matthew who reports the life of the Child who preached the Kingdom and died beneath the inscription "This is Jesus, King of the Jews," and who on the Mount of Ascension bid His disciples to preach the Gospel to all the world.

Shadow and Substance III: Missing the Point

Still the shadows move across the wall of time in the text. When it became evident that the star was moving toward Jerusalem, the Wise Men said among themselves, "Of course, where else should a king be born?" and the star disappeared. If the wisemen were going to do this thing on their own, they didn't need the guiding star. It's that way in substance, too. People want religion. Great! God has made His Holy Word, His message to the world, available. The Bible is still the best seller. The Bible is in innumerable hotel rooms, in 2000 languages, in countless homes. But the guru has more appeal, the self-appointed prophet is more enticing than the static book. Who needs that Light?

Matthew strengthens his shadow of how God operates—and how men fail to hear. Herod called the theologians, the Sanhedrin, together to ascertain where the Messiah was to be born. They return their answer—quoting Scripture!—"In Bethlehem of Judea." That close to the Holy Word! That close and the theologians missed it! How like the tens of thousands who hear the Christmas story on the air and in periodicals, and don't really hear it at all. How like the tens of thousands who are within arms length of Scripture, and do not reach for it or open it! How like the tens of thousands who could tell you the story of the manger or would recognize the Epiphany star, yet are unmoved by its import.

Remember the Christmas carols on the department store loud-speakers? "Silent Night" and "Rudolf the Red Nose Reindeer," "Jingle Bells" and "Hark! the Herald Angels Sing" moved in silent and meaningless progression. The twinkling lights on outdoor Christmas trees proclaimed Christmas, but not Christ's birth, to many passers-by. Churches had services for empty pews, or worse—no service at all—on Christ's birthday! The shadows were everywhere, but the seekers of the substance were few.

Shadow and Substance IV: Epiphany Now

Epiphany is the manifestation of Christ to the world. The Wise Men's account is regarded as the first recorded Epiphany, for the Wise Men clearly represent the world for whom Christ had come. When the world was redeemed and heaven became a possibility for everyone, Christ ascended into glory. The Epiphany, the great one, was over and past. Where is Epiphany now? How shall Christ be manifested to the world so that people may know and believe? Ah, good friends, you are the twentieth-century Epiphany; you are the light of Christ in the world. By your deeds they shall know Him. By your witness to the Christ in you, Christ walks the earth again. In the metaphor of these words, you are the shadow of Christ. St. Paul's "which are a shadow of things to come; but the body is of Christ" (Col. 2:17 KJV) might as well have been said of Christ's people (rather than of holidays and holy days). It is by your cups of cold water (in the name of Christ), your soft word (in the name of Christ), your temperament (for the sake of Christ), your love (in emulation of Christ), your forgiving heart (because of Christ), that Christ's Epiphany happens today.

Mrs. M., a promiscuous grandmother, asked Mrs. Z. what made her so different. Mrs. Z. told Mrs. M. about the Christ in her life, and what her church meant to her. Mrs. M. eventually joined the church, and after a year or so gave up her promiscuity. So the shadow gave way to the substance; thus a woman was led to know Jesus.

Often medical missionaries treat the native sick and ailing without a word of the Christ who motivates them, unless by their deeds the question—"Why are you here among us?"—is raised. Only then is it time to move from shadow to substance, to the "Christ in me."

Substance and Shadow V: The Church

The church is shadow; heaven is the substance. The present is shadow, for this world is terminal. Eternity is substance because it is forever. The church in the present foreshadows the fellowship, the community of saints in glory. The bride of Christ is being prepared for the marriage and the wedding feast in the mansions. Thus the church is a viable part of the twentieth-century Epiphany. Church buildings stand in the center of little communities and villages and are scattered through cities. Their spires lift the cross of Christ high above the roof tops. Whether they are little frame buildings or soaring cathedrals, they speak of people's trust in God and faith in Christ. They are the gathering places of the faithful. Week after week sinners come seeking forgiveness, the weak come to be strengthened, the burdened come to be relieved, the committed come for direction. Where two or three are gathered in the name of Christ, He is in the midst of them. He grants the sinner forgiveness, the weak new strength, the burdened comfort, the committed renewed zeal. They worship Him in prayer and song; they lift up holy hands in adoration. In the gathering, through Word and Sacrament, through the promise of Christ Himself, through the Christ in each of the sinner/saints, a twentieth-century Epiphany happens for the faithful.

All the while this little (or large) gathering of God's people is knowingly (or unknowingly) a shadow of things to come. One by one, even now, the greater gathering is happening as the trumpet announces the arrival of another saint in glory where the eternal Epiphany at the throne is a certainty. One great day the trumpets will sound the end of time, and all the saints in time will be translated to join the congregation of the faithful in glory forever. The church now, with all its scars and warts, is a shadow of things to come, when all the saints will be the Church Triumphant without spot or blemish and with Christ forever.

Reprise

So the Wise Men, who for a paragraph or two appear in the sacred record, mount their "ships of the desert" and softly pad off toward home, richer by far for their experience at their very personal Epiphany event. Little could they know that their visit to worship the newborn King would be recorded by Matthew, that it would cause endless speculation as to their origin, purpose and destiny, or that here in this place we would be talking about them on this day. Nor could they ever have guessed what their visit would mean for the church. They are shadows of history, men without substance—except as they gain substance from the Christ whom they visited, the baby Jesus whom they worshiped.

Yet for us their very shadow has become the substance out of which Matthew begins his eloquent call to his peers to know and accept the crucified and risen Christ as Savior and Lord. The Holy Spirit used their shadow to bridge the testaments from prophecy to fulfillment. And I pray that the same Spirit was present in the use of their shadow as we proclaimed Christ at this year's Christmas celebration, the Christ who motivates and moves us as individuals and as an assembly of God's people. Our congregation in this little corner of the world and the Kingdom is a shadow, too. Remember well that Christ can only be known in our century through you who are a shadow of things to come for any soul to see that lives without Christ.

His Baptism and Ours—Ordination to Mission

THE BAPTISM OF OUR LORD
FIRST SUNDAY AFTER THE EPIPHANY
MATTHEW 3:13-17

Frederick W. Kemper

Only rarely in Scripture is there an appearance, or theophany, of the blessed Trinity. One visible visit of God occurred at the baptism of Jesus at the Jordan. Even then the appearance of God is behind a veil, as it were, for only the Father's voice is heard; the Son is vested in human flesh; the Spirit appears as a dove. Far from being clarified, the mystery of the Trinity, the essence of God, the question of God's appearance, and many more intriguing problems remain, not to be answered until we are at last face to face with our Lord. As small a tidbit of the mystery of the Trinity that it is, it is enough for Matthew to introduce the appearance of the Spirit and that of the Father with a well placed and much needed "Lo!" If Matthew had carried the thought a sentence further, he probably would have introduced the third person of the Trinity, Jesus, still dripping from His baptism, with a third "Lo!" He leaves that to the reader, for his whole purpose is to introduce the very Son of God, who had come to reclaim a people for God. The baptism of Jesus, Son of God, is of such import that it dare not be neglected; its position in this First Sunday after the Epiphany celebration is a truly remarkable insight on the part of the church.

The Baptism of Jesus

Jesus' baptism is His "ordination" into His mission as Savior of the world. The manger story, the arrival of the Wise Men, the twelve-year-old in the temple are prologue. Now the hour for His ministry had come, and on the schedule of God's timetable He appeared at the Jordan where John was baptizing. Matthew tells us that John had been preaching, warning people of the "wrath to come" and calling for repentance and baptism. He reports that John hesitated about baptizing Jesus, for he should rather be baptized by Jesus. But, Matthew explains, Jesus must be baptized with John's baptism in order to fulfill all righteousness—for the "wrath to come"(v. 7) could not be stayed except as the righteousness, the will of the Father, was accomplished. So Jesus stepped into the water, and John, however reluctantly, baptized Him.

Then the appearance of the Trinity! The Spirit as a dove, the voice of the Father, Jesus, Son of God, manifesting themselves to all who were present! The announcement of the Father is all important. "This is My beloved Son, in whom I am well pleased." The relation of the Father's announcement to the fulfillment of all righteousness is crucial to understanding Jesus' baptism. Sonship grants privileges and imposes purpose. Jesus, as Son, will have immediate access to the Father—to His house and His heart. But He will be at the Father's disposal, bound by His Sonship to do the Father's will—in this case to "fulfill all righteousness," or, more specifically, to interpose Himself between the "wrath to come" and the sinful world. No wonder God, who "so loved the world" that He was not willing that any should perish, was pleased to make the announcement and pleased as well with His Son who in His baptism had accepted Sonship with attendant privileges and responsibilities. "*This* is My beloved Son" (as opposed to Mark and Luke who record the Voice as saying *"You"*) is Matthew's way of announcing to the world who this Jesus is.

Jesus did not need Baptism. He was the sinless Son of God. Yet He deigns to be baptized with John's baptism of repentance, that He might identify Himself with all of humanity. By this opening act of His ministry He is proclaiming His oneness with all people. He thus makes Himself sinner with us. As sinner He, too, would have to face the wrath to come. As sinner He would endure the wrath of God for all sinners' sakes. He would place Himself under the very judgment of the Father in all sinners' stead, and suffer the terrible and terrifying sentence pronounced against them. Thus He will save mankind from perdition and make possible a citizenry for heaven.

We must understand the nature of Jesus' involvement in our humanity as He steps into the Jordan. In the play *The Deputy* by Rolf Hochhuth, a young priest discovers the truth about the Jewish extermination camps. He makes it his mission to stop the awful orders that set and are keeping in motion the slow extermination of a whole people. He appeals to everyone in authority, finally even to the pope, but all turn a deaf ear to him or plead excuses that remove them from any responsibility. When all avenues of protest have been exhausted, the hero of the play sews the identifying six-pointed star on his sleeve and presents himself at an extermination camp, where he moves to the ovens with the people whose cause he had taken on himself. So Jesus, being baptized by John, identifies Himself with sinners. He will accept their punishment, their death. Unlike Hochhuth's hero, Jesus will go into His death that all sinners could have life, and have it more abundantly.

Jesus' baptism at the Jordan set Him on a course that would not be completed until He had survived the Passion. The Jordan baptism necessitated His suffering under the judgment of the Father and could not be separated from the cross. Later He spoke of His baptism on several occasions as the suffering He would experience in Jerusalem. The purpose of His Sonship, the fulfilling of all righteousness, the will of the Father to redeem Himself a people, was never far from His mind.

So the Jordan event becomes the official beginning, the "ordination" as it were, of Jesus for His mission. There are other words we could use. It is His "Christing," that is, His anointing, to be our Prophet, Priest, and King. It is the moment of His commissioning in a public place, for all the world to know. From this moment on He will be about the Father's business, doing the Father's will, fulfilling the Father's plan for the world's redemption. He will be the Son of God and a Man in mission.

The Purpose: Our Baptism

When Jesus' mission had been accomplished—when all righteousness had been fulfilled and the wall of partition between people and God had been broken down—on the Mount of Ascension Jesus gave mandate to teach and baptize all nations. Pentecost saw 3,000 people baptized. Baptism for them meant son- and daughtership. It meant they had access to the Father, and that they had accepted the responsibility of their adoption into the Father's family. Their baptism brought forgiveness from the sin in which they were born and from their sins of ommission and commission. By their baptism they were grafted into the body of Christ, that is, they became members of the communion of saints, of the new and holy Christian church. They were ordained, as it were, into the royal priesthood with its privileges of the Father's house and with the responsibility of being at the Father's disposal. They were people on a mission with the mandate to preach the Gospel of repentance and faith in Christ and to baptize into His Kingdom.

They went out, those sons and daughters of the King, in obedience and in joy. Their mission took them across streets, across nations, across continents, across time—until in a quiet, wondrous moment they came to you. The water and the Word of baptism conveyed to you the great blessings and the same responsibility that all who are baptized are given. You, in Baptism, had "the washing of regeneration and renewing in the Holy Spirit." You received the Holy Spirit. You were received into the community of believers. You were ordained into the royal priesthood. You, like Jesus, were given a commission and mission that would maintain the kingdom of God and push back its boundaries.

Jesus' baptism led to His cross and death—and resurrection. Your baptism identifies you with Christ—who identified Himself with you. With Him, in Him, in Baptism, you died and were buried; you were quickened; you rose to newness of life. His baptism led Him under the judgment, the wrath, of God. Yours leads to the mansions. The same Spirit who led Jesus leads and blesses, guides and sustains you. Do not discount the wonder, the miracle, of your baptism; do not ignore the responsibility it has placed upon you.

The Purpose: If Only . . .

The celebration of the Epiphany, the story of the presentation of the Christ to the Wise Men and to the world, is over. In these Sundays following the Epiphany the church stresses the twentieth-century epiphany—the presentation of Christ to our world through evangelism and mission. It is these aspects of the Church's responsibility that we will speak in the weeks that lie ahead. It will be our purpose to speak of the various aspects and involvements of God's people in the evangelizing and "christing" of the church in the world. If Baptism is ordination to the priesthood, to mission, then this text and the kind of thinking we have been doing this morning summons us without harsh transition to think a moment or two on some aspects of the Church's mission as a prelude to the Sundays that will follow.

The gifts of the Holy Spirit are varied. Some are given a gift that enables them to acquire new languages; some can preach, others teach. Some receive willingness or time, patience or courage. All, under the Holy Spirit, can be bent to the Father's will and purposes. If only we would let the Spirit lead. If only we would follow. Some do, and they are working for the kingdom in foreign lands. They are the vanguard of the church, taking Christ to old and new mission stations around the globe. They learn new languages, endure hardships, keep books, fly airplanes, work shortwave sets—whatever is required of them to make disciples of and baptize the nations. Many are a backup at home, contributing, publicizing, praying, and encouraging their fellow Christians in far off lands.

Many are in mission in our own land. To some is given the wondrous patience to work with the mentally and physically handicapped. There are Sunday schools for the mentally retarded in many churches. Materials for teaching are produced by our own synodical Board for Parish Services. Men enlist for the chaplaincy in our armed forces. Men and women serve in our hospitals and correctional institutions. Others find opportunities for service in homes for the aged and in mission activities in the inner city. Some serve the deaf, bringing the Gospel to them in sign language. Others sit tedious hous making little raised dots on special paper for the benefit of the blind.

Many Christian people are involved in "bringing Christ to the nations" via radio and presenting Him to them through television. Others have expanded their vision and find their mission in collecting mites, saving stamps, clipping coupons—in order to advance the cause of the King. And we haven't even mentioned the teachers of the Sunday schools, the day schools, the high schools, and the colleges. We haven't touched on those who have been called into the holy ministry from this parish (area), or the young women who have become deaconesses to serve the Lord.

To each of us, because the Christ is in us, has been given the gift of loving and caring, precious to those who need our care. Who of us cannot speak a word of comfort to someone in distress, or the saving Word to some troubled conscience? Who of us has no reason to smile when Christ and the Spirit are in us? The King's great speech in the parable of the Last Judgment—"I was hungry . . . in prison . . . naked . . . persecuted"—has set goals for those who respond to Christ and live out their baptismal mission.

If only every one brought one soul to Christ in a year—in a decade—simple mathematics tells us if no one is brought to Christ, the Christian church could disappear from the face of the earth in a single generation! If only . . .

The End Result

Our creeds have nobly embodied the results of Jesus' baptism (remembering that His baptism includes the Jordan waters and the cross). The ancient creed fragment quoted in Philippians (2:9-10 KJV) confessed: "Wherefore God also hath highly exalted Him and given Him a name which is above every name, that at the name of Jesus every knee should bow . . . ." In the ecumenical creeds we confess our belief that "the third day He rose again . . . . and sits at the right hand of the Father." When His mission was completed, Christ returned in radiant splendor to His throne in glory.

But mankind has been the recipient of forgiveness, faith, and new life in Christ. Out of mankind has come a faithful community of believers in Christ—His body, His bride, the church. While the church as we see it may be pockmarked and ailing, but *the* church, the communion of saints, called together by the Holy Spirit, is nothing less than perfect, a bride fit for the holy Bridegroom. The church is the joy of Christ. It was made possible by the shedding of His holy precious blood and by His innocent suffering and death. It is His prized possession.

We are in the church by the power of the Spirit. By our baptism into Christ we were placed into it—and the heavens rejoiced. We were set into mission to the world for our three score years and ten. When at last the divine summons comes for us to cross the deep abyss, we, by virtue of our baptismal faith, will join the ranks of saints and angels to sing the songs of eternity. Do not discount that solemn yet glorious moment of your baptism when the blessed Trinity came to you, gave you the guarantee of the Holy Spirit, and claimed you for eternity.

When the record of our Lord's baptism is heard again, think of these things. In fact, why don't we read it again, remembering these great truths about our Lord and about ourselves. (Reread text.)

Evangelism Is a Pod of Ps

SECOND SUNDAY AFTER THE EPIPHANY
JOHN 1:29-41

Oscar A. Gerken

One of the disadvantages of prepackaged and frozen foods is that we no longer experience the satisfaction of growing, harvesting, and preparing the vegetables we eat. I remember especially the joy of prying a pea pod open with my thumbnails and watching the peas spill out into the pan. I thought of this childhood experience as I began to prepare this sermon, for the text illustrates the two types of evangelism still in use in the church today, the minister's sermon and the hearers' witness; for me they form a delightful (please pardon the pun) pod of Ps.

First, we read in our text about the ministry of John, which I like to describe as "Public Professional Preaching"; and then we are given an example of "Private Personal Proclamation" by one of John's hearers, Andrew. We have, then, the pod of P s we summarize with the word "evangelism":

1. Public Professional Preaching
2. Private Personal Proclamation

I. Public Professional Preaching

To begin, I'd better deal with the objection in your mind to my reference to John as a professional. According to the dictionary, the word *professional* pertains to a profession, and the word *profession* means "the occupation to which one devotes oneself, a calling." According to this, John the Baptizer was a professional even though he received no pay, for he devoted his life to the preaching of God's message.

Before John was born, the angel Gabriel spelled out John's profession by telling his father that his "miracle baby" would "make ready a people prepared for the Lord" (Luke 1:17). John himself summarizes his mission in life by saying in our text, "I came baptizing with water, that [Jesus] might be revealed to Israel." Yes, John was a professional preacher! He dedicated his life to getting people ready for Jesus.

The public preaching of John was evangelism in its purest form, for the climax of his brief ministry is summed up in the *evangel,* the good news, he voices twice in our text. After telling his opponents on the previous day that he was the messenger of the Christ, John calls the attention of his followers to Jesus by declaring, "Look, the Lamb of God, who takes away the sin of the world!" And a day later, John repeats this wonderful witness to Andrew and another disciple: "Look, the Lamb of God!"

By referring to Jesus as "the Lamb of God," John was telling his followers that Jesus was the promised Rescuer, the only One who could free them from the eternal consequences of their sinfulness. John was echoing the evangel found in the well-known 53rd chapter of Isaiah which describes the Messiah as one who was led like "a lamb to the slaughter" (Is. 53:7). Later, preachers Paul and Peter would use the same figure of speech in referring to Jesus as "our Passover lamb" (I Cor. 5:7) and reminding us: ". . . you were redeemed . . . with the precious blood of Christ, a lamb without blemish or defect" (1 Peter 1:18-19).

Some Bible students do not believe that John was always as confident about the truth of his message as we generally think, and they document this view by citing the incident of John's sending his disciples to Jesus with the question, "Are you the one who was to come, or should we expect someone else?" (Matt. 11:3) and the fact that John says twice in our text: "I myself did not know him."

Others believe that John was a good psychologist and sent his followers to Jesus with a question about His messiahship because he knew they would be convinced by their contact with Jesus. Those who lean toward this interpretation (and I must confess I am among them) regard John's declaration in our text, "I myself did not know him," as John's way of saying that his listeners should not accept this testimony as John's, but as the testimony God had given to John to be passed on to them. Thus, John declares in our text, "I saw the Spirit come down from heaven as a dove and remain on him. I would not have known him, except that the one who sent me to baptize with water told me, 'The man on whom you see the Spirit come down and remain is he who will baptize with the Holy Spirit.' I have seen and I testify that this is the Son of God."

Regardless of which interpretation we prefer, there certainly was no doubt in John's mind as he spoke these words. He *knew* that Jesus was the eternal God come to rescue mankind. Not once, but twice in this chapter the baptizer says that Jesus was "before" him (vv. 15 & 30), that—as the evangelist John says in the initial words of this book—"In the beginning was the Word." Jesus, *the* Son of God, existed already when time began!

This evangel about the Lamb of God who removes all our sins by His perfect life, substitutionary death, and triumphant resurrection is still the message heard from countless Christian pulpits. "We Preach Christ Crucified," the well-known Lutheran Hour slogan, is still by the grace of God a true description of our congregation and Synod. And that's essential, for this Lamb of God is the only One in whom and through whom we can receive forgiveness and life.

I'll never forget the first words the sainted Dr. John Fritz spoke to our class in our first session with him at the seminary. The course was homiletics, a course in preaching, and Dean Fritz's words of greeting to our class were "Gentlemen, I'm here to teach you how to preach, and the one thing I don't want you to ever forget is 'Preach the Gospel!' If you don't preach the Gospel, your congregations don't need you; they can go to hell without you!"

That's why John told two of his followers, "Look, the Lamb of God!" Those two didn't wind up in hell, for we read, "When the two disciples heard him say this, they followed Jesus." They were on the road to heaven. John's "Public Professional Preaching" had been successful!

II. Private Personal Proclamation

The other half of our evangelism pod of Ps described in our text can be referred to as "Private Personal Proclamation." I realize that Andrew and the other one who followed Jesus (probably John the Evangelist) both became professionals in the same sense that the baptizer was a professional—they also devoted all of their energies to being public witnesses to the Gospel.

But at this point they were still uneducated fishermen from Galilee. Andrew worked with his brother, Simon Peter, and John was associated in the fishing business with his father Zebedee and brother James. They probably did not give up their fishing business until a year or so later (we'll talk about that next week), and during this period combined their fishing with following Jesus. Thus, they were laymen in our modern sense of the word.

What was the first thing Andrew did after John told him that Jesus was the Lamb of God who rescues from sin? Our text answers, "The first thing Andrew did was to find his brother Simon and tell him, 'We have found the Messiah.'" Notice that word "first"! Andrew didn't waste any time. He wanted to share this good news with someone he cared about, his brother Simon. That took priority over everything else, and we can sense Andrew's urgency and excitement in John's record of his witness to Peter.

Notice also that there's nothing fancy or involved in Andrew's witness for Jesus. He and John had stayed overnight with Jesus and had undoubtedly listened for many hours to Christ's words of deliverance. There was no doubt in their minds that Jesus was the promised Savior. That's what the Hebrew word "Messiah" and the Greek title "Christ" mean. Literally, both words mean "the anointed one" and focus attention upon this Old Testament ritual. When a person began an important work, a costly perfume or oil was poured over his head (Remember that Samuel anointed David to be king?) as a symbol of God's power to fulfill his mission. Therefore, when Andrew told his brother that he had found the Messiah, he was telling Peter that Jesus was the promised Savior.

Andrew's simple witness, "We have found the Messiah," was blessed by the Lord, for the words immediately following today's Gospel go on to say, "He brought Simon to Jesus." Just five simple words, and yet they tell a glorious fact. Little is said about Andrew in the Bible. He alone of the two sets of brothers—Andrew and Peter, James and John—was not one of Christ's intimate inner circle. We repeatedly read that Jesus took Peter, James, and John with him, Andrew wasn't included.

And yet Andrew is the one who was responsible for Peter's becoming an apostle of the Lord Jesus. Andrew was no theological giant. When Jesus confronted his associates with the problem of a hungry crowd prior to the feeding of the 5,000, Andrew could only say that there was a little boy with five loaves of bread and two fish (John 6:9). He didn't have the answer. But Andrew was interested in people, and it's significant that Philip on a later ocasion told Andrew about some Greeks who wanted to see Jesus, and Andrew was the one who brought them also to the Savior (John 12:22). Andrew wasn't a great leader, but he cared about people enough to give his private witness in his personal life.

We can learn from Andrew to simply tell people that we have found the Savior. If nothing else, we can tell them that our faith is centered around the truth Jesus Himself expressed and which we memorized long ago, that "God so loved the world that he gave his one and only Son, that whoever believes in him shall not perish but have eternal life" (John 3:16).

Mary was, as she herself put it, "just a housewife." That, however, is a great understatement, for Mary knew Jesus as her Savior and, like Andrew, couldn't help but speak about her joy in Christ. It wasn't long before the neighbors who lived on both sides of her, and also a family down the street, were brought to church by Mary and learned to know their Savior.

George was a retired businessman who had been a nominal member of a Christian church. Then something happened, and George not only spoke about Jesus but gave generously of his time to help anyone who needed help. It wasn't so much what he said, but the way he lived, that prompted his friends and acquaintances to take a long look at the ministry of George's church.

Krista was a teenager, and her joy and enthusiasm radiated in her face as she told her family that she had gotten a part-time job at a local fast-foods restaurant. Her parents were happy to hear that Krista gave such a witness at work that her fellow workers began to watch their language when they worked with Krista. And the icing on the cake was provided when her unchurched boss got in touch with Krista's pastor to find out what the church believed and taught. He and his wife eventually joined that congregation.

These are just three of many true stories from the lives of God's people which demonstrate that powerful sermons are proclaimed in the private personal lives of God's people as well as in our Christian pulpits.

Yes, evangelism is a pod of Ps, and these Ps are "Public Proessional Preaching" and "Private Personal Proclamation."

To God alone be all glory!

Let's Go Fishing!

THIRD SUNDAY AFTER THE EPIPHANY
MATTHEW 4:12-23

Oscar A. Gerken

Today's Gospel describes the call to discipleship extended by Jesus to two sets of brothers—Peter and Andrew, James and John. Actually, this was the second time Jesus called them. The first call, which we discussed last Sunday, is narrated in the first chapter of John's gospel and took place perhaps as much as 18 months prior to the call described in our text.

John the Baptizer was now in prison, and Jesus had returned to Capernaum to put His ministry into high gear. This narrative indicates that during the previous year and a half Jesus had not done any extensive preaching, for it states, "From that time on Jesus began to preach, 'Repent, for the kingdom of heaven is near.'"

Much had happened during those first 18 months of "low intensity ministry." The first miracle at Cana, the first cleansing of the temple, an interview with Nicodemus, the encounter with the Samaritan woman at Jacob's well, the healing of the nobleman's son at Capernaum, a second trip to Jerusalem, the healing of the lame man at the Pool of Bethesda, His rejection at Nazareth and the move to Capernaum—all this had taken place since the first call we studied last Sunday.

Evidently Jesus had permitted His disciples to combine their discipleship with their fishing business or had excused them to go back to their nets, for we read, "As Jesus was walking beside the Sea of Galilee, he saw two brothers, Simon called Peter and his brother Andrew. They were casting a net into the lake, for they were fishermen." Then Matthew reports, "Going on from there, he saw two other brothers, James son of Zebedee and his brother John. They were in a boat with their father Zebedee, preparing their nets."

These four Galilean fishermen were summoned to discipleship. What was this call all about? What was involved in following Jesus? What is the application and meaning of this call for us today? Let's take a look at the call and the challenge it presents.

I. THE CALL

The call itself is simple and direct. Jesus merely said, "Follow

Me!" Luke gives us a more extensive description of the event by reporting a miraculous catch of fish which immediately preceded the call. He reports that Peter's response to that miracle was to fall down at Jesus' feet and exclaim, "Go away from me, Lord; I am a sinful man!" (Luke 5:8). We're not told what else Jesus said to Peter and the other three, but it's reasonable to assume that He told them why they didn't have to be afraid, for He was "preaching the good news of the kingdom."

Jesus frequently spoke of His kingdom and told many parables to illustrate the good news that we do not have to be afraid because God has provided forgiveness and life through His Son. Although all four men Jesus called to discipleship often failed miserably to comprehend and confess "the good news of the kingdom," they did grow in their discipleship. Peter learned to confess with enthusiasm, "You are the Christ, the Son of the living God" (Matt. 16:16). And John was led to write near the end of his narrative of Jesus' life, "These are written that you may believe that Jesus is the Christ, the Son of God, and that by believing you may have life in his name" (John 20:31).

Jesus has also called us to follow Him. For most of us, this took place when we were baptized in infancy. Although we were not fully aware of what was taking place, the Holy Spirit through Baptism began His work in us, bringing us to trust in Jesus as our Savior and teaching us to rejoice in the life salvation God freely gives in His son. We followed Jesus as we learned to lisp our childhood prayers, as we were reminded of God's love by our parents, as we attended Sunday school and perhaps a Christian day school, as we grew spiritually as well as physically. For others, this call came later in life as we heard the invitation of Jesus, "Come to me, all you who are weary and burdened, and I will give you rest" (Matt. 11:28).

Whether we began to follow Jesus as infants or later in life, we are here this morning because we have learned to know and appreciate the love, forgiveness, and life God gives us in Jesus Christ. Jesus was speaking of this when He said, "My sheep listen to my voice . . . and they follow me" (John 10:27).

A woman was anxious and afraid as she lay in the hospital bed and talked about her illness with her pastor. And yet it wasn't her illness that bothered her most; it was the feeling of guilt that haunted her as she remembered her past. "Does God love and forgive me, pastor, in spite of what I've done?" she asked. To this the pastor quietly responded, "Now you're beginning to understand what the Gospel is all about. Neither you nor I deserve it, but God still loves, forgives, heals, and gives life."

This is the call Jesus extended to Peter and Andrew, James and John, for today's Gospel concludes, "Jesus went throughout

Galilee, teaching in their synagogues, preaching the good news of the kingdom, and healing every disease and sickness among the people."

II. The Challenge

Although discipleship begins with following Jesus, it doesn't end there, for Jesus adds the following challenge to His call: "I will make you fishers of men." This is an interesting figure of speech, for fishing requires commitment and concentration. Jesus expected these fishermen to demonstrate to demonstrate the same intensity in fishing for people as they had in fishing for fish. They were to follow Him and learn from Him how to use the bait of the Gospel in rescuing people.

Notice that the challenge Jesus attaches to the call is to be *fishers* of men, not *catchers* of men. We speak and worry too much about winning souls for Christ and tend to forget that we cannot make Christians of anyone; the Holy Spirit alone can convert people by creating faith. It's true that Luke reports in his account that Jesus told Peter, "From now on you will catch men" (Luke 5:10), but the catching was not Peter's responsibility or accomplishment. Peter himself was quick to point out, when he healed the lame man in the temple (cf. Acts 3:12-16), that the power and credit was God's.

This period of the church year is traditionally the time when Jesus' fishing challenge is emphasized. The Epiphany season stresses that Jesus is the almighty God and the Savior of all people. Jan. 25 is observed in the liturgical calendar as "The Conversion of St. Paul." All too often, however, we speak of evangelism *results* rather than of the evangelism *process*—the matter of witnessing, of sharing our joy in Christ, of fishing for people.

Maybe I can express best what happens with a humorous story I read several years ago. A minister was asked how many active members there were in his 1,000-member congregation. Without hesitating, he replied, "I have 1,000 active members. About 200 are active for the Lord, and the other 800 are active for Satan." Although all of us, as disciples of Jesus, are to fish for people, we sometimes are so concerned about what might or might not happen when we witness that we "cop out" and let someone else do the witnessing.

Actually, we can't help witnessing, but our witness may be a negative witness which repels rather than attracts people to the Gospel. That problem existed in the Corinthian congregation. St. Paul discusses it in today's Epistle (1 Cor. 1:10-17). He had organized the congregation and spent 18 months as pastor in Corinth (cf. Acts 18:11). He was succeeded by Apollos, a young man, and soon the congregation was dividing into factions. Some declared themselves still faithful to "Pastor Paul" while others preferred younger Apollos and still others wanted Cephas (another name for Peter) to come and straighten out the problem. Added to this was a fourth faction which had no use for preachers and recognized only Jesus Christ.

Does this sound familiar? It reminds me of the time a member of my congregation told me of eating in a restaurant in another city and hearing the people at the next table lamenting loudly the funds spent in a building program in their Lutheran congregation. The individual who told me about this commented, "I didn't feel like going to that church."

Our fishing doesn't have to be a polished presentation. One of our hymns expresses it very well by saying:

> If you cannot speak like angels,
> If you cannot preach like Paul,
> You can tell the love of Jesus;
> You can say he died for all. (*LW* 318)

And our fishing may not be verbal. In His sermon on the mount Jesus admonished, "Let your light shine before men, that they may see your good deeds and praise your Father in heaven" (Matt. 5:16). Often people tell pastors they were attracted to the church by the attitudes and lives of church members, and I'll never forget the new church member who told me a number of years ago in Michigan, "Every Sunday during this past winter, my neighbor would get up early and shovel the snow out of his driveway so he and his family could go to church. I decided to find out what's so important here to make him do that."

The same call to discipleship Jesus spoke to these four fishermen by the Sea of Galilee still sounds today through the Gospel. It is, first of all, a call to follow Him, to listen to His Word, to trust in Him for forgiveness and life, to build our lives around the Gospel. But it is also a challenge to proclaim this good news by word, by attitude, by actions, by our lives—to be fishers of men.

Let's go fishing!

Blessed by the Beatitudes

FOURTH SUNDAY AFTER THE EPIPHANY
MATTHEW 5:1-12

Richard G. Kapfer

Today we consider the opening words that Jesus spoke in His Sermon on the Mount: "Now when he saw the crowds, he went up on a mountainside and sat down. His disciples came to him, and he began to teach them." Then He shared the Beatitudes, the "blesseds," with His disciples.

Don't let the quiet of this scene dominate too much. Don't let the words of beauty—and the Beatitudes *are* beautiful—lull you into a romantic never-never land where you "dream the impossible dream." Don't let the lofty goals expressed become so lofty that they never land in the place where you live.

In many ways the Beatitudes are the most misunderstood, misapplied words in Scripture. If they are read wrongly by the unwary, they suddenly snap shut on our unbelief with the strong jaws of God's unrelenting law. If they are romanticized into a pretty slogan appropriate for a wall poster, they suddenly leap from the page and engage us in battle over who we are and who God is.

But if they are read rightly and understood through the eyes of humble faith, they describe the life of blessedness that God has already bestowed on us, His beloved children.

I. The Beatitudes: A Trap for Self-Righteousness

If we read only the words of the Beatitudes, they appear to present a simple formula, the formula of "If-Then." *If* you are poor in spirit, *then* yours is the kingdom of heaven; *if* you are meek, *then* you shall inherit the earth; *if* you are pure in heart, *then* you will see God.

With that reading the Christian faith becomes a religion of payoffs. "God, this morning I was really humble and contrite and sorry. Just look at my face! Now will You give me what I'm asking for?" "God, I pray each day; I study hard; I'm so humble that I could author the book *Humility and How I Achieved It.* Now will you give me an 'A' on the exam?" "God, I thank Thee that I am not like others—proud, happy, overbearing, rich. Most of the time I am actually quite miserable. But I have the kingdom, don't I?"

We may not be as crass as this, but the fact is that often we live the Christian life grudgingly, but with the goal in mind of getting a payoff from God. *If* I do these things, *then* I'll be blessed by God.

It is at that point that the words suddenly snap closed on us, for Jesus told His disciples how they were to keep these and all other words and commands of God. "Be perfect, therefore, as your heavenly Father is perfect" (Matt. 5:48). The words are no longer words of blessing, but words that curse. The "If-Then" formula condemns us, for no one can live by that formula.

II. The Beatitudes: Fighting Words

At least if we read the Beatitudes as a formula, we take them seriously. Although they can trap us, we are only a step removed from their blessing, as we shall see. But if we read them as mere suggestions, frosting on the cake, or romantic slogans to adorn the outward Christian life, we are really in worse shape. We aren't being honest with ourselves or with God.

If the Beatitudes are just slogans placed into a religious compartment and stored away, as nice sayings usually are, then a person is trying to live in two worlds. One is the world of Sunday religion, a spiritual, nonpractical world that doesn't really happen, and the other is the real world where the practice is "Blessed are the rich in things, for their is the prosperity. Blessed are the ones who laugh and seek pleasure, for they will always be happy. Blessed are the proud, for they are the movers and shakers. Blessed are those who hunger and thirst for more at any cost, for they shall succeed. Blessed are the powerful, for they will never need anything from anyone. Blessed are the impure in heart, for they will keep one step ahead of everyone else. Blessed are the warriors, for they are the winners."

That is clearly the choice in the Beatitudes as Jesus gave them—either be blessed by the world's standards or be blessed by the Lord. A war is being waged between the Preacher of the Beatitudes and the world and its promised blessings. The Beatitudes, then, are fighting words. They have to do with attitudes, with our style of life, with the way we live. It is a war against the proud, against the self-idolators, against the forces of evil that bless sin and rebellion against God.

III. The Beatitudes: Where God Can Break Through

In either case, when the Beatitudes are misread or misapplied, they lead us to a sense of helplessness. That is Point 1 for understanding the Beatitudes. *They are meant for those who know they are helpless!* By helpless, we should not substitute "faint-hearted," "cowardly," "weak," as in saying, "If you become fainthearted, cowardly, and weak, then you will be able to do the Beatitudes and be blessed for it." Rather, the Beatitudes are meant for those who know they are helpless, and, Point 2, *they know where their Help is!* Then and only then do the Beatitudes become blessings.

The witness of the New Testament is that the Preacher who speaks the Beatitudes *is* the Beatitude. He is the poor in spirit. He is the one who mourns for the earth. He is the meek and humble Jesus of Nazareth, God's Son in the flesh. He is the one who hungers and thirsts for righteousness, for only as He fulfills all righteousness as our Substitute can we be blessed. He is the merciful one, for only by God's mercy can sin be forgiven and conquered. He is the pure in heart who is holy, perfect, and without blemish. He is the Peacemaker who brings peace with God. He is the persecuted one.

Persecution and death—that is the outcome of the Beatitudes, of facing the chanters of the devil's beatitudes. That is where the war ends—at a cross, where Jesus is despised, mocked, forsaken.

Under the cross we cannot help but call out, "This is the blessed life? This is where it all ends? This is the outcome of the Beatitudes, with Jesus hanging on a cursed cross of shame and defeat?"

No, this is where the Beatitudes begin! Rising out of an empty tomb a blessed victory song is sung: "He is risen! He rules! He has obtained the victory! He has won the battle! He awaits the blessed ones in heaven, and He is with them always!"

At the tomb of victory we realize that the Preacher on the mountain was not a mere teacher who spoke fine words. He is the Word, the Savior, who spoke and acted for our blessing that we might receive the Beatitude, Himself! Through Him we receive every blessing.

The Beatitudes are the promises of the Kingdom, and they are ours already now. Blessed is the person who knows and believes this! Happy and content in the deepest sense is the person who lives under God's blessings!

The Beatitudes describe the life of those who have life in Jesus' name. They are not perfect yet. The battle over the Beatitudes still rages. But the battle that we face daily is over the first part of each Beatitude: "the poor in spirit," "those who mourn," "the meek," "those who hunger and thirst for righteousness," "the merciful," "the pure in heart," "the peacemakers," and "those who are persecuted because of righteousness." The battle is one that we fight in the Spirit each day. It is fought every time we are confronted with the seemingly more attractive and immediate blessings that the world offers—promises that run counter to the will of God and the example of Jesus.

It is fought by the mother who wonders where the blessings are in doing the tasks of running a home, perhaps in addition to working at a job eight hours each day. No one in her family seems to appreciate her work or consider her a blessing, except perhaps on Mother's Day. Yet she is one of those who are blessed now!

It is fought by the teenager who must somehow deal with the pressures and expectations of his friends alongside the expectations of his parents and church and God. It isn't easy, and his friends will not "bless" him for unpopular choices. Yet he is one of those who are blessed now!

Blessed now? Yes, for the second part of each Beatitude is ours now, and that makes all the difference. By faith in Jesus Christ we are blessed now. Our is the Kingdom and the comfort and the inheritance and Christ's righteousness now. Ours is the mercy and sonship and, in God's good time, the blessed event of seeing God.

The Preacher did not speak the Beatitudes apart from His mission that took Him to the cross. He spoke them *because* of His mission. Now He steps into the middle of each Beatitude with the word of blessing: "Be faithful, even to the point of death, and I will give you the crown of life" (Rev. 2:10). We can *live* the Beatitudes now, for we *have* the Beatitudes now! You are a beatitude of life!

To this the blessed ones can only respond in gladness, "Amen! Blessing and glory and wisdom and thanksgiving and honor and power and might be to our God forever and ever! Amen."

"The Standouts"

FIFTH SUNDAY AFTER THE EPIPHANY
MATTHEW 5:13-20

John D. Fritz

Sticks and stones may break my bones, but names will never hurt me!

Have you ever noticed that there is a tremendous amount of name-calling in the Bible? But name-calling in the Bible is completely different from the kind of put-down name-calling we experience from childhood on. When God calls us names, He does it for the purpose of building up, not tearing down. He does it for the purpose of encouraging and strengthening and comforting. He does it to show us how much He loves us, how important we are to Him. So He calls us a "chosen people, a royal priesthood, a holy nation, a people belonging to God" (1 Peter 2:9), and He does that to let us know we are what we are so we can witness our salvation to other people. In that way we praise Him for His grace to us in Jesus.

The Salt of the Earth

In today's Gospel selection Jesus is doing some name-calling in order to let His disciples and us know what our chief functions are in this world. "You are the salt of the earth," said Jesus. "But if the salt loses its saltiness, how can it be made salty again? It is no longer good for anything, except to be throw out and trampled by men" (Matt. 5:13).

Although all of us are well acquainted with salt, there are a number of things we might find profitable to remember in order to see the meaning of the term for our own lives. First, we ought remember that salt occurs universally under varying conditions. It is found in solution in all ocean water; it is distributed also throughout many rivers and inland lakes and seas, the concentration varying from .002 percent in the Mississippi River to 12 percent in the Great Salt Lake in Utah. Salt occurs in the form of a surface crust or layer in swamps and dry lake bottoms, especially in arid regions.

Salt has been important to man as a seasoning and preserving agent since prehistoric times. It was commonly used in the altar offerings of the ancient Greeks and Romans, as well as the Hebrews. It was an important medium of exchange in commercial ventures throughout the Mediterranean area. Because of its usefulness in preserving foods, it was used by the ancients as a symbol of enduring faith. In the form of salt cakes, it served as money in ancient Ethiopia and Tibet. The English word *salary* formerly represented a soldier's money allowance for salt. It was derived from the Latin word *salarium,* the term denoting the salt allotment issued to soldiers in the ancient Roman army. So a phrase has been handed down to us that means a person is really earning the money he makes. We say, "He is really worth his salt."

Salt has four main qualities. It is white and pure; it prevents rapid decay; it preserves food; and it renders the food palatable. But it can lose its saltiness. That was particularly true of salt in the Holy Land which underwent a chemical change, either by being exposed to rain or being stored for some length of time. A certain bituminous salt found in Judea very rapidly became flat and tasteless. It was then used in the court of the temple in wet weather to prevent worshipers from slipping and falling.

Christians are the salt of the earth, said Jesus. Their business is to counteract the moral rot and spiritual decay so prevalent in the world. We do not have far to look to see the rottenness and decay. Our daily papers, our newscasts, and our monthly magazines bring us reports of murder, rape, adultery, graft, robbery, and slander. The producers of movies and television tell us that the open portrayal of adultery and fornication, violence and homosexuality, is exactly what the public wants. In offices, in factories, in restaurants, in places of education, in stores, and even on elementary school playgrounds the name of God is used in vain in the form of cursing and frivolous swearing. Cartoon characters in comic strips frequently lampoon the Christian stand on moral issues in our time. And all of that is only a brief glimpse of the seamy side of our so-called "Christian America" and should suffice to depict the rottenness and decay of our civilization in the sight of God.

To preserve the world, God has distributed Christians as universally as salt. We are to be an influence for good. Having experienced the cleansing power of the Gospel, we are to live a Christian life in the midst of a perverse and crooked generation. Redeemed from sin through our Lord Jesus Christ, we want to influence others so they too may believe and be saved. We strive to set an example of Christian morality and living in our homes, in our businesses, in our schools, and in our recreation.

If we don't do that, we are salt that has lost its taste. Insipid, saltless salt is really a contradiction in terms. Christians who have lost their distinctive Christian character and attitudes will cease to influence their surroundings for good. They no longer live as disciples. Just as savorless salt has no value and is treated as refuse, so Christians who have ceased to fulfill their role of acting as a moral power in the world, will cease to be of any value to God.

Not only are Christians the salt of the earth, but, Jesus says, they are also

The Light of the World

With this picture Jesus is teaching us the same truth He did with the salt. He is giving the same admonition.

Strictly speaking, Christ is the only true Light of the world. It is through Him that we learn of God's love to us in the high price Jesus paid—His life, His suffering and death on the cross—to redeem us. In His teaching we learn God's will for us and see clearly the way back to the Father through Christ. In the light which Christ gives we become changed persons. And as changed persons we have power from Him to give light to others. As our Christian faith works, people will hear of Him from our lips and see Him in our lives.

"A city on a hill cannot be hidden. Neither do people light a lamp and put it under a bowl. Instead they put it on its stand, and it gives light to everyone in the house."

Notice that Jesus said we are the light of the world, not just of the immediate neighborhood. To emphasize that, Jesus refers to something well known to His hearers. Many cities of the Holy Land were located on the tops of hills and mountains. Some of them were probably visible from the place where he had gathered with the disciples. Those who heard Him that day were certainly acquainted with Mount Zion. Cities situated on hilltops or mountaintops would not be hidden. They were the most conspicuous objects in the entire landscape.

Christians, by virtue of their discipleship, are like such a city. Their faith makes them different people—different in motivation, different in opinion, different in goals, different in life-style. And being different makes Christians marked people—standouts. That is as it should be. It agrees with the nature and the object of our calling as His disciples.

To light a lamp and put it under an overturned measuring device—here an earthenware bowl holding a little more than a peck—made no sense at all. One lit a lamp to put it on a stand. Maybe the lampstand was just a stone sticking out of the wall in the house, or a lampstand in the form of a tripod which could easily be moved from room to room. But the lamp went on the stand to give light to the people in the house. That's how the light fulfilled its purpose.

It's the same with us Christians. Jesus Himself applies the conclusion: "Let your light shine before men, that they may see your good deeds and praise your Father in heaven." There is too often a tendency to hide belief and convictions. We generally try to keep our Christian views to ourselves because we fear unpleasant consequences much more than we fear offending someone else. To think and act that way is disloyal to Christ. The light of faith we have is given to us from God to shine. It is to shine, not so that people might admire us, but so that they will eventually come to the conclusion that God is behind the good works, that He is the Power from which the good works flow. And so the glory and the honor will go properly where it should—to the Father in heaven. All glory must be God's. And that will be true in Jesus' life as well, for He will

Fulfill the Law and the Prophets

"Do not think that I have come to abolish the Law or the Prophets; I have not come to abolish them but to fulfill them."

The good works by which the Christian leads others to glorify the Father are done in faith according to God's law. That law, says Jesus, will not change or pass away or be bent in the slightest. So long as the earth stands, not even one iota, the smallest letter of the Hebrew alphabet, nor one little dot, the slight little point on a Hebrew letter which can change the meaning of a word, shall change. Every claim of the Law will be fulfilled by Him. Every punishment of the Law will be borne by Him. Every prophetic utterance and promise of God in the Old Testament prophets will be fulfilled in Him.

Meanwhile, everyone should know that no one abrogates any commandment, no matter how small it might be, without falling under the judgment of God. "Anyone who breaks one of the least of these commandments and teaches others to do the same will be called least in the kingdom of heaven, but whoever practices and teaches these commands will be called great in the kingdom of heaven." Every particle of the Law, every commandment—even the Fifth Commandment which contains only three syllables in Hebrew—must stand as God gave it and be fulfilled perfectly. Those who change the meaning for accommodation to self and who teach others this may be done, will be rejected from the Kingdom. But he who teaches them and lives them in faithful conformity to the Old Testament Scriptures shall receive the reward of faithfulness and be great in the kingdom of heaven.

The scribes and Pharisees of Jesus' time prided themselves on a keeping of the Law, but it was nothing but a slavish observing of externals. They put on a great show of righteousness in the eyes of the people, an impression they were careful to nourish, but it would avail them nothing for entry into the kingdom of heaven. "For I tell you," said Jesus, "that unless your righteousness surpasses that of the Pharisees and the teachers of the law, you will certainly not enter the kingdom of heaven."

Only the righteousness of Christ will do. By faith the Christian accepts and believes and trusts in Christ whose perfect life becomes our righteousness and whose death atones for every sin and makes us holy before God. It is in that faith that the Christian is light and salt for the world. He reflects in his homelife a sacrificial love like Christ's; in his business the honesty and credibility of someone who in his chosen profession serves God and man; in his social life the avoidance of every appearance of evil because of the name of Christ he carries; and in his religious life the faithful worship of the God who through the Word has brought us out of darkness into His marvelous light.

Yes, God has made us standouts—people who by His grace are different, not just in name, but also in life. "You are the salt of the earth and the light of the world." Salt and light, working silently and almost unnoticeably, seem so commonplace. But their influence and usefulness are beyond estimate. God's standouts also work silently and often remain unnoticed, but they exert a tremendous influence for God in the world. God help us be salt! God help us be light!

The Righteousness That Counts Before God

SIXTH SUNDAY AFTER THE EPIPHANY
MATTHEW 5:20-37

John D. Fritz

Mistakes can be fatal. A nurse reached for a bottle of medicine, thinking she had the drug prescribed by the physician, and gave it to her patient. The patient became violently ill. A drug which was harmful to her patient had been placed in a bottle the same size and shape. In her haste she had not read the label.

Mistaken notions about religion can be ever so much more dangerous. Eternity is at stake. Innocent as certain teachings may seem on the surface, they are soul-destroying unless they are prescribed by our Lord Himself. The words of Jesus are a warning about being religious and yet not being saved. "For I tell you," says Jesus, "that unless your righteousness surpasses that of the Pharisees and the teachers of the law, you will certainly not enter the kingdom of heaven." On the basis of those words we need to be clear on the kind of

Righteousness That Counts Before God

Righteousness is another name for blamelessness or holiness. Jesus was speaking to a group of His disciples and was clearly pointing out that their own righteousness or holiness would count for nothing before God. They would not enter into the kingdom of heaven unless their righteousness exceeded that of the scribes and Pharisees.

The Righteousness of Scribes and Pharisees

Scribes were men who made copies of the Scriptures. They also studied the law of Moses and the prophets very thoroughly, interpreted that law for the people, and applied it to everyday life. They were the authorities on historical and doctrinal matters. The highest court among the Jews, the Sanhedrin, counted many of them as members. They insisted on a strict observance of the laws of Moses and were outwardly a highly moral group of religious leaders.

The Pharisees were a sect in the Jewish community whose belief was that God's grace and heaven comes only to such as keep the law of God. They were pillars of morality. They went beyond the letter of the law in keeping feasts and fasts, giving tithes and observing ceremonies. They prided themselves on their religious scrupulousness and clean living and pinned their hopes for eternity on them. They looked with disdain on those they considered less pious and with contempt on Jesus because He ate with common sinners. They derided Jesus with the words, "This man receives sinners and eats with them!"

Of these two groups of Jewish religious leaders Jesus said, "For I tell you that unless your righteousness surpasses that of the Pharisees and the teachers of the law, you will certainly not enter the kingdom of heaven."

What was wrong with the "righteousness" of the scribes and Pharisees? It was a veneer. Jesus looked into their hearts and found them wanting. He called them hypocrites. He called them "white-washed tombs . . . full of dead men's bones." They resembled the tombs on the hillsides of Palestine, many of which were decorated beautifully on the outside, but obviously inside were full of rot and decay.

The Righteousness God Demands

What did the scribes and Pharisees lack? The words of Jesus in the succeeding verses give us a clue. Jesus uses five examples to show how man's own righteousness is faulty. The first is the Fifth Commandment, "Thou shalt not kill." The scribes and Pharisees taught that murder was sin. But Jesus reminds His disciples that God's protection of human life extends not only over physical life, but over the whole of life. Life can be threatened by another's angry thought or sneering word. So Jesus said, "But I tell you that anyone who is angry with his brother will be subject to judgment. Again, anyone who says to his brother, 'Raca,' is answerable to the Sanhedrin. But anyone who says, 'You fool!' will be in danger of the fire of hell." Why? Because whoever hates his fellowman is a murderer, and no murderer has eternal life abiding in him. God looks at the heart. Evil thoughts and words are sin already, and the soul that sins, dies. Bearing a grudge or wronging someone without making an effort to make it all right will damn a person despite all outward piety and righteousness.

"Therefore, if you are offering your gift at the altar and there remember that your brother has something against you, leave your gift there in front of the altar. First go and be reconciled to your brother; then come and offer your gift." More important than the performance of religious rituals and ceremonies is being at peace with each other and having a forgiving spirit. The fact that Jesus urges us to make friends quickly with our accuser indicates that every day should be considered as the possible last day and should be filled with an urgency to reconcile. For if God's grace and love to us in Jesus have not led us to practice love and mercy and forgiveness, we may not look for mercy in the Last Judgment.

The sixth commandment is also used by Jesus for an example of what righteousness truly calls for. "You have heard that it was said, 'Do not commit adultery.' But I tell you that anyone who looks at a woman lustfully has already committed adultery with her in his heart. . . . It has been said, 'Anyone who divorces his wife must give her a certificate of divorce.' But I tell you that anyone who divorces his wife, except for marital unfaithfulness, causes her to commit adultery, and anyone who marries a woman so divorced, commits adultery." God is witness to the marriage covenant. In Mal. 2:14-16 we are told that God hates divorce as much as bloody violence. Both the lustful look and divorce violate the marriage covenant. While the Law in Deuteronomy (24:1-4) conceded divorce and prescribed the certificate of divorce, it was because the Law could not overcome man's hardness of heart.

God's intention at creation was lifelong and indissoluble union between man and woman. The scribes and Pharisees felt that if they refrained from acts of immorality they were pure. No, said Jesus, God looks at the heart, and lustfilled eyes reveal the heart's evil intent. While the Pharisees interpreted Moses' prescription concerning divorce very liberally, and a man could divorce his wife for almost any cause, Jesus championed her cause because she was left helpless and without honor by such a procedure. But the wife can no more violate marriage than the husband.

Can you and I say that our hearts are clean? Has no evil thought ever lodged in our mind? no lustfilled desire? Does no evil word ever cross our lips? Sinful thoughts, desires, words, and deeds must be eradicated. In Biblical thought various parts of the body are the means man uses to express his will and desire and may stand for the whole man in action. So Jesus said, "If your right eye causes you to sin, gouge it out and throw it away. It is better for you to lose one part of your body than for your whole body to be thrown in hell. And if your right hand causes you to sin, cut it off and throw it away. It is better for you to lose one part of your body than for your whole body to go into hell." To pluck out the eye and cut off the hand are expressions used by Jesus to show how resolutely we must fight and repress the sinful desire, no matter how painful the effort may be.

Another illustration is used by Jesus to indicate the kind of perfection and righteousness God requires. It has to do with oaths: "Again, you have heard that it was said to the people long ago, 'Do not break your oath, but keep the oaths you have made to the Lord.' But I tell you, Do not swear at all: either by heaven, for it is God's throne; or by the earth, for it is his footstool; or by Jerusalem, for it is the city of the Great King. And do not swear by your head, for you cannot make even one hair white or black. Simply let your 'Yes' be 'Yes,' and your 'No,' 'No'; anything beyond this comes from the evil one."

In the case of the fifth and sixth commandments Jesus applies them to the nth degree. In this instance, however, he goes beyond the mere letter of the Law so that its intention can be fully realized. What the Law says loudly and Jesus makes abundantly clear is that when a man speaks he is speaking *always* in the presence of his God, not simply on one occasion or the other. Jesus removes the oath so that every "Yes" and every "No" a person speaks is spoken as in the presence of God. Anything other than that comes from the evil one, the Devil, who is the father of lies. It is his influence that makes an oath a necessity in the courtroom.

From all of what Jesus has said it is obvious that man's righteousness, even if one is a scrupulous scribe or a pious Pharisee, is of no use at all to gain the favor of God or to enter the kingdom of heaven.

The Righteousness God Gives

But thank God we are not compelled to stop here. Jesus came into the world, not to bring about its condemnation, but that through Him it would be saved. Thanks be to God that Jesus' righteousness is ours. He came to live our life for us, in our place, from conception to resurrection. He came to be our stand-in. He took our place in every respect. He did it perfectly. He kept every command of God in the minutest detail. And having done all that, He suffered the punishment of hell on the cross for each human being. There the job was finished for all time and for eternity.

Our hope is in Him and in Him alone. The apostle Paul, writing by inspiration of the Holy Spirit, proclaims, "God made him who had no sin to be sin for us, so that in him we might become the righteousness of God" (2 Cor. 5:21). Although all our righteousnesses are as filthy rags (Is. 64:6), Jesus' righteousness, and therefore the very holiness of God, becomes our righteousness and holiness. Paul said that for Jesus' sake he suffered the loss of all things in order that "I may gain Christ and be found in him, not having a righteousness of my own that comes from the law, but that which is through faith in Christ—the righteousness that comes from God and is by faith" (Phil. 3:8-9). There is forgiveness from God through Christ. He makes the sinful heart clean, and His righteousness becomes our righteousness through faith. And that is the only righteousness that counts before God.

"For I tell you," says Jesus, "that unless your righteousness surpasses that of the Pharisees and the teachers of the law, you will certainly not enter the kingdom of heaven." Well, it does! It does because of this Christ who takes us to Himself and says, "Your sins are forgiven." With that glorious Gospel we can go forth from this church, striding shoulder to shoulder with Him, knowing that everything we do now by the power of the Spirit will be done in faith in Him who loves us and who gave Himself for us.

Love Turns the Cheek

SEVENTH SUNDAY AFTER THE EPIPHANY
MATTHEW 5:38-48

Richard G. Kapfer

The text for today is one of those portions of Scripture that I suspect we read through, scratch our head, and say, "Well, that doesn't make sense." Then we go on to something else without really thinking about what those words mean for us and what Jesus intended by them.

Some years ago we visited in the home of a family we had known for years. They shared with us a serious problem that they were facing. It had to do with this command of Jesus. They had taught their son, who was a strong and healthy fourth grader, that he was always to turn the other cheek. He tried his best to practice this. Then one day the bully of the school found out that he had someone he could use as a punching bag. So every day on the way home from school the bully would pick on this boy, and he wouldn't fight back. Day after day for several weeks, he would come home hurt because of what the bully had done. His parents shared with us this anguish-filled question: "Here are the words of Jesus; here is our boy; what do we do?"

I'm afraid that my answer was not very good. I mumbled—I usually mumble when I don't know what I'm talking about—something like, "Well, you have to defend yourself. Jesus didn't intend that your son get hurt. Why don't you just tell your boy to haul off and slug the bully? Even if he loses the fight, the bully will probably leave him alone, because bullies are generally cowards anyway."

Afterward, I wasn't very satisfied with my answer. You and I as Christians are called to be different people, but I had given the same answer that the world would have given.

If you read through the rest of the passage you will see other potential dilemmas lurking there, such as not only giving your coat to someone who asks, but your cloak also, and going two miles for someone nasty who forces you to go one mile, and not refusing anyone (anyone?) who would borrow from you. On top of this, you are to love your enemy and pray for your persecutor! Those words are extremely difficult, and we need to look more closely at what Jesus was saying.

I. Three Ways of Dealing with This Command

I suspect that we deal with "cheek turning" and all the other commands of Jesus listed here in at least three ways. The first way is that we follow them when it is convenient, but when they become difficult, we ignore them. Actually, we do follow Jesus' directive to turn the other cheek much of the time.

Parents will go to the room of their teenager, open the door, put a hand across their eyes, and say, "Oh, what a mess!" Instead of waiting until the teen gets home and saying, "Clean it up!" the parents simply go ahead and clean up the mess themselves. That's a form of cheek turning. Husbands and wives couldn't have a marriage that would last more than 30 days if they weren't turning the cheek almost constantly. If you are employed in a place where many people work closely with one another, you know you need to turn your cheek many times. Someone borrows something from you and never returns the item. You get angry, but you turn the other cheek. You students may have a roommate who, during final exam week, insists on gathering practically the whole hall in your room for a party. Yet you turn the other cheek.

At least you do for awhile. Suddenly one day you explode violently with your mouth or maybe even with your hands, because all that accumulated anger and bitterness finally has to get out.

Still, the words of Jesus are there. "Do not resist an evil person. If someone strikes you on the right cheek, turn to him the other also."

A second option is that we try hard and fail. That is what this family was doing. The mother and father were extremely frustrated and angry. They were angry at the bully. I suspect that they were also angry with Jesus for having given this command. They lived in a sinful world, and they knew that. There are people who will take advantage of Christians, and Jesus knew that, too, as He spoke these words. Maybe the family thought the bully would reform, that he would see the conduct of their son and would say, "There is a Christian. I'm going to change my life." However, that wasn't happening. They took this word, this law, to its conclusion, and the conclusion wasn't working well for them.

We lived far away from the couple, so we never learned the outcome, but I think I can predict it, and it isn't nice. One day the boy will get tired of being hurt and will punch the bully. The bully will go away and leave him alone. The conclusion that the boy will draw from this is disastrous for the Christian faith. He is going to say, "Well, the things in the Bible are fine, but they belong to a special, spiritual world. In the *real* world, they don't work." So on Sunday he will join his fellow Christians in singing, "Take my life and let it be consecrated, Lord, to Thee," but during the rest of the week he is going to live without the Word of God informing his daily actions. He may even conclude, "This is a dog-eat-dog world. I've got to look out for number one. Do it to them before they do it to you." Faith and life will be totally separated in this young person's life. It happens all the time!

A third option in dealing with the command to turn the other cheek is to admit that we can't keep that word of Jesus. Our Lord concluded this section of the Sermon on the Mount with words that simply won't let us dismiss His commands nor allow us to keep them only partially. After all of these hard sayings, Jesus concluded, "Be perfect, therefore"—and the standard for perfection is—"as your heavenly Father is perfect."

II. The Command Still Stands

Those words of Jesus eliminate the first option, that of ignoring His command. They also eliminate the second option of putting religion into a compartment. The will of God is unbending. It enters into every area of life. Its function is to show us our sins. It can never provide a solution; it can only show us that there is no solution found in keeping the Law. It reveals our complete helplessness.

That is why Jesus came into our world. He came not to remove the Law, but to keep the Law for us. "While we were yet sinners," the Bible says; while we *weren't* cheek turners, God's Son came for us sinners. He was reviled, but He did not revile back again. He is the greatest cheek turner in the world! His death on the cross as the innocent and blameless Son of God is the ultimate example. In Jesus Christ God turns *His* cheek for us and our sins.

Yet the family who had this dilemma was a Christian family. They were looking at the command of Jesus from this side of the cross. They weren't saying, "*if* we keep this Law, *then* we will be saved." They knew they were saved only by faith in Jesus Christ. They were saying, rather, "*Because* we are Christians, *therefore* we ought to turn the other cheek." Only Christians can say that.

Still, there was something wrong. This family was making the rule the final word. To live only by rules and laws in our lives as Christians is to say that nothing else matters, nothing else needs to be considered. The situation doesn't matter, I don't matter, the bully doesn't matter, God doesn't matter, faith doesn't matter, the Gospel doesn't matter. All that matters is the rule.

Several years ago a famous playright and his wife were mugged on a street corner in New York City. The wife was horribly beaten by the attackers. Afterward, she praised her husband who had done nothing to help her, because he had remained true to his pacifist beliefs. The rule that he lived by not only prevented him from doing something he considered to be wrong, but at the same time it prevented him from doing good for someone in need. There is something wrong with that. There is also something wrong with what the family we have been discussing was doing to their little boy. They were breaking other rules in order to keep this rule.

III. The Command Is Part of Another Command

The apostle Paul writes something that is very instructive for us in Romans. "The commandments, 'Do not commit adultery,' 'Do not murder,' 'Do not steal,' 'Do not covet,' and whatever other commandments there may be, are summed up in this one rule: Love your neighbor as yourself.' Love does no harm to its neighbor. Therefore love is the fulfillment of the law" (Rom. 13:9-10).

Love is the rule! The rule is not the rule! Love is the rule, and the command of Jesus is part of the rule of love!

Love's question is this: What good is my love doing to and for the other person? What is the goal of my cheek turning? Here we have to be careful. I am getting hurt by turning my cheek. The bully is not stopping. Therefore, I'll "love" the bully by hitting him. That's the old nature talking, not the new nature. Our love needs direction and power so that we love in the fullest sense of that beautifully Christ-like way.

In the First Epistle of John, the apostle writes of love, "This is love: not that we loved God, but that he loved us and sent his Son as an atoning sacrifice for our sins. Dear friends, since God so loved us, we also ought to love one another" (1 John 4:10-11). Love is found not in us, nor in a command, but in Jesus Christ. We love *because* of His love and *through* His love for us. In other words, we are at the cross. Jesus is there for us. He values us. Because He values us with that kind of love, we can realize something else. He values those who want to do us harm. He died for them, too. Christian love, then, is cross-shaped.

Cross-shaped love doesn't ask, "When do I stop turning the other cheek?" That is a law question. Rather, the question for the cheek turner is, "How can I love this person all the way to the cross?" Sometimes, in fact most of the time, the most loving response is to turn the other cheek, so that the mark of the cross can be seen on our cheek. At other times Christian love requires us to stop turning the cheek and to say, in one way or another, "I have been turning my cheek because in Jesus Christ I love you. I have turned my cheek so that you may see Christ through me." But there are times when we must in love hold the bully at arm's length and say, "Enough! I love my Lord too much to let you go on doing that to yourself and to me!"

It was perhaps high time for that family to have said that to their son. In love for the bully who was persisting in evil they needed to love in another way, for *love* is the fulfilling of the law, not cheek turning all by itself.

What if we are wrong? What if we lose patience and "punch" the bully long before we should? What if we don't turn the cheek at all? If we live by the rule, we have no place to go except the rule. But we live by the Gospel, and so we know where to go. We go to the Source of love, Jesus Christ. He comes to us through Word and Sacrament to fill us anew with His love and forgiveness, that we might live lives that are cross-shaped in His love. Then we pray. We talk to God about those difficult situations. We reflect with God about those who persecute us and despitefully use us. We pray for them. Then, when love requires it, we will turn the other cheek gladly and willingly.

We will do it for the sake of love, whose name is Jesus Christ our Lord.

An Alternate to Anxiety

EIGHTH SUNDAY AFTER THE EPIPHANY
MATTHEW 6:24-34

Lyle D. Muller

To live in the twentieth century, to be an American, and to be anxious appear to be synonymous. The subjects of our newscasts are gun-control, nuclear waste, armament buildup, violence, depleted resources, and economic insecurity. Dubbed "An Age of Anxiety," the time in which we live contains a paradox. Our material and scientific progress has accelerated at an unprecedented rate, but we are not more content or happier. Anxiety strikes all of us in the church, too. That's our concern today. What is anxiety doing to us who follow Jesus? To our trust in God? To the abundant and joyful life He desires for us? To the first-place position He and His kingdom seek in our lives?

Success-Oriented

There's no doubt that our society is success-oriented. Our children quickly learn our system of competition and awards in the classroom, in music, in sports, in being popular, and in gaining recognition from their peers. Such individual striving for success can be a salutary thing, of course, when it means that we are seeking to do the best with the abilities and resources God has given us, and when it results in giving honor to Him and becoming a channel of loving service to others. Too often, however, success becomes identified with self-worth and self-esteem. The result is anxiety over "keeping up" and "getting ahead" and "having it made."

Material Worth

Our success is measured most of all in the salary we make, the material things we possess, and the buying power we have. Our anxiety focuses on the concerns Jesus raises about what we shall eat, what we shall drink, and what we shall wear. Billions are spent in advertising to prompt consumers to desire what they don't need.

Marshall McLuhan reminded us in *Understanding Media* of the immense investment in research, in gathering and processing social data about people's experiences and feelings, and in creating an anxiety over not having the new car, appliance, or apparel. We're always feasting our eyes on something that is just out of our reach. Our affluence dictates that the more we have, the more we want.

Results of Anxiety

The anxiety over money and what it represents festers and grows in the human mind and heart, and it creates new anxiety about our whole life. We become envious of those who have more, bitter toward those who seemingly used us to get ahead, selfish toward those who are in need, and fearful of the future. Joy and strength are sapped from our lives. Days are weary and nights are sleepless when worry and fretting take over. One out of every three illnesses are anxiety-related, doctors and psychologists remind us.

Most dramatically, we who shake our heads in bewilderment over those who still bow down before idols of wood and stone may have forgotten Jesus' warning that we can be sacrificing our lives at the altar of "mammon," or "riches." Our energies and time can become offerings laid down at the shrines of worldly success. Our hearts can trust in money and possessions alone to "give us this day our daily bread" and to "deliver us from evil."

The tragedy occurs when trust is no longer placed in God for all things and we disobey the very first commandment of God, "You shall have no other gods before me." Jesus lays it on the line. "No one can serve two masters. Either he will hate the one and love the other, or he will be devoted to the one and despise the other. You cannot serve God and money" (Matt. 6:24).

Jesus' Concern

Jesus expresses concern about many kinds of anxieties. "Therefore I tell you, do not worry about your life, what you will eat or drink; or about your body, what you will wear" (v. 25). "Who of you by worrying can add a single hour to his life? And why do you worry about clothes?" (v. 27-28). "Therefore do not worry about tomorrow, for tomorrow will worry about itself" (v. 34). "For where your treasure is, there your heart will be also" (v. 21). We should not be surprised at Jesus' frequent references to anxiety, for He was only observing what people were like.

A person at that time could become just as anxious about a new camel as a new car, or about a new shawl as a new fur, or a carpenter's shop as an office or factory, or over shekels as dollars. What anxiety does to us, it did to people then. That's why Jesus' words cannot be set aside as simply beautiful imagery about the birds of the air or the lilies and grass of the field. They are more relevant than we care to admit.

Don't Distort Jesus' Words

But we sinners are always uncomfortable with the direct, uncompromising words of our Lord that portray us as we really are. How many want to hear sermons about their money and possessions? As the saying goes, "You can touch anything, but not my pocketbook!" How many of us really welcome a stewardship caller challenging us to evaluate our financial priorities in the light of God's Word?

It is not surprising what many have done to these words from Jesus' Sermon on the Mount. Some say Jesus is advocating a first-century hippie philosophy: "Get out of the rat race. Don't adorn yourelf with middle- and upper-class comforts. Drop out of school. Sell the house; put your goods up for auction. Join a commune. The business world and its institutions are corrupt. Don't be inhibited. Leave it all behind; love people freely; get in touch with nature and life again."

Others see in this text the medieval desire to leave the world and join religious orders behind cloistered walls, to be untainted by the world, to take a vow of poverty and be rid of worldly comforts once and for all. Still others see in Jesus' words a ground for noncompetition and nonachievement, or a rebuke of capitalism and a plea for socialism.

Look At Jesus' Life and Words

But Jesus did not live by or proclaim such views. His disciples carried a purse to buy food; they neither gave away all that they had nor begged for everything. While on the cross, He thoughtfully provided for His mother. He walked among the poor, often having no place to lay His head, yet did not refuse the luxuries of the rich. He could provide festive wine for a wedding, eat at the table of a rich

Pharisee or tax collector, and not begrudge a woman using expensive ointment for washing His feet.

His life recognized and praised the heavenly Father as the source of all the daily bread and all the riches and kingdoms of this world. He served only Him and lived not by bread alone, but by God's Word (Matt. 4:1-11). He does not say that we should not plan or be careful or make provision for the future. He does say that we should not be anxious.

The Care of God

The antidote for anxiety lies not in getting more things, or in protecting ourselves, but in the loving care of God for His children. John writes, "There is no fear in love. But perfect love drives out fear" (1 John 4:18). He who feeds the birds of the air, which neither sow nor reap nor gather into barns, and He who clothes the lilies of the field, which neither spin nor toil, will care even more bountifully for us. He is our Shepherd who knows all our needs, and we will not want. Tomorrow belongs to God. We have nothing to fear, as Franklin D. Roosevelt said, but fear itself.

The Kingdom of God

We can trust the care of God and believe that His love is perfect because of His Son Jesus Christ. In Him the kingdom of God is manifested and comes to us. Anxious and fretful sinners though we are, preoccupied with ourselves and things money can buy, He loved us so much that He came into a world that worships creatures and not the Creator. Jesus came into the world He made to turn us back to God by being the Way Himself. In Him God draws near to us with the blessings of forgiveness and new life in which Christ is Lord and King, in which we can trust and serve God and not ourselves or things.

A new self-worth and self-esteem takes over which He bestows on us as His redeemed children. We are not economic pawns of cruel fate and bad luck, but people of great worth and dignity bought with the price of Jesus' blood. His righteousness, as a garment of inestimable value, covers us and makes us beautiful to God.

We have nothing to be anxious about as long as as we are dressed in His righteousness and basking in His grace. There is nothing to fret about, because His Word, filled with promises of care and love, is trustworthy and sure. There is nothing to be discouraged about because our life now is truly worth more than food or drink or clothing.

A New Alternative

Daily the choice is ours—seek Christ's kingdom and His

righteousness or turn from God and become part of an anxious world. We can think and plan about our problems, or we can worry and be fearful about them. We can pray about them and draw upon God's strength and care, or we can fret over what we will do by ourselves.

We can express a joyful exuberance about life's todays and tomorrows that are in God's hands, or we can complain about what we're going through and what is ahead. We can work and gratefully accept whatever fruits God gives, or we can work and be unhappy that we have little to show for it. We can be cowards in the face of life, or we can do all things through Christ who strengthens us.

Nothing tests our character as much as anxiety. It can paralyze the child of God, or it can turn us to the freeing and uplifting power and love of God. The choice is ours.

The Ecstasy and the Agony

THE TRANSFIGURATION OF OUR LORD
LAST SUNDAY AFTER THE EPIPHANY
MATTHEW 17:1-9

Lyle D. Muller

Some years ago a movie entitled "The Agony and the Ecstasy" portrayed the life of Michelangelo. This fifteenth-century artist experienced many struggles with poverty, capricious popes, and dishonest rulers. He labored for years on his back, painting the ceiling of the Sistine Chapel in Rome, a feat that brought him glory.

Such stories have popular appeal among us. We admire those who go from rags to riches, from lowliness to the heights of glory. Today we remember that most of our Lord's earthly life showed just the reverse. He went from ecstasy to agony. He chose that way for our sakes, to reassure us of His redemptive purpose in our lives and to lift us to glory.

A Glorious Day

Jesus was born into our world with the multitude of the heavenly host giving glory to God. Wise Men came from afar to honor Him with their gifts and adoration. His ministry began with the awesome voice of the heavenly Father and the descending presence of the Holy Spirit commissioning Him at his baptism. To be sure, Jesus knew lowliness and once remarked that He had no place to lay His head. But the first years of His ministry drew large crowds and the acclaim of many (Luke 4:15).

A more glorious day is described in today's Gospel. For a brief moment the Lord Jesus shines in all the brightness of the glory and all the fulness of the majesty that He enjoyed in heaven with the Father before He came to earth. The holy splendor of God breaks through the human frame of Jesus of Nazareth, Jesus the son of Mary, Jesus the healer, Jesus the teacher, and Jesus the preacher. All the things He had been saying and doing were giving glory to God, but now His face and clothes were shining with His own glory. Now we see the splendor that surrounds God in heaven, which Jesus set aside to come to us (John 17:5).

Witnesses to His Glory

Others are witnesses to this spectacular event. Two heroes of the Old Testament appear on the mountain with Jesus and speak with Him. One is Moses, the great giver of the Law. He must have felt right at home on this mountaintop with the bright cloud, the voice, and the glory of God around Him. The other person is Elijah, the fiery prophet.

These two representatives of the Old Covenant, revealed in the Law and the Prophets, now stand at the side of Him to whom they pointed. Present again is the Voice, the heavenly Father identifying Jesus as His own beloved Son. Also there are Peter, James, and John, three disciples Jesus chose to hear and see this event. They would tell the world, "We were eyewitnesses of his majesty. For he received honor and glory from God the Father when the voice came to him from the Majestic Glory, saying 'This is my Son, whom I love; with him I am well pleased.' We ourselves heard this voice that came from heaven when we were with him on the sacred mountain" (2 Peter 1:16-18). God's great acts in history have their witnesses.

The Turning Point

The Gospel writers indicate that this act was to become a crucial turning point in Jesus' ministry. Luke tells us that Moses and Elijah are speaking to Jesus about His "Exodus," His departure about to occur in Jerusalem (Luke 9:31). Matthew and Mark indicate that the Transfiguration represents a change of course in Jesus' ministry that will end in Jerusalem. The ecstasy on the mountain will not continue, even though Jesus must have enjoyed it.

The three disciples want to remain on the mountain to build tabernacles and somehow to bottle up the glorious day and retain it for themselves, but Jesus takes them with Him down into the valley. A father with a very sick boy was waiting in agony in the valley below. Others would come who were afraid, guilt-ridden, hurting, and dying.

But the greatest agony ahead was to belong to Jesus. He had been telling His disciples that He must go to Jerusalem and suffer and be put to death (Matt. 16:21). He would reinforce that prediction in the coming days (17:12, 22-23). In our worship this Lenten season, we will sense the distress Jesus' disciples experienced (v. 23). He must have felt it a great deal more.

A Day of Reassurance

Reassurance for Jesus

Yet the Transfiguration strengthened Jesus for what was ahead. The presence of Moses and Elijah signaled their affirming support. The Old Testament is being fulfilled in Jesus. The New Covenant is falling into place, based on His impending sacrifice on Calvary for the sins of the world. The old gives way to the new with a glory that far surpasses that of the old (2 Cor. 3:9-11).

The voice of the Father reassures Jesus that He is still the beloved Son as declared earlier at His baptism. The eternal plan for the salvation of the world has not changed. It is proceeding according to the Father's will. In all the agony ahead, Jesus could remember this day and be bolstered. The Father was with Him.

Reassurance for the Disciples

The disciples would be troubled in the days ahead as well. There would be moments when they would attempt to compromise and deny their relationship to Jesus. They would flee in the face of danger and question Jesus' very existence. But they could look back and remember how "The Word became flesh and lived for a while among us. We have seen his glory, glory of the one and only Son, who came from the Father, full of grace and truth" (John 1:14).

The glory of God could be hidden from their view for a time and mocked by sinners, but it was no less present. God was in Christ reconciling the world, including them, to Himself. The Beloved was not going to desert them. Soon they would see the Father's plan completed "to the praise of his glorious grace, which he has freely given us in the One he loves" (Eph. 1:6).

Our Agony

This need for reassurance applies equally to us. Some of our fellow Christians are in deep valleys of trouble and discouragement today. We all join them from time to time. Illness can rob us of the will to live. Loss of work and income can destroy confidence and courage. Family arguments and divisions can turn daily living into a nightmare. Unfaithful friends can cause scars that never leave.

The agonies of life can also be destructive to our faith. The story is told of one demon in hell who had great success in eroding the faith of Jesus' followers. Other demons tried to discover the tool he used and to buy it at great price, but to no avail. Finally he named the tool. "It is discouragement," he said, "and it is successful because it gives up on God."

Reassurance for Us

After reminding us of the glory he saw on the mountain, Peter declares that we are no less favored. "And we have the word of the prophets made more certain, and you will do well to pay attention to it, as to a light shining in a dark place" (2 Peter 1:19). The voice had told him, "Listen to him!" (Matt. 17:5), and Peter discovered that his doubts and discouragements increased when he no longer listened to Jesus.

Our joy is that the same Jesus says to us, "Don't be afraid." As we go to the Holy Scriptures, God's high mountain for us, Jesus Christ is there to be transfigured before us in all His glory, to lift us up to the Father, to bolster us for the walk through the valley below, and to reassure us that His plan of salvation includes us.

What a privilege we have as we begin another Lenten pilgrimage. When it's done, we also can say, "We have seen his glory." Receive all the strength and encouragement from it that you possibly can for your own valleys ahead. Remember that Jesus has never left you. Even if you don't feel His presence, even if the glory of His countenance is hidden for a time, remember from this day that He is still the beloved Son of God and your Savior. You see, He was glorified in His death and resurrection! The world's darkest day became it's brightest.

A Day to Proclaim

Witnesses Needed

You and I also have the privilege of being witnesses of God's great acts to those who are hurting, afraid, guilt-ridden, and dying today. This is Jesus' way of showing His glory to the world today (John 17:10). Tell in your own words what you know of Jesus from the Scriptures and of His goodness and grace to you in your lifetime. The Father's counsel is still to be given, "Listen to him!" Direct your relatives and friends to Him.

Surveys indicate that our nation has 100 million people who have not worshiped Jesus in the last six months. Over one-half of them have never been visited and personally invited to worship by a church in their community, yet 51 percent envision joining a church someday if someone gives them a good reason to do so. We have the reason! We have beheld His glory so often in the Scriptures and in our lives. Share the good news! It's too good to keep to ourselves.

Another Day of Glory

I trust that we will also look ahead, to another day of glory. We await the day when Jesus will come, as He said, in the glory of His Father with His angels (Matt. 16:27). He looks forward to it also. "Father, I want those you have given me to be with me where I am, and to see my glory, the glory you have given me" (John 17:24). Then we'll know why the sufferings of this present time are not worth comparing to the glory that will be revealed in us. What a Transfiguration Day that will be!

When We Are Tempted

FIRST SUNDAY IN LENT
MATTHEW 4:1-11

George W. Bornemann

Children of God over and over pray, "Lead us not into temptation; but deliver us from evil." As we so pray we ask that God would watch over us, His dear children, and keep us, so that the devil, the world, and our own sinful self would not deceive us and so draw us into misbelief, despair, or any other great shame and sin. And we pray that God would deliver us from every evil of body and soul, and especially from the evil one, that when our final hour comes in His mercy God would take us to Himself in heaven.

The entire Lenten narrative, as we remember our Lord's encounter with evil—the evil of the men who condemned and crucified Him, but even more our own evil which sent Him to the cross—we give thanks to our Lord for giving Himself in our place. It is by such grace that we can stand in our own hour of temptation. When we are tempted, we have more than an example. In Christ we have a Victor, the only One who could overcome the devil and all he stood for.

For nearly 1,600 years this lesson on Jesus' temptations has been the opening text for Christians celebrating Lent. Lent has become a 40-day period set aside to recall our Lord's conquest of Satan. On Calvary and even during this 40-day period He fought with our greatest foe. Few artists have attempted to capture this scene on canvas. Few icons depict this incident. Yet three of the gospel writers begin the narrative of our Lord's ministry describing it.

When our Lord was baptized in the Jordan by His forerunner John, a great pronouncement was made by our heavenly Father that this indeed was His beloved Son. Three years later, as His ministry moved toward its final conflict, on the Mount of Transfiguration our heavenly Father again spoke, "This is my Son, whom I love; with him I am well pleased. Listen to him!" Both pronouncements preceded great conflicts, one in the wilderness with Satan and the other at Calvary with all the consequences brought about by Satan, namely, sin and death. Wherever and whenever Satan is at work, it always results in testing, in sins, in failures, in mistakes, in death and dying. It is for this very reason that Jesus Christ came in the world to save sinners by overcoming Satan and destroying our last enemy, death. No wonder such pronouncements from the heavenly Father are made before these conflicts.

Both pronouncements were followed by great confessions of faith—from John the Baptizer and from Peter the Fisherman. John called Christ the Lamb of God, and Peter asserted that He was the Christ, the Son of the living God.

Both pronouncements prepare us to know that for Christ and for us the conflict with Satan is primary. He came to give His very life in vicarious atonement for the sins of the world. His struggle against His and our archenemy assures us of final triumphant victory.

As we see the temptation unfold, we note that

When We're Tempted, We Are Tempted As God's Own

It was as a humble and obedient servant that our Lord Jesus went to Calvary. He was condemned because He was God's Son, even as He claimed. And it is now, as God's Son, that He is led into temptation in the wilderness. As a lamb led to the slaughter so He is led into the wilderness.

It is significant and no mistake that He is led there by the Holy Spirit. As God's Son this was His role—to be tempted in all things as we are, to face the very foe who destroyed all relationships between God and man, to be our Representative and Pioneer, to overcome as our Victor any testing which the evil one might bring forth.

When Satan said, "If you are the Son of God," there was no question in his mind that indeed He was God's Son. Satan was a product of God's creation. Before he fell in rebellion against God, He knew God. He knew that by Him who came in the flesh all things were made and without Him was not anything made which was made. When He inhabited some children of men here on earth and

Jesus told him to leave, the devil responded, "We know who you are. Are you come to destroy us before our time?"

"*If* you are the Son of God"? It was *because* He was God's Son that He was tempted. He was the Seed of the woman who was to crush the serpent's head. Satan recognized that the final crushing would come some day. He knew who Jesus was.

"*Since* you are God's Son! Since You have all power; since You are hungry from fasting 40 days and nights; since you are God's Son, why not make bread from these stones? You can do it!"

That is how our enemy works. Our foe knows that we are God's children. He knows that by the power of the Holy Spirit we have been born anew. "Ah, now," he says, "now that you are God's children, let's see what you can do in and with that new relationship. Will God really take care of you? Will He feed you as He did the children of Israel in the wilderness? Will He take care of you as He did a hungry Elijah? You say He can do all things—a miracle! Can you now call on Him and He'll give you bread? Or will He give you stones instead of bread? Remember His promises—He told you all things are yours, and all things are possible if you but believe in Him."

Temptations like these are trying, not for the unbeliever or scoffer, but for the child of God who has tasted and knows the goodness of the Lord, especially for the sinner who has found grace and pardon with God in Jesus Christ. Temptations like these are most difficult and trying for the young, the new Christian who just recently came to faith. "Now that you are God's child"—and then the temptations come—"will He answer your prayer? Will He take care of you? Will He not only forgive sins but will He forget them? Will He keep His promises? Really?"

Confidence in God at times is shaken. Trust is often most difficult at the very moment when God Himself is directing our lives. Remember how God tested Abraham? Abraham believed God, and it was that faith which declared him to be God's child, a true friend of God. Abraham believed that God's gift, a child, would be the one through whom God's blessing would come to himself and others. But then God asked him to climb Mount Moriah to offer his son as a sacrifice. Isaac wondered about this, too, but on the way Abraham kept saying, "The Lord will provide. In the mountain of the Lord it shall be seen. Have faith. The Lord will provide." His confidence remained firm in the testing and trial. God indeed did provide, for a ram caught in the thicket became the substitute for Isaac.

When trials come our way, we ask, "Will the Lord take care?" And indeed He does. He always delivers us in our hour of trial and testing. We, too, have a substitute which He provided, One whose head was crowned with thorns, whose limbs were nailed to a tree. God selected Him long before we came to His altar. Christ on Calvary's cross is God's answer to a trust which can say as did Abraham, "The Lord will provide," for the Lord indeed has provided.

Peter expressed confidence that Jesus was the Messiah, the Christ of God. At another time Jesus reminded Peter that he was in danger of denying his Lord. "No, never," was his response. He meant it. Jesus told him that Satan would be tempting him. God would allow His disciple Peter to endure temptation and testing, just as Abraham and Jesus Himself. "But," says Jesus to Peter, "I have prayed for you, Simon, that your faith may not fail. And when you have turned back, strengthen your brothers" (Luke 22:32). The Lord Himself will be with the child of God who faces temptations.

We, too, aware of our dangers, cry to God, "lead us not into temptation," but we also know His power and grace, and so we continue, "but deliver us from evil," or as some translations have it, "deliver us from the evil one."

In our hungers and needs, however great or devastating; in our longings and hopes, as dear and strong as they may be; in our despairs and doubts, the devil would whisper in our ear, "but you are God's child, how can He do this to you? You are God's child; has He abandoned you? You are God's child; how can He let this happen?" Call on Him and see if He responds. Since you are His, let the miracle happen!

Our Saviour, who had more reason to know the power of God and His miracles than any of us, responded, "Man does not live on bread alone, but on every word that comes from the mouth of God." Man's life does not consist in the things he possesses but in the will of God. It is not what we put in our mouths but what comes from the mouth of God. It is not what man wants; it is what God wants. Trust God and discover that He does not abandon His children, His creation, His redeemed ones, His very own.

Jesus faced temptation as God's very own. He understands and knows well our plight, recognizing it from ages of conflict with the old evil foe. His intercession for us, the sending of His holy angels, His constant care is ever with us. In Him is life indeed.

Jesus quoted the Holy Scriptures, the shield for our defense against our enemy, the Word which proceeds from God's mouth and which not only gives but maintains life and faith, trust and assurance. It is that revelation which furnishes us with power from on high. But there comes a time in our lives, even as Jesus experienced, that

We Can Be Tempted with God's Word

Satan knows that when God speaks, it is done, that faith comes by hearing and hearing by the Word. Satan knows that God's will is for good, that His will is recorded for learning and instruction. It was for that very reason that in the beginning he said to our first parents, "Yea, has God said that? Now really, you will not die. Rather you will have your eyes opened and know more and more even as God Himself."

The very promise of God's salvation in Christ at the cross, the very assurances that Christ has overcome death, devil, and sin are used by Satan to question our trust in those words. "Look," he says, "all around you is death. Everyone dies. How can you say that in Christ there is no death, but only life? Look, all around you is sin; the world is torn apart by sin. How can you say that in Christ there is victory over sin? Can you trust God and His word?"

He said that to our Lord also, tempting Him with the very Word of God. "If you are going to rely on the principle that man lives by God's Word, follow me." He took Jesus to a place where He might let Himself fall. Suppose you were to take a young bird and place it on the wing of a giant eagle, carried aloft as the space shuttle *Columbia* is carried on the wings of a 747 airplane. Fly high! You might even nudge the bird away from the body of the eagle where it would be quite safe, and place it a little further out, even all the way to the very edge of the feathers (as the Roman writers would say "to the *pinnaculum,"* pinnacle in English). Way out there, can the bird trust its parent? Will the parent really care? And Jesus was taken to the pinnacle of the holy place of God as spoken of in Psalm 91, a Psalm which the devil misquoted: "under his wings you will find refuge . . . no harm will befall you . . . he will command his angels concerning you . . . they will lift you up in their hands, so that you will not strike your foot against a stone." "Is not that what God says in His Word?" asked the devil. Trust God. You will not be crushed. You will not be dashed. Can we rely on what He says? We, too, face those very challenges.

Then Jesus said to him, "Do not put the Lord your God to the test." The devil was not asking Jesus to trust God's Word; he was asking for mistrust. The devil was not testing Jesus' faith; he was testing God's promises. To trust God is not to test Him but to believe Him. To trust God is to believe His Word, His promises. The father of the demon-possessed boy cried out in response to Jesus' call for faith, "I believe; help my unbelief."

Over and over God has given us precious promises—that He will take care of us, that He will be at our side, that He will be our Strength and Stay. Mary, mother of our Lord, sang, "His mercy extends to those who fear him, from generation to generation. He has performed mighty deeds with his arm; he has . . . lifted up the humble. He has filled the hungry with good things, . . . He has helped his servant Israel, remembering to be merciful . . . as he said to our fathers." Simeon, when he saw and held the Child Jesus, praised God for the salvation which He had "prepared in the sight of all people." When David was delivered from the hands of his enemies (2 Samuel 22), he admitted to God, "With my God I can scale a wall. As for God, his way is perfect; the word of the Lord is flawless." The psalmist urges us, "Wait for the Lord; be strong and take heart and wait for the Lord." In the midst of his lamentations, Jeremiah could say, "The steadfast love of the Lord never ceases, His mercies never come to an end; they are new every morning; great is Thy faithfulness. 'The Lord is my portion,' says my soul, 'therefore I will hope in Him' " (Lam. 3:22-24 RSV). And Jude could end his letter with a blessing, "To Him who is able to keep you from falling and to present you without blemish before the presence of His glory with rejoicing, to the only God, our Savior through Jesus Christ our Lord, be glory, majesty, dominion, and authority, before all time and now and for ever" (Jude 24-25 RSV).

Trusting in all God's promises we walk by faith and not by sight. One of Jesus' early disciples, Thomas, had difficulty with this, for He could not accept the promise of His Lord nor the witness of others to that promise. The kind and caring, generous and gracious Lord reached out to him, "Put your finger here; see my hands. Reach out your hand and put it in my side. Stop doubting and believe. . . . blessed are those who have not seen and yet have believed."

It is not always easy to believe. When you see your little baby being baptized you ask, "How is it possible that water can do such great things as to make this child God's very own, a child to inherit all God's promises?" But it is His Word; on that you can rely. "Whoever believes and is baptized will be saved." When we lay our loved ones to rest in the sod of the cemetery, we wonder how is it possible for our loved one to come back to life, even another life in the hereafter. But it is His word, not man's, "He who believes in me will live, even though he dies; and whoever lives and believes in me will never die. Do you believe this?"—Mary, Martha, Andrew, Peter, John, you?

When we're tempted, and God's very own promises are before us, then is the time to grasp them by the hand of a God-given faith and to trust Him all the way, for He will give us only the best and nothing else. He did that in His gift of Jesus Christ on Calvary's cross.

But the devil was not finished with Jesus, for temptation involves more than faith in promises. It is to face the reality of life itself, the reality of this very world. And like Jesus, when we're tempted,

We Are Tempted in God's Very World

The devil brought Jesus to see all the kingdoms, riches, and power of this world. "All this," says Satan, "I will give you, if you will bow down and worship me." What arrogance! Not only had Satan spoiled God's world when he caused Paradise to become a wilderness, but now he enters that wilderness and says to our Lord, "All this is mine to do with as I please, to share its treasures with whomsoever I will, if I am recognized as the world's ruler."

This was not his world. It is God's world, created and sustained by Him, precious in his sight. This is God's world which has been groaning in pain until now waiting for its redemption, its freedom from this tyrant who masks himself as ruler. This is the world in which God called man to have dominion and to rule. But the usurper, both God's and man's, tells the very Creator, "It is mine, and those who worship me can have it." Truly a liar, as Jesus once identified him!

He brought to this world his mark, and it was the mark of sin. He is like one who believes that if he were to put a scratch on a painting, the whole painting would belong to him. He is like one who believes that if he tears a limb from a tree, the entire tree now belongs to him. He is like one who throws mud on the wall of a home and says, "The entire house is now mine."

God will not and does not abandon His creation. He loves the world, all of His creatures, and above all the people who were made in His image. He loves the world so much that He gave His only son into death for its salvation. God wants man to be what He intended him to be in the very beginning—His very own, trusting His word, as he lives in His world.

So again Jesus says to Satan, and again from His very words, "Worship the Lord your God, and serve him only." There is no other course our Lord can assume but to say to His foe and to our enemy, "Begone, Satan!"

It is at this very point that we, too, tempted to believe that this world might be ours or belong to those who would work evil, tempted to hear the voice of those who would tell us how to get ahead in this world, are reminded, "Ah, but there is One who is above you and me, and He is the Lord our God. He Himself is Lord. There is none other. And Him we worship."

So, beloved, when we are tempted as God's own children, just as Jesus, God's Son, was tempted, we flee to our heavenly Father and find help in His promises.

And when we are tempted to doubt God's promises or to twist

them for the wrong, we turn again to His promises, and pray the Holy Spirit to increase and keep us in the faith.

And even though the whole world seems against us or we are tempted to believe it is ours, may the Lord by His Word keep reminding us there is none other but Him our Lord.

Christ won the victory for us, paying for our doubts and failures, rescuing us from our mistakes and wrongs, overcoming our foolish ways, freeing us from guilt and punishment by His sacrifice. Yes, He won the victory over our evil foe, the devil.

Though devils all the world should fill,
All eager to devour us,
We tremble not, we fear no ill,
They shall not overpower us.
This world's prince may still
Scowl fierce as he will,
He can harm us none,
He's judged; the deed is done;
One little word can fell him. (*LW* 298:3)

Christ, the Living Water

SECOND SUNDAY IN LENT
JOHN 4:5-26

George W. Bornemann

Imagine a spring of water which, like an artesian well, bubbles up constantly, not merely to refresh us in life but to give us eternal life, life which never ends. Moreover, the water would give us refreshment for all the varying needs of our earthly existence. We know of no such living water in this world. But there is One, namely Jesus Christ, who in Himself was such a spring of living water, and whoever would drink Him and embrace Him, would receive the best of life hereafter and also the best of life in this world.

Our text tells us that He came to the well at Sychar, to teach the Samaritan woman and all of us that He is that Living Water. Some of us know Jesus Christ as the way to eternal life. He is not merely the one who would show us the way, but He Himself is the Way. Some of us know Jesus Christ as one who could guide us in this life and in the life hereafter. But He is not only the teacher of life, but He is the very Life Himself. He is not only the dispenser of the water of life, but He Himself is the very Living Water.

When the Lord Jesus sat down at the well, He did so because He was tired and thirsty. When the woman of Samaria came to the well, she came because she was thirsty. And our Lord said to her, "If you knew the gift of God and who it is that asks you for a drink, you would have asked him and he would have given you living water."

As we review the story of this encounter, it is not difficult for us to imagine who this woman might be, but we need to ask

Who Is This Person Who Offers Living Water?

In appearance Jesus does not seem to be the kind of person who could offer any kind of water to the woman at the well. He came as a tired traveler. He came from the southern portion of the land to this fork in the road inside Samaria. He was in a strange territory where Jews did not often come, one which they purposely avoided. His traveling companions, the disciples, had gone into the nearby town to buy food.

It was noontime, the sixth hour of the day, when the woman also came to the well for water. Jesus asked her, "Will you give me a drink?" He who later said He had a spring of water within Him which welled to eternal life is the one who asks her for a drink of water.

It was another day, and also at the sixth hour, when at another city, Jerusalem, Jesus also cried out, "I am thirsty." He who has the living water for eternal life was dying on the cross of Calvary and cried for some refreshment for His parched body. It was more than a human being who was tired and hurting at Calvary when He cried out for something to drink. It was the Savior of the world, who was giving up everything—all His life, all His powers—for the salvation of the world. He set aside His very self, taking our place at Calvary, thirsty that we might never go thirsty either in this life or in the life to come. He would satisfy our every need, not merely for a cup of cold water but for water to wash away our filth, our dirt, our sins, our failures, our mistakes.

When we behold Him at Calvary as our substitute crying out in thirst, we would not think of Him as one who could give us any kind of help. And the maid at the well did not see Jesus as the kind of person who could give her water, living or otherwise. She saw Him in His humanness, a traveler, one not from Samaria but a stranger, a foreigner, a Jew. Obviously He was most incapable of giving her water. He did not even have a bucket or jar.

From the rest of the story in John's gospel we realize He had all power in heaven and on earth. He is the Creator Himself. He can calm troubled waters. Not too many days prior to this He had told an old man that by water and the Spirit he could be born again to a new life. But before the woman, He appears as one who is thirsty, a man who was not only born but who will die.

Jesus did come into our world, born of a woman, to redeem us. And He certainly is human, one with us in all things, except that He knew no sin. He came to be with us, alongside of us, tenting among us. He came in our flesh and took on Himself our nature. He also took on Himself our sins and wrongs and carried them to Calvary's cross. He came to our world—a world we wrecked and corrupted. And in His humanness He said to the woman, "I am thirsty."

The village woman did not know Him, but soon she would discover for herself who He really was. He showed Himself ultimately to be the Messiah, the Lord, the promised Savior of mankind. He was the One who gave up everything for us that we might have a blessed life here and the promise of eternity. He endured the drought of death that we might have everlasting springs of the water of life.

The Nile River by its gift of water has created a ribbon of green in the upper portion of Egypt. On both sides is the Sahara Desert, a land of the dead. Wherever the water comes, there is life. Into the midst of a dying world, and to us as dying persons because of our sins, comes the greatest Person of all, God's Son. He gives life to everything He touches. He is the Living Water.

When Jesus sat down at the well, He said, "I am thirsty," but the conversation soon turned to the woman and living water.

What Is This Plea for Living Water?

Yes, the woman recognized Jesus in all His humanity. He was a Jew and she a Samaritan. And Jews and Samaritans "do not associate" with each other. But Jesus, a Jew, is more than a Jew. He is above earthly prejudice. He is not limited to human judgments. He does not separate people. He has no favorites. It is sin which has divided people from one another. Sin is responsible for the remark that the woman made, "You are a Jew and I am a Samaritan woman. How can you ask me for a drink?"

It is sin which prevents a man from knowing God, His rules and His love, His power and His promises of mercy. Sin has indeed separated us from one another and from God.

And so this request of Jesus, which surprises the woman because it leaps over the barrier between them, is now turned around by Jesus. "If you knew the gift of God, and who it is that asks you for a drink, you would have asked him and he would have given you living water." Had she known Him, she would have approached Him with the plea for the water of life instead of waiting for His plea to her, "I am thirsty." In her weariness and in her need she would have cried out.

Too often in what we consider a religious life we want to be the givers to God. We give Him a few moments of our days in prayer, a few moments of our week at church, a few moments to read His Word, a few mites for His mission. And we think we have given our very best. But it is God who is the Giver. It is God who provides for our needs daily, constantly. It is God who reaches out and guides our life. It is He who gives us salvation and forgiveness. It is He who provides for our protection. If we were to recognize Him as the Giver of all things, we would not always be saying to Him, "Lord, what do you want me to do?" We would be constantly coming to Him as beggars, receiving. We would come to Him with our empty cups to have them filled with the water of everlasting life. We would drink of Him and of His pleasures constantly and forever. We have so little. He offers so very much. What we have perishes and dies. What He has saves and makes us live.

What can we really offer Him? We have nothing to give. We have nothing to back up our pleas that suggest we deserve His grace or goodness. "Nothing in my hand I bring; simply to Thy cross I cling. Naked, come to Thee for dress; Helpless, look to Thee for grace; Foul, I to the fountain fly; Wash me, Savior, or I die." He pays the price for our guilt. He bears the shame of our wrongs. He suffers the consequences of our failures. He gives and gives and gives. His mercy is constant, ever flowing, a well which springs up to eternal life.

The woman said, "You have nothing to draw with." Jacob at least could dig a well and offer his cattle and children something to drink, but this man had nothing, not even a bucket to draw water from a well which was already dug. How could He possibly offer her anything?

As the man said to Jesus, "Heal my son, if you can." "'If you can'?" said Jesus. "All things are possible to him who believes." "Yes, Lord, I believe; help me when my faith falls short." And Jesus healed the child because He could and because He wanted to.

Jesus turns the situation all around. His request, "Give me a drink," becomes the promise, "I will give you a drink." He offers us more than we could ever offer Him.

And when the eye of faith is dimmed and can not see Him as the Giver and Provider, He still mercifully and kindly reaches out to all of us. It is at the cross of Christ that we put it all together and say over and over, "There it is. It really happened. The thirsty one at the cross is the one from whose side flows living water to give me life now and hereafter."

The plea of Jesus did not fall on deaf ears. The woman heard Him. She indeed wanted and needed life. But where could such a well be found?

Where Is This Place Where Living Water Is Found?

He said to her, "Everyone who drinks this water will be thirsty again, but whoever drinks the water I give him will never thirst.

Indeed, the water I give him will become in him a spring of water welling up to eternal life."

"That," said the woman, "I'll take. I'll never thirst again. I'll never need to come here again to draw water." She was still on that human level, not rising to the divine. She was still in the temporal arena and had not yet entered the eternal one. But she was ready to accept His offer, even if she did not fully understand it.

Was she inwardly hoping for mercy, for grace, for release from some inner torture or pain? Was she, as so many of us, longing for some ray of hope, a drop of mercy instead of justice, a word of love in the midst of punishment, a desire for life surrounded by death?

It was then, when the law of readiness was applied, that He aimed straight at the target, "Go, call your husband."

I'm sure we all realize that each of us has what someone has called, "our own ladder down to hell—some sin, some haunting memory of a past transgression, some tiring temptation which plagues us. We have our weaknesses and worries. We know there is a spot where we hurt and need help, all the possible help we can get. Perhaps we, too, have pleaded, "Lord, give me the help I need, the inner power and strength to aid me in my crisis, to make me firm in my temptation, to keep me safe in my danger, to deliver me in my suffering, to free me from the horrible consequences of my own sins."

"Go," said our Lord, "call your husband." What a heavy word for her! "I have no husband," she quickly replied. "You are right when you say you have no husband. The fact is, you have had five husbands, and the man you now have is not your husband. What you have just said is quite true." Whether He spoke in harsh or kind tone, it matters not. The subject was there. He knew her, for He was God. She knew herself, as indeed all of us must ultimately learn to know ourselves for what we are. Only Jesus has insight to be able to pierce into our hearts and minds, our lives and ways. He understands our thoughts afar off. He knows where we hurt, where we are touchy, and why we hurt. He knows our troubles, our mistakes, our failures, our sins.

And He also knows what it is that will wash away those sins. He knows what it is that will give comfort to our dried-up hopes. He knows what will give life instead of death, forgiveness instead of justice, hope instead of despair. He not only can say, "Here is life," but offers Himself to us. "I am the living water. If you drink of me, you never thirst again."

"Sir," she answered, "I can see that you are a prophet," a man of God who understands and knows. She who had one problem brings another to Him, as she asks, "Where can we go to God? Where can we find Him? Where is the place to drink of this spring of water for eternal life?" Some have said she tried to turn Him away from her problems when she remarked, "Our fathers worshiped on this mountain, but you [Jews] claim that the place where we must worship is in Jerusalem."

He replied that the place to find God is not in Jerusalem, although salvation is from the Jews. It is not on Mt. Gerizim. The hour was coming when neither on that mountain nor in Jerusalem would people worship the Father. "You Samaritans worship what you do not know; we worship what we do know, for salvation is from the Jews. Yet a time is coming and has now come when the true worshipers will worship the Father in spirit and truth, for they are the kind of worshipers the Father seeks. God is spirit, and his worshipers must worship in spirit and in truth."

Come, just as you are. Come in truth. God is not limited to time or space. He is spirit. He sees and knows our wrongs and mistakes. He knows and understands our ways and words and deeds. He cares for us in love. Salvation, forgiveness, freedom, and life come from the Jews, not because God is the God only of the Jews, but because the Savior is the *full*-fillment and (turn it around) the "filling full" of all the promises given to mankind through the Jewish people. He is the One who is the Living Water. The place of the living water is not in Jerusalem or at Gerizim; it is in God.

"I know," said the woman, "that Messiah is coming. When He comes, He will explain everything to us." The Messiah will give the guidance and show her where that water of life is. "I," said our Lord Jesus, "who speak to you am he."

The place where you find the living water is in Christ. The place where you find water of life for eternity is in Jesus who comes in the flesh to give His very life and His very being on Calvary for the sins of all mankind, Jews or Samaritans, Greeks or Romans, all afar off and those who are near.

Yes, she saw in Him a *Person* who was a tired and traveling wayfarer, a Jew who wanted a drink. But He showed to her, as He shows to all of us, that He is one who is offering us sinners the water of eternal life, for in His very person He is the Water of Life.

She heard His *plea* for a drink of water, but indeed there was a greater plea. He reaches out to all of us, offering His grace and mercy, His continuing, unending love and kindness.

She came to that *place* at the well and wondered if there were another place to get better water. He showed her that there was only one place, and that was in Himself. "Drink of Me! For I am the well of water not only for life here but life forever."

She left there and told others. The disciples returned and were amazed at what they saw. The story reminds us that all people—the friends of the woman, you and I—will find in Him grace and joy for life now and life forever.

Getting and Keeping 20/20 Vision

THIRD SUNDAY IN LENT
JOHN 9:13-17, 34-39

Arthur O. Kaul

Some years ago I was a pastor in one of our larger cities. It was Good Friday. I was invited to conduct worship services in a large state institution for the blind. About 400 blind people, most of them in their 20s and 30s, attended the service.

It was an experience I shall never forget. There was a mixture of joy and sadness in my heart. It was a joy to see so many blind people singing the great gospel songs of Lent. I had never experienced this before. There was also sadness in my heart. All these people sitting before me were blind. They could not see the beauty of the flowers or the changing of the seasons. They could not communicate quite like seeing people.

I. The Plight of the Handicapped

John 9 tells of a young man born blind. It describes his contact with his parents, his neighbors, the Pharisees, and especially his eventual union with Jesus.

To be handicapped in any way is always difficult. Only too frequently handicapped people are misunderstood and sometimes even resented.

To be handicapped at the time of Christ, and especially to be blind, was a severe blow to one's personal and social life. There were no doctors to whom such people could turn. Institutions for the blind were nonexistent. Many of these blessings came because of Christ and the Gospel. There was no chance of employment for such an individual. The result was that the blind could easily lose their self-esteem.

Perhaps the most cutting blow to a blind person at that time was that few people seemed to care. They became society's outcasts. The only source of livelihood was begging. There were many beggars because there were many handicapped people. Blindness then and now seems to be very prevalent among many people in the Middle East.

However, today we have means of caring for such people. Modern medicine and surgery have done miraculous things for the blind. Currently, new techniques and glasses have been developed.

These have restored eyesight to many people so that they can even read.

Institutions dot our countryside, all caring for handicapped people. It can be said that we are a caring people. Much is being done for many forms of illness and blindness. The young man in the Gospel had none of these advantages.

II. The Gift of Sight

Thanks to the power and mercy of Jesus, the young man got and no doubt kept his 20/20 vision. This young man had met Jesus. Things happen when we meet Jesus.

The attitude of many people at the time of Christ was that being born with a handicap was a sign that the person or his parents had committed some grievous sin. Today, this attitude sometimes still prevails. Our home was blessed with a mentally retarded son. My wife and I have had to counsel other parents in similar situations who were asking, "What did we do that God should send this affliction on us?"

Even our Lord's disciples accepted this notion, They asked Jesus, "Rabbi, who sinned, this man or his parents, that he was born blind?" Jesus told His disciples that neither the young man nor his parents had sinned. Rather, Jesus was going to demonstrate the majesty, power, and mercy of God in and through the young man's healing.

He made some clay with dirt and spit and placed it on the man's eyelids. He told him to go and wash in the pool at Siloam. When he had washed, he returned seeing. We can be sure it was 20/20 vision. Jesus never does things halfway. The young man was healed that God would be glorified even among His critics.

Jesus healed many people during His ministry on earth, yet there are no healing movements recorded in the Bible. St. Paul, through the power of God, healed many people, but not all people. In 2 Tim. 4:20 he writes, "I left Trophimus sick in Miletus." Three times he asked God to heal his own affliction. God, however, as much as told Paul he could use him better sick than well. To the Corinthians he wrote, "Three times I pleaded with the Lord to take it away from me. But he said to me, 'My grace is sufficient for you: for my power is made perfect in weakness'" (2 Cor. 12:8-9).

Yet God wants us to go to Him with all our heartaches, problems, and sicknesses. Perhaps some people are sick because they have forgotten God and prayer and are relying only on their own strength and ability. The Bible makes it clear that often we have not because we ask not. The hymn states it this way, "Oh, what peace we often forfeit; Oh, what needless pain we bear—All because we do not carry Everything to God in prayer!"

Sometimes our own guilt or feelings that we keep hidden can cause sleeplessness, headaches, and other symptoms.

Jesus wants us to go to Him with all of our needs. He is the same yesterday, today, and forever. Are you ill? Go to Jesus. Talk to Him in prayer. Draw strength from His eternal Word. Read the Psalms. They are for you, and in them you will also find your needs met, as the Psalmist found his needs met, by a merciful and all-powerful God.

Opposition arose to Christ's healing because it was done on the Sabbath Day. The Pharisees, religious leaders, opposed this healing when they, of all people, should have known better. They lived only by the Law. They were guided by rules and regulations. There's nothing wrong with that in the right context. However, the laws, rules, and regulations became ends in themselves. Jesus had said, "The Sabbath was made for man, not man for the Sabbath" (Mark 2:27). The Pharisees turned this statement around. They would rather see a man sick, suffering, or dying on the Sabbath Day than to lift one finger to help such a person, because they thought obedience to their understanding of the Law came first. They were blind to love, mercy, and justice. These were the very attitudes that Jesus was teaching and demonstrating. They hated Him for that. Religion can become a very dangerous thing when it is twisted and corrupted. Man has done many sinful things in the name of religion.

Mark's gospel in the New Testament gives illustration after illustration of the confrontations Jesus had with the Pharisees. It was always on their misuse of the Law.

The Pharisees had no love for this young man who had been healed. They asked him how he had received his sight. He explained to them how Jesus had healed him. The Pharisees became angry. To them this incident was proof that Jesus was not from God, especially because He healed on the Sabbath Day. That was a disgrace and violation of the Law. They couldn't understand how a person could do such a miraculous thing and disobey the Law at the same time.

There is some Pharisee in all of us, and we need constantly to be on guard against it. Parents make rules for their children and that can be good. But when those rules become only a rod, with no love and affection, they can destroy and lead to anarchy.

We all have the temptation to think of ourselves more highly than we ought. This was the problem of the Pharisees and led them into becoming cold, hard, and legalistic.

III. The Gift of Faith

The young man who was healed by Jesus not only received

20/20 physical vision, but he also received 20/20 spiritual vision.

At first, the man thought of Jesus as only a prophet. He said so. Many people today look upon Jesus as only a prophet. Most religions outside of Christianity place Jesus into this category. They say that Jesus, along with Moses, Abraham, Buddha, and others, were great teachers, and that's as far as it goes.

What little social standing the young man had was completely lost when the Pharisees cast him out of the church. He had told the Pharisees that if Jesus were not from God he wouldn't have been healed. In anger they told him he was born in sin and had no credentials to tell them anything. When Jesus heard that the young man had been cast out, He sought him. What a confrontation He had! Jesus asked him, "Do you believe in the Son of Man?" He answered, "Who is he, sir? Tell me so that I may believe in him." Jesus answered, "You have now seen him; in fact he is the one speaking with you." The young man answered, "Lord, I believe," and he worshiped Him.

Jesus was then and is today the seeking Savior. He is seeking the lost. He is seeking the straying and the erring. God's people are His voice calling people to repentance and faith in Him.

The young man made a great confession of faith, "Lord, I believe." Is that your confession? Can you say from your heart what Luther stated in his explanation of the Second Article of the Apostle's Creed, "I believe that Jesus Christ, true God, begotten of the Father from eternity, and also true man, born of the Virgin Mary, is my Lord, who has redeemed me, a lost and condemned creature, purchased and won me from all sins, from death, and from the power of the devil; not with gold or silver, but with His holy, precious blood and with His innocent suffering and death . . ."? Can you say with Luther, "This is most certainly true"? If you can, thank God for the gift of faith He has given you. You are then a spiritual brother or sister to the man born blind.

Not only did the young man believe in Jesus as His Lord and Savior. We are told that he also worshiped Him. Without worship our faith can die. Do you worship regularly and faithfully? Far too many people worship Him on Easter and perhaps at Christmas. They then think that they have done their duty. There are others who say they believe, but are never in God's house. The young man in our text not only believed but he worshiped Jesus. We can be sure he regularly worshiped the Lord who healed him in body, mind, and soul.

Jesus did not forgive only some of this young man's sins. He did not partly save him. Jesus gave this man 20/20 spiritual vision. He was completely healed and completely forgiven.

How does one get 20/20 spiritual vision? God's Word says, "If you confess with your mouth, 'Jesus is Lord,' and believe in your heart that God raised him from the dead, you will be saved" (Rom. 10:9). Jesus must be received by faith. "Yet to all who received him, to those who believed in his name, he gave the right to become children of God" (John 1:12).

With Martin Luther again we all must confess, "I believe that I cannot by my own reason or strength believe in Jesus Christ, my Lord, or come to Him; but the Holy Ghost has called me by the Gospel." It is the Holy Spirit who works this faith in our hearts. Let's thank God it's not our work, but His.

The young man no doubt kept his 20/20 spiritual vision. Are we keeping ours? Is it 20/20 vision? We are all tempted to say what the little poem says, "Jesus paid a part, and I a part, you know; sin had left a little stain, we washed it white as snow."

The Good News is that God loves us in Jesus Christ, that Jesus died for our sins, that He arose, that He promises eternal life to all who trust in Him. These precious truths are all revealed to us in the Word of God. We need to be faithful to that Word. Our faithfulness should lead us to read His Word. In Bible classes we can grow in that Word, and in our worship we can praise God for that Word.

In the Sacrament of Holy Communion God comes to us in a very personal way. He takes each one of us aside and says, "My body broken for you, My blood shed for you, that you may be forgiven and strengthened." This Word and Sacrament can give you 20/20 spiritual vision.

This text not only tells us that Jesus is a prophet, but that He is more than a prophet. He is the Savior, the Healer, and the Helper. It tells us that He is the Christ who cares and who loves. He would tell us today, "Flee to Me, cling to Me, and you will have 20/20 vision."

What Makes Christians Different?

FOURTH SUNDAY IN LENT
MATTHEW 20:17-18

Arthur O. Kaul

The drug culture has a language all its own, like "taking a trip," or "I had a bad trip."

A few years ago there were Jesus youth movements. They spoke about "taking a trip with Jesus." Most of it was very personal, emotional, and subjective.

During Lent we talk about another trip. It's a trip that Jesus took for us.

In the Gospel Jesus brought the disciples on a trip to Jerusalem. It wasn't a long trip, but a trip in which they could go with Him only as far as Jerusalem. The rest of the way He had to go alone.

Jesus took the disciples aside and had a private talk with them. He told them what was lying ahead. It wasn't good. He said the church's leaders would condemn Him to death. He would be mocked, beaten, and crucified. Then our Lord added what would become the touchstone of Christianity, His resurrection—"On the third day he will be raised to life." This was not just a neat little phrase tacked on at the end. The resurrection of Christ is crucial. St. Paul devotes a good portion of his epistle to the Corinthians to the subject of Christ's resurrection. He states that if Christ did not rise, we are wasting our time in worship, and our faith is useless. He proclaims that Christ did rise, and he gives evidence and recalls eyewitnesses.

In Matthew's account we look at these acts of Jesus for our redemption and at some of the actors surrounding Him for guidance in this Lenten season. From this holy and hellish drama let us gain renewed faith, forgiveness, and hope. Lent will sharpen our spiritual focus so we can ask the question, "What Makes Christians Different?"

I. The Difference Hidden

Christians are different. When Christ entered the heart and life of St. Paul, he was changed. In fact, he became so different that people around him were at first suspicious of him. Later he could write, "If anyone is in Christ, he is a new creation; the old has gone, the new has come!" (2 Cor. 5:17).

James and John did not understand life in the Kingdom. They wanted to be big shots. Their mother was encouraging them in this effort. They wanted seats of prominence. Why take the back seat when you can have the front? was their attitude. Jesus knew that neither James, John, nor their mother were ready to sit where Jesus sat, nor was it His to give them.

The height of their pride showed when they told Jesus that they were qualified and able to sit as His right and left sides. They spoke in ignorance. They didn't realize what was involved in drinking His cup.

The rest of the disciples were no better. They reprimanded James and John for their behavior. They probably only regretted that they hadn't thought of it first. This later became clear in their behavior during the trial and suffering of their Lord.

The problem that afflicted James and John is the same problem that we have to fight every day. It's our proud and egotistical nature. As Luther put it, this self-centered nature has to be drowned every day, and every day a new man, a new nature, must arise in us. And that is something that is possible for us because of our Baptism.

Perhaps it would be good to ask ourselves some rather personal and penetrating questions from time to time. Am I either knowingly or unknowingly creating the impression that I think I am a better person than I really am? Am I honest in all my words and acts? Is there the suspicion of hypocrisy in my life? Do I exaggerate? Am I reliable? Can I be trusted? Am I jealous, impure, irritable, touchy, distrustful? Am I self-pitying, self-justifying? Am I proud? Do I thank God that I am not as other people? If so, what am I doing about it? I recall once visiting a man in a hospital. He told me, "I became a Christian several years ago, then after that I was sanctified, and now I am completely free from sin." I told him that he had gotten further in a few years than I had progressed in a lifetime. At the end of his story Paul could only say that he was the chief of sinners. Pride is the stepping-stone to self-righteousness.

Jesus immediately set out to correct the thinking of James and John. They had indicated they could endure the same suffering and abuse that Jesus was about to experience. Jesus told them, "You will indeed drink from my cup." They would suffer for the sake of the Gospel. However, to be concerned about a place of prominence in His kingdom was completely out of line with its nature.

These disciples did eventually have to pay the price for following Christ. John was exiled to a lonely island where he wrote the Book of Revelation, and James was murdered, as were most of the other disciples.

When Jesus said, "You will indeed drink from my cup," He identified the sufferings of all of His disciples—endured for the sake of the Gospel—with His own sufferings. Peter the apostle writes, "Rejoice that you participate in the sufferings of Christ" (1 Peter 4:13). The suffering of Christ was a suffering for the salvation of the world. The suffering of His followers was a confessional suffering, as they confessed His name in a hostile world.

There is a price to pay for being a Christian. Through the centuries men and women have had to give their lives for their faith. Today in many parts of the world the Christian life is not easy. Some governments are downright hostile to Christians and make every effort to thwart mission work and to stamp out Christianity. I have some messages that were spoken by a pastor of the Russian Orthodox Church. They were smuggled out of Russia by dissident intellectuals. In these messages he gives a good testimony to the Christian faith. What happened to him? The secret police removed him from his pulpit near Moscow and sent him to Siberia. When people come out of a background of another religion and embrace the Christian faith, they are sometimes disowned by their own families.

We in America are fortunate. We have religious freedom. Some people even behave as though it means freedom from religion. Yet even in America Christ's words apply, "You will indeed drink from my cup."

Christian youth often find it hard to live their Christian faith surrounded by multiple temptations. "Most of my friends use drugs, why shouldn't I?" "Many of my friends are having sex; maybe I'm missing something." These are only several of the items Satan flings at our youth. To keep the Christian faith through a myriad of temptations is not easy. But to those whom He has called in Christ, God will give strength to meet every temptation.

In His conversation with the disciples Jesus said, "You know that the rulers of the Gentiles lord it over them, and their high officials exercise authority over them" (Matt. 20:25). The disciples were misconceiving Christ's kingdom and following a wrong principle about greatness. They were degrading His kingdom to the level of heathen kingdoms. Jesus pointed out the vast difference. Heathen rulers oppress their subjects. They use authority to maintain their greatness. In Christ's kingdom love is the compelling force.

II. The Difference Revealed

Christians are different in many ways. God has redeemed us and made us His children. We are new creatures through the forgiveness won for us in Christ. He even calls us "salt." We are to influence our society as salt gives flavor to food.

A few years ago a choir from one of our synodical schools gave a concert in a congregation. One of the frequent comments after they left was, "These young people seemed different, such fine Christians." Why not? Christians are different.

James and John and all the disciples became different. After Christ had died, risen, and ascended into heaven, the Holy Spirit came upon them. They were given a new direction and sense of urgency. The Holy Spirit comes to us even today to empower us through Word and Sacrament, to renew us and form us into His kind of people. The distinguishing mark of a Christian is servanthood. Jesus told the disciples, "Whoever wants to be great among you must be your servant, and whoever wants to be first must be your slave—just as the Son of Man did not come to be served, but to serve, and to give his life as a ransom for many" (Matt. 20:26-28).

In the Old Testament the prophet Isaiah had described Jesus as the suffering servant of Jehovah. His entire life was a life of service. We are told that He came not to be served but to serve people. When

He instituted the Lord's Supper, He also washed the disciples' feet. At that meal there was not only bread and wine, but towel and basin—symbols of service.

It must have been quite a shock for the disciples to learn that they were not to seek worldly greatness. They were to become servants and slaves, helping people spiritually and physically. This, He said, is the mark of true greatness. As we are renewed by His love and forgiveness, we also learn to demonstrate our faith by serving others. There is so much to do. There is a world outside in trouble. Millions in America and in our world do not know Jesus Christ as their Lord and Savior; they must be told.

Nursing homes are filled with lonely people. They need a word of love from us. Many teenagers are searching for the meaning of life, but searching in the wrong places. Broken homes and broken lives everywhere call us to service. Let us ask God to open our spiritual eyes to see and give us the power to make ourselves available for help when it is needed. In times of sickness someone may be needed to lend a hand, to send over some food or watch a child. In times of discouragement people need to know we will try to understand and share the burden. As people who know how much we have been helped, we become the ones whom people will call on when help is needed.

Jesus was straightforward. He points us to the source of faith and motivation for servanthood. The bottom line is that He came "to give his life as a ransom for many." St. Paul captured the meaning for us when he wrote, "He died for all, that those who live should no longer live for themselves but for him who died for them and was raised again" (2 Cor. 5:15). When St. Paul met the risen Christ, he asked, "Who are you, Lord?" Jesus responded by identifying Himself and telling Paul He had a job for Him (Acts 9:5-6). His message is the same for us.

Jesus is God's very Son. He took the form of man. He never sinned. He was holy. He died to pay for every sin you and I have committed. He arose from the grave. He promises all who believe in Him a new and eternal life. It's a precious promise that changes our lives so that the world can see a difference in us. The first century Christians showed their faith by their deeds. This faith in action is something all of us possess as He lives in us.

St. John wrote, "All men will know that you are my disciples if you love one another" (John 13:35).

National Emergency: What Shall We Do with Jesus?

FIFTH SUNDAY IN LENT
JOHN 11:45-53

Arthur J. Spomer

This is an emergency session. There is clear and present danger to national security. The Sanhedrin, the Jewish Supreme High Council, comes to order. The atmosphere bristles, charged with the electricity of united feeling due to the common threat. The subject on the agenda: "What are we accomplishing? Here is this man performing many miraculous signs. If we let him go on like this, everyone will believe in him, and then the Romans will come and take away both our place and our nation" (John 11:47b-48).

The concern was rooted in an unusual recent occurrence. Jesus had raised Lazarus from the dead. This meant that no longer could they imagine they were dealing with an escaped mental hospital inmate, nor a "messiah" who had mere words. So now, what shall they do with Jesus? If He is left to do as He chooses, everyone will come to believe, and then what?

Their responsibility cannot be avoided, because Jesus is always provocative wherever He goes, whatever He does. It cannot be avoided because the situation demands a response. The alternatives are too painfully clear. Something must be done.

I. Jesus Is Provocative

Jesus provokes response. Seldom, if ever, does one leave with a neutral reaction. It is like a controversial piece of sculpture in the city square. To some it seems out of place; it does not blend in with the surroundings. It appears offensive to some, and may be despised by many. Yet it is loved and acclaimed by others. It "makes a statement" that is either wholeheartedly embraced or rejected in disgust. Few can remain neutral. So it is with Jesus.

His World Had to Deal with Him

The Sanhedrin, His Jewish contemporaries, even Pontius Pilate had to come to grips with Jesus. They had no choice but to be making choices. "What shall we do with him? If we let him go on like this, then what?"

The gathered Sanhedrin looked at the situation and wrote a script of the future that went something like: "If we let him go, everyone will follow him. That will bring social unrest. If there is unrest, then Rome will come and crush us, destroying our institutions, our temple and finally the national identity we have struggled through the centuries of persecution to maintain."

Although a something in Pilate desperately wanted to let Jesus go, the consequences of doing so were not acceptable. Political pressures demanded that he both keep a lid on Judea and still let the people have their way. It was a political tightrope. A loud and powerful minority wanted to be rid of Jesus. "Cooperate or else," was the message, and they could make good on their threats.

Our World Must Deal with Him

The world of the twentieth century must come to grips with Jesus, too. He poses a threat to the status quo. Jesus appears to many as one who could come and "spoil all the fun." The evangelist John makes this kind of observation about the confrontation between Jesus and the current order of things:

> He who does not believe is condemned already, because he has not believed in the name of the only Son of God. And this is the judgment, that the light has come into the world, and men loved darkness rather than light, because their deeds were evil. For everyone who does evil hates the light, and does not come to the light, lest his deeds should be exposed (John 3:18b-20 RSV).

Light breaks into the darkness of dishonesty, lies, coverups, and all forms of sin. Light threatens the bondage of greed, lust, power, and self-imposed loneliness. In the natural state people hate their prisons and yet choose to remain in them. The hold of sin is threatened by Jesus. The world today, like Caiaphas, the Sanhedrin, and the populace in general, instinctively recognizes that you cannot let Jesus "go on" and have business as usual.

People certainly will tolerate "religion." A certain nostalgic reverence of holy things out of the distant past is permitted, as is civil religion, humanism, secularism, even "God, guns, and guts to keep America strong." But Jesus on his own terms as Savior and as Lord is not so easily tolerated. His active presence makes people slightly uneasy. He causes sweaty palms. He exposes the shabbiness of self-righteousness—the filthy rags of man's desire to earn God's respect and acceptance. He offers salvation not like some celestial vending machine that dispenses quantity for value received, but as a free gift. This is offensive. Where the world is content with instant intimacies and disposable loyalties, Jesus commands a radical followership of devoted disciples literally ready to lay down their lives. The world sees the bottom side of things and says "this side up." Jesus turns it the other way around, the right way. If we let Him go on as he chooses, the conventional conduct of the world is fundamentally challenged.

We Must Deal with Him

The provocative nature of Jesus cannot be tamed by us who claim to be religious.He is not like some petty deity who could be placated with formula prayers and a nicely scheduled 60-minute Sunday sacrifice. He reserves the right to invade the sanctuaries of our temple and cast out everything that is wrong. It seems safer to maintain an arm's-length relationship with Him. We might wonder, "What will happen if we let Him go?"—in our lives—in our church? Perhaps He will not find everything to His liking. It is all too easy to make decisions, operate our administration, and focus time and resources in the church for our convenience and pet programs rather than in ways that let Jesus "go on."

The story is told of the day a tornado hit town. The news report of the event stated, "We are happy to report that the storm which destroyed St. Matthew's Church did no damage to our town." When the Gospel has become domesticated to fit into the comfortable plans of the ecclesiastical institution, the absence of such a church will have no negative impact on the community. But the church where Jesus Christ is actively working in the lives of His people will have the same impact on the world as Jesus had when He walked among people 2,000 years ago.

II. Reality Requiring Response

Not only does the person of Jesus provoke response, and that rarely neutral, but also the ministry and "signs" (as the evangelist John puts it) require some sort of verdict on the part of the person who sees or hears the evidence. Either we have here some form of colossal deception, or we have no less than the Savior of humankind. A piously fuzzy middle ground is not one of the options.

No Messiah of Mere Talk

Jesus was not the first "messiah" ever to come around the bend of a Judean road. History documents many so-called "christs," charismatic figures, exorcists, teachers, miracle workers, rabble-rousers troubling that area. Its history, culture, and current political situation were ripe for such figures. But here was One who had more than talk, tricks, and crowd appeal.

Living Lazarus Cannot Be Ignored

Jesus did many signs, all of which challenged people to faith. But now there was one piece of evidence that was so dangerous that Jesus must be done away with and the evidence literally covered up. "The chief priests made plans to kill Lazarus as well, for on account of him many of the Jews were going over to Jesus and putting their faith in him" (John 12:10-11). It's easy to see the threat in letting Jesus go on as he had been. Even the impenetrable wall of death, heretofore unbreached, was now falling at a word of command from Jesus. A walking, breathing Lazarus is evidence the populace cannot ignore. They had seen the corpse, even smelled it in death. Now it walks. The alternatives are becoming more and more clear.

A Confronting, Living Word Today

The first century was faced with an acting Messiah; we are no less faced by a living Jesus. Years after the earthly ministry, crucifixion, resurrection, and ascension of Jesus the writer to the Hebrews speaks of Him as "the same yesterday and today and forever" (Heb. 13:8). Jesus not only intruded upon the first-century Judean landscape, but He also intrudes where people are today. He is more than talk and words, more than nice memories and delightful stories for children. Jesus is liberating action today. He gives a word that is more than words. "The words I have spoken to you are spirit and they are life" (John 6:63).

Just as Jesus called out and said "Lazarus, come out," he now speaks in the Word and personally addresses each of us by name "come out." "Come out of death, guilt, and bondage and into life." He has come that we might have life and have it abundantly. He offers and literally gives peace and joy and everything that we need but can find nowhere else. He offers and He gives forgiveness for the undeserving and fellowship with outcast sinners. He responds to the questioning soul who asks, "Am I worth anything? Am I loved? Do I belong anywhere?"

Jesus not only gives an answer, Jesus IS the answer. He identifies so closely with the human situation that He put Himself in the place of each of us on the cross. The hammer of justice nailed him where we should have been. He became sin for us. The high priest didn't know it, but he was more than right when he said, "It is better for you that one man die for the people, than that the whole nation perish" (John 11:50). Either we have a fanciful tale too good to be true, too fantastic for serious consideration, or we are looking eternal salvation literally in the face. The alternatives are becoming more clear.

III. Clear Alternatives: Sacrifice Jesus or Let Him Go On

Neutrality Is Not Possible

Either Jesus must be sacrificed to preserve the status quo, or he is allowed to go on. The people Jesus encountered had to take a stand. They could not be neutral, theoretical, or theological for long. Think of the woman at the well. Think of Nicodemus, the rich young ruler, and others. The choices are clear today.

Preserve Business as Usual

The Sanhedrin was decisive: "Get rid of him!"—not only that, but "Get rid of Lazarus as well." Not many people even among unbelievers are so blatant. The main problem in the so-called free world today is not so much active opposition as benign neglect. It is not communism, atheism, or humanism. The church too can sacrifice Jesus to preserve business as usual. He can so easily, without our realizing it, be relegated to an inconsequential fenced-in play yard somewhere in the universe. He can be fenced in to "Come, Lord Jesus" before the meal, the polite prayer to open the PTA and the City Council, or the heresy "religion is a private matter." The sharp, hard edges get softened, and the embarrassing aspects of Jesus allowed to "go on thus," are amputated. "Stop here"—at the edge of our "sacred" life. "Go no further!" In the process our witness is dwarfed and truncated; our experience of the gift of salvation is filtered through narrow slits of our limited vision; and the Jesus who is so large astride the universe is made into a small plastic figurine kept with all our other "meaningful" objects in life. Jesus either is everything, or He is nothing. He never seems to tolerate our attempts to keep Him in between.

Let Him Go On

When Jesus is permitted to "go on," He can accomplish what He comes to do. He once came to pay the price of sin on the cross. He came by His Spirit in the water and Word to claim you as His. He comes by Word and Spirit to build active, conscious faith that lays hold of God's promises and builds our sanctification. He so orders things by His providence in the universe that everything works for our good to the end that we might be conformed to the image of his Son (Rom. 8:28-29). He sends us into the world with a life to live and a message to speak. He wants the redeemed to look redeemed, to be ready to give an account of the hope that is in them. If we have begun by the Spirit, let us not end in the flesh (Gal. 3:3). "Since we live by the Spirit, let us keep in step with the Spirit" (Gal. 5:25).

Let Him go on. The result: the world will come to know God sent His Son. The only evangelization program and staff that God has is us. Jesus desires to live His life today in His body on earth—in us and through us. It is through us that He can demonstrate to the world His love and power. No, we cannot both let Jesus go on and have business as usual. He never intended anything like that. The Sanhedrin asked, "What shall we do?" We, too, face the question.

"What shall we do with Him?" The destiny of many hangs on

how we will answer the question and live out our answer. The choices: stop Him, ignore Him, diminish Him, or let Him go on.

Choice and decision apart from action are of little value. There are five frogs sitting on a log. One of the frogs decides to jump off the log into the water. How many frogs remain on the log? Most people would say "four." But there are still five. He is still ON the log until he jumps. The choice to jump does not automatically remove him. "What shall we do with Jesus?" Our mental decisions mean very little. Hearers of the Word are effective in the doing.

Confusion, Rejection, or Faith?

PALM SUNDAY
SUNDAY OF THE PASSION
MATTHEW 27:11-54

Arthur J. Spomer

The narrative of our Lord's passion has always been fascinating and compelling drama. Even in a secular age like ours, thousands of tourists and millions of dollars flow into such communities as Oberammergau in connection with the presentation of the Passion Play. The story is compelling, especially when portrayed with skillful acting and theatrics that can draw people into the event.

The dramatic impact of the original event is punctuated and underlined by St. Matthew by means of questions and statements that crisscross through the story like currents of electricity. "Are you the king of the Jews?" "Which do you want . . . Barabbas, or Jesus?" "What shall I do, then, with Jesus who is called Christ?" "Don't have anything to do with that innocent man!" "Surely he was the Son of God!" These statements focus the spotlight on Jesus. Through them and the reactions to them it is shown that he was sometimes the object of confusion, sometimes of rejection, but also often the subject of faith.

I. Object of Confusion

While Jesus endures the ordeal of the events with calm assurance about His identity, mission, and future, around Him swirls a frenetic confusion.

Correct Titles, Incorrect Understanding

The other characters in the drama, especially those who stood in opposition to Jesus often are confused, using the correct titles for Him, but in ignorance and confusion. They really did not know who He was.

Christ

Twice during the course of the hearings Pontius Pilate used the title "Christ" in reference to Jesus, but he came short of acknowledging that Jesus truly IS the Christ. He asked, "what shall I do, then, with Jesus who is called Christ?" (Matt. 27:22). Mere human eyes cannot see a Christ (or "Messiah") here. They cannot discern that before them is the Chosen, the Anointed, the Savior and Deliverer of mankind promised ages ago in the Scriptures. What they see can only confuse them. Many people today stand in a confused state with reference to Jesus. When Peter correctly identified Jesus as the Christ at Caesarea Philippi, Jesus told Peter, "This was not revealed to you by man, but by my Father in heaven" (Matt. 16:17).

King of the Jews

"King of the Jews" is another title used in a confused way. While many of Jesus' fellow Jews feel certain in their own minds that Jesus is anything but their king, Pilate begins his interrogation that Friday morning with the question: "Are you the king of the Jews?" He is confused when Jesus answers, "Yes, it is as you say."

Jesus did not look like a king to Pilate. Where was His territory? All Jewish territory was under Caesar, governed by Pilate or by Herod. He had no army. He bore no marks of a king. What was it to have a kingdom "not of this world?" Was this a madman perhaps? Yet the title is correct. Jesus is the promised King, the true Heir of David who would sit on his throne forever and reign over the true sons of Israel. But the kingliness is disguised because Jesus wears a servant's apron.

"King of the Jews," the accusation attached to the cross by Pilate, is a title they used to ridicule Him. They place on Him a robe, a crown made of thorns, and, for a scepter, a reed. Then they mock Him. Little did they know there was truth in what they said. The air is filled with confusion. The irony is that they will kneel one day with all creatures before King Jesus when He returns to claim His kingdom and will say to their utter amazement, "Jesus IS Lord."

Son of God

To ridicule Jesus they use another of His holy titles, "Son of God." "If you are the Son of God, come down!" They were not the first to taunt and challenge, "If you are . . . ." Satan had done so in the wilderness. They were confused if they thought they could lightly use that title. The laughing crowds did not know what that one pagan centurion attending the execution saw—Jesus truly was the Son of God.

That Righteous Man

Yet one more title comes off the pages of the drama: "That righteous Man." Pilate's wife shares her superstitious confusion, "Have nothing to do with that righteous man" (Matt. 27:19 RSV). She said this about Jesus, but did not know the full truth she was speaking. She and her husband thought only in terms of Roman law. In reference to that, Jesus was innocent. But Jesus was far more than that. He came to fulfill all righteousness, the just requirements of the Law which the rest of mankind had failed to meet. Because he successfully did that, and did it in our stead, he is the Savior of mankind. St. John refers to Jesus by that title when describing his saving activity for the penitent sinner. "We have one who speaks to the Father in our defense—Jesus Christ, the Righteous One" (1 John 2:1).

Compounded Confusion: Jesus Exceeds All Frames of Reference

Confusion is compounded when what is happening around you does not fit into your frame of reference. Jesus came to complete the mission the Father had for Him, not to fit into man's categories of thought. Someone from a Stone Age society cannot understand a computer. It is beyond his frame of reference. The narrow confines of sinful man place the real Jesus outside his frame of reference. He is confused until the light of the Spirit breaks through to give him understanding.

I am reminded how, in my childhood, our family had a favorite card game. I was eager to be old enough to participate, and in time I observed enough to know how to deal, how to score the points, and most of the rest. Yet there was one crucial exception to my knowledge in the rules of the game. As a result, I went through all the motions of the game on the surface, but never really knew what made it tick until a flash of insight one day. From that time on I could win. I enjoyed the game. I suddenly knew what it was all about.

Many today can be playing the "religion" game, doing the "spiritual" thing. There is even a fascination with Jesus, but often the crucial, central point of it all is missing, and confusion is bred. For example, there are popular books with ennobling, quasi-religious themes and with "Christ figures." The author leads the reader through spiritual pilgrimages, but to a destination of confusion. There is also frequently a confusion between occult accents and the things of God. These confusions, sadly, are to be noted in the person in the pew at times. Hardly is there a pastor who, upon explaining and opening the Scriptures one-to-one in a counseling situation and sharing the Gospel, sees a mouth drop open, eyes widen, and the excited reaction, "so THAT'S what it's all about." The real work and purpose of Jesus had been an object of confusion.

Rome As Frame of Reference

Pilate could only look at things through Roman eyes. When he saw Jesus and heard words like "king," he compared Jesus with Caesar. Across his mind flowed images of palaces, territory, armies, bureaucracy, and the like. When he heard "Son of God," he thought again of the emperor who was said to be an incarnation of one of the gods. He would visualize opulent ritual and genuflecting before the image of Caesar. He might even become slightly misty-eyed if he had more of a mind for nostalgia.

But the word "Christ" or "Messiah" turned him away in disgust. Had not this country seen enough trouble because of religious fanatics? At least im Rome people did not take their religion so seriously. When his wife spoke of the Righteous Man, his frame of reference was Roman Law. Is the man innocent? Has he met the demands of Caesar? Somehow, Jesus could not fit into Pilate's frame of reference.

Legalistic Judaism

Nor could Jesus fit the frames of reference of current Judaism. There should have been a proper frame of reference there. Judaism had the covenants, the promise, the Scriptures, and the Law, all of which bore witness that Jesus was the Christ, the Son of God, the true King of Israel who would sit on the throne of his father David forever. Yet, confusion reigns. The spiritual leaders of Israel at Jesus' time completely missed the point of the Scriptures. They saw only law and regulation. They lost the frame of reference for promise, and so confused was the result that no two teachers could agree. It was like a group of blind men in a room with an elephant, each trying to describe what he perceives. Confusion reigned and Jesus was rejected.

20th-Century Man

Does twentieth-century man have a sufficient frame of reference for Jesus? With continual multiplications of the mass of human knowledge, one might think that man is approaching a time when he can find ultimate truth through his mind and machines. Yet the frustration is that we are no closer than Jesus' confused contemporaries. The possession of knowledge does not lead man to God. "Where is the wise man? Where is the scholar? Where is the philosopher of this age? Has not God made foolish the wisdom of the world? For since in the wisdom of God the world through its wisdom did not know him, God was pleased through the foolishness of what was preached to save those who believe" (1 Cor. 1:20-21). Systems do not quite know how to handle Jesus on His own terms. He is still much larger than man's systems. So confusion still reigns, and Jesus is rejected.

II. Object of Rejection

Thus far we have seen Jesus as an object of diverse and confused opinion. This confused ignorance finally resulted in overt rejection. That he was and is rejected would come as no surprise to us since Isaiah had characterized the Messiah as a Suffering Servant who was "despised and rejected by men, . . . one from whom men hid their faces" (Is. 53:3).

The Choice Clearly Stated

There might be a confusing multitude of choices about Jesus, but Pilate reduces them to two: "Which one do you want . . . Barabbas or Jesus?" (Matt. 27:17). The choice is clear—is it Jesus or something else?

Barabbas: Everything Other Than Jesus

Who is Barabbas? He is whatever there is other than Jesus. The world is full of a bewildering variety of things but it all comes down to "Jesus or something else." Even Christians are tempted to try to have both Barabbas and Jesus.

Let's imagine that you can acquire Christianity at a store. A customer approaches the clerk with the following shopping list: "Give me three pounds of God, six yards of the path of obedience, and one pint of faith." Modest portions of religion are taken to fit spaces fashioned by a lifestyle that can use Jesus as an afterthought—a bit of Jesus and a bit of Barabbas.

But the question is "Barabbas or Jesus?" We might want to have the salvation of Jesus plus some merit from our works. We might want to have the grace that there is in Jesus for the gift of heaven, but not want to move on to sanctification and holiness in our living. We might want Jesus plus the things of the world as objects of worship and highest affection. While we want to muddy the choices, God seems to turn up the contrast between Jesus and Barabbas.

Jesus: Everything the World Is Not

St. John warns about loving the world and the things of the world, "For everything in the world—the cravings of sinful man, the lust of his eyes and the boasting of what he has and does—comes not from the Father but from the world" (1 John 2:16). Jesus gives the gift the world cannot give. He gives the peace the world cannot give. He is willing to come in the scandal of failure and weakness through a cross. He is willing to be faithful to His Word and promise in the midst of a world of disposable commitments and relationships. He is willing to heal the disease (Ps. 103:3), and not just treat a few symptoms. Jesus became an object of rejection as the people chose the world, chose Barabbas over Him.

Rejection That Leads to Ridicule

What else can you do with someone you have rejected than finally to ridicule him? Like children at play, they taunt and they laugh as they say, "Hail, King of the Jews!" They dress Him up—robe, crown, scepter—as if He were a doll. They laugh as they make up new jokes like, "If you are the Son of God, come down from the cross."

Laughter often is a cover-up for emptiness and the pressure of tears behind the eyes. The volume of the voices increases, but still the emptiness is there. Maybe they can give each other courage with shouts and catcalls. They reject him and confirm that rejection by ridicule.

In our own times many who have rejected Jesus express that rejection by open and shameless ridicule. For a long time already the entertainment industry has been broadcasting examples of it into our homes. As our sense of outrage diminishes and our level of tolerance increases, we are in danger of subtly joining the forces of ridicule.

III. Object of Faith

Finally, there is a third sort of object that Jesus is to many—the object of faith.

Who Is He to Us?

We might correctly answer who Jesus is—Son of God, King of the Jews, the Christ, the Righteous One. But who is he to US? Our answer to that question determines what we do with Jesus, whether he is an object of confusion, rejection, or faith. When Jesus asked Peter the informational question, "Who do people say the son of Man is?" He followed Peter's answer with a direct and personal question, "Who do YOU say that I am?" The question of Jesus' identity is never dispassionate; it always confronts—"What does this mean to *you*?"

Our Reliance Demonstrates Our Evaluation

A faith is only as good as its object. It can be no stronger than its base. If the object of our faith is strong enough, then we move onto that object in trust. Many years ago as a pioneer man was walking from a distant town to his home, it was necessary to cross a wide river. Since it was early winter, the river was covered with ice, but the man was fearful that it might not be thick enough to support his weight. To minimize the risk he lay flat on the ice to distribute his weight and slowly crawled across. Though his faith in the ice was weak, he took the risk. The ice was strong enough to support him. He it not been, even the most courageous faith would have been of no value. Moments after he arrived on the opposite bank he heard shouts and the noise of hoof beats. Turning he saw a team of horses pull a loaded sled safely across the river. The object of faith was more than strong enough. So also is Jesus, our Savior, strong enough to support our faith.

True faith does not say, "*If* you are the Son of God . . . ." Knowing Jesus moves us to say, "*Because* you are the Son of God . . . ." I can rest my weight entirely on Jesus. There is no more confusion, no mere dispassionate and theoretical reflection, but a reliance on Jesus alone because life depends on it. When we have met Him and our eyes are opened to see and know Him, the only worthwhile quest of life is at an end. A centurion of Rome had traveled many a mile in his life, had seen many a battle, attended many an execution. He had seen the world and had no doubt often wondered what it was really all about. Certainly there had to be more than the Roman system. And now, as he stood by the cross and saw this man crucified and die, God opened his eyes and removed the confusion. Jesus was no longer an object of confusion or rejection but of faith. He could believe and trust and say, "Surely he was the Son of God!"

Cleaning Up

MAUNDY THURSDAY
JOHN 13:1-17, 34

Kenneth Rogahn

The way people spend their last hours before death indicates a great deal about the kind of life they have lived. More often than not, we expect people to use their time to "prepare to meet your Maker." This preparation may include repentance and recognition of sin, confession, and the experience of absolution or forgiveness. In special cases the Sacrament of Baptism or other church ceremonies may be employed in an effort to prepare for death. People tend to get their affairs in order and complete unfinished business. Given these common attitudes, it is striking indeed to see our Lord, on the night in which He was betrayed and in the face of death, using His time otherwise. In a sense He was "cleaning up his affairs" and "tying up all the loose ends." But He was doing more. His actions with His disciples show us very clearly that *Jesus used His last hour to prepare us to help others get ready for God.*

Jesus Cleanses Us

Jesus' intention overcomes our objection. He cleanses us. Everyone needs to do some preparation to face God. Only Jesus can make us ready for that moment when we stand before the Father. Indeed, each moment of our life is a moment of judgment, and we always need Christ's help to be ready.

Washed and Made Clean

Jesus washes us and makes us clean before God. As Jesus evaluated His disciples on the night before His death, He knew, although they did not, that there was much He had to do for them. His words, as recorded in John 13—17, were one way in which He would make them ready for what was to come. They contain His beautiful explanations of how they would be enabled to carry on after He had left them.

His is a cleansing action. Jesus did more than just talk. His intentions and the desires of His heart were demonstrated. The love that was the bond between Him and them was not diminished by His recognition and acceptance of the impending cross. "He now showed them the full extent of his love" (John 13:1). He washed their feet!

Each disciple was washed. Picture the scene as he moved around the table from one disciple to another. What surprise! What astonishment! But also, what relief and joy that Jesus would wash them and make them clean. Perhaps they were unaware of all the implications of His action at first. What He did was unusual behavior indeed. But he washed their feet anyway. He made them clean. And they were different because of what He did.

We, too, are cleansed. We are also washed by Jesus. His act of cleansing was not completed when He made the disciples' feet spotless and took away the dust of the road that had clung to them. His cleansing is total and for all. He accomplished a full cleansing not only with basin and towel, but by the giving of His life on the cross. His blood increased the cleansing power of water, like a powerful detergent added to cut through the deep-seated grease and grime. He removes the "stubborn stains" that are deep beneath the surface and resist ur lick-and-a-prayer efforts to remove. He is the total cleansing power for all that soils and darkens our lives. Where we have dirtied ourselves, He cleanses us. Where we need new life, He offers His own.

Our baptism is Christ's washing of us. In the water of our baptism, His Spirit conveys the Word of forgiveness that came true at Calvary. We are bathed, "washed in the blood of the Lamb," as God marks and seals us with the name of Jesus. Our inborn and deep-seated sin is rooted out and washed away. The contamination that threatens our holiness each following day cannot withstand the scrubbing action of His cross. He scours and brightens every inch of my life, for I belong totally to Him. He wipes between the toes, into every hidden part of my body. He removes the sin that lies heavy upon me and is concealed in me. As He gave Himself for me and for all in His death, He sanctifies and cleanses me and everyone for all time.

God sees me as cleansed by Christ. Now I share in His salvation. By the water of my baptism I have received the blessing of God's grace. I inherit all that Jesus bestowed upon His heirs when He died. Life and salvation are mine, for I am His. In the judgment of God—now and forever—I stand pure and holy as Christ Himself. I have part of Christ, the free gift which He offers to all. It is a heavenly washing that was characterized by His action around the table in the circle of the disciples, that night when He first washed their feet.

Objection to Cleansing

Why would anyone object to His cleansing action? God's marvelous grace and Jesus' gracious cleansing are necessary and beneficial. But our natural condition is such that we may object to what God is doing in Christ. Instead of receiving and rejoicing, our human tendency (like that of His other disciples) is to correct and question Him.

Peter considered Jesus' action demeaning. He is at one extreme. He was offended by the thought that Jesus would wash him. The action seemed beneath Jesus. Or perhaps Peter considered himself to be above such an act by His Savior. It was not that Peter thought he was perfect. He was very much aware of his failures and shortcomings. More than once his error was revealed to himself and to others so plainly that he couldn't overlook it. But he was just not prepared for the remedy that Jesus proposed. He wasn't comfortable with what Jesus wanted to do. And we can understand his feelings, if we reflect a moment on our own attitude. We, too, confess that we are not perfect, that the work of God is not complete in us. But it hardly seems appropriate to us that Jesus must stoop so low to correct our situation.

We are ready to improve; we are trying to do better. We want to increase in godly character and quality, but we want to do it our way and on our terms. It is, after all, rather humiliating to be served by a humble Savior. We would rather claim a perfect and powerful Lord. We try to keep Him on a pedestal above us and excuse Him from the cross He chooses to bear. But He insists on humbling Himself, serving, even dying and emptying Himself, in His efforts to cleanse us. To use Luke's phrase, "it is necessary" for Christ to suffer and to die, to lower Himself to that extent, to sacrifice the last drop of self-respect, to place Himself at our feet and beneath us, so that we might be saved. To reject His way of washing, then, is to reject Him. He saves in His own ignominious (but exalted) fashion, or not at all.

Peter tried to improve Jesus' technique. "All right then," he muttered (when he had been put to shame), "clean me. But make me clean enough to pass my own inspection. Don't just wash my feet." Not content with one insult, He seemed to accept Jesus' action, but then he sought grudgingly to improve on it. We, too, are tempted to transfer our attention from the uncomfortable image of a crucified Redeemer to a critical inspection of how He operates. Like Peter, we think we can understand the logic and rationale of the work of God in Christ. Then we want to add something more to what He is doing. We are dissatisfied perhaps with the pace or scope of our sanctification. We want God to do more. We see areas of our life that do not suit us. So we insist that our Lord deal with them also, on our terms. "If you must change me, Lord, do it my way" is our prayer. He doesn't seem to be doing enough to satisfy our expectations. We aren't satisfied with the extent of His cleansing. We know better than He (we think), what He ought to do with us and for us.

It is not impossible, even in the face of Jesus and the generous forgiveness He embodies, to so distort His intention and work that it no longer helps us. Judas is an example of people who reject the action of God in Jesus. The washing does no good for one who prefers to be dirty. Like Peter, Judas had his own "better idea," and it did not center in Jesus as the one who cleansed him. The devil put it in his heart. Judas was the betrayer. He was not washed. He was not clean, not at all. And though he seems at first to be the exception, he is really not so different from us or Peter.

Judas is simply at the other extreme, the point where one's own will and mind have *completely* separated him from the grace of God. His sin was no greater than Peter's, for they both objected to the way in which Jesus did His loving work. But his objections were not overcome by the grace of God. Jesus did not respond to his objection as He did in the case of Peter. Perhaps it was because He knew Judas could not stand to be seen in his weakness and to receive power from Him as Peter did. So Judas went out and away from Jesus. He was lost. He had no cleansing.

Jesus Calls Us to Love

Jesus adds another dimension for our attention—love as He does. Maundy Thursday can be a sad occasion if our attention remains on Judas or Peter in their weakness. All the gloom of Good Friday threatens already to invade our situation when we recognize how unclean we humans are in the sight of God. We need to focus anew on the Jesus who is on center stage this night, for He alone can bring a new dimension to our existence as His followers. He isthe bearer of the New Testament in His blood, so He does not leave us in our weak condition.

In Control

Jesus knows what He is doing. Those around Him may misunderstand or challenge His loving actions, but He remains in control of the situation. In His Word from the cross He shows that He is aware of our ignorance and the failure of all people. "Father, forgive them," He prays, "for they do not know what they are doing" (Luke 23:34). By His resurrection, He proves Himself to be Lord in power. But He knew all along that God had sent Him. He always knew that He was going to the Father. He knew when the hour had come to glorify His Father. He taught His disciples all that He knew. He knew that He was the Teacher of the truth of God, so He knew that the Father's will required that others would go out in His name. He knew He was the Sender as well as the Sent One.

Giving an Example

He demonstrates His love as an example for our activity. Others may not know what He does, but we who are included in the new covenant of God have received wisdom from above through Christ. We know that we have one Master, and we are not on our own. We are servants and slaves of Christ. We confess that now we are sent by Him into the world to carry on His loving service.

Our task is to clean up others in this world in the style and manner of Jesus. Our job is not as great or difficult as His, for He has conquered the enemy and removed the great uncleanness that entered the world by sin. He has won the victory over death and the devil, which corrupt and contaminate the people that God created to praise Him. He has overcome all evil. The decisive battle is over, and ours is a mopping up action. We have been called by Christ and are now sent by Him to wipe out the vestiges of sin that remain in the world. The marks of the battle, the leftover traces of the struggle that Christ waged on the cross, are for us to wipe away and cleanse. If the world is a sink into which all the dirty dishes are placed, and the water and work of Christ have washed them clean, then we who have also been cleansed by Him are like a dishrag that tidies up after the dishes are done. Christ uses us to wipe out the remaining dirt marks, to make sure there is no ring left in the sink and no traces of dirt remaining. We are sent to people who are soiled by sin and need to be cleaned. Christ cleans them through us. We are cleaned so that we can help clean others. That is Jesus' way. With His word, by the water of Baptism, in loving service, we are God's agents to remove sin.

Since He has provided the cleansing of sin by His righteousness earned and won on the cross, and because He is risen in power to be Lord and Savior, He can use us to bear the message to others. Through the ministers of His church—and that should be every Christian—He speaks the word of absolution which wipes away all sin. He gives us the right and ability to speak and act in His name. Without Him we can do nothing. With Him, in Him, for Him, the least of Christians can bear the "power of God for salvation" (Rom. 1:16) in an effective way. Not by our own doing, of course, but with the means of grace the Lord has entrusted to us.

Power and Blessing

Jesus gives power and blessing to do as He did. Maundy Thursday received its name because Jesus gave us His command (in Latin *mandatum* from which the word "Maundy" developed) that we love one another as He loved us. On that same night He promised and provided the power to do it when He passed out bread and wine that He had blessed. "This is my body . . . . this is my blood," He said. The Holy Supper is given for us to eat and drink, so that we will never forget what He has done and will be able to do what He wants us to do. As He promised to the first disciples, so He assures us that He dies and rises in order to send His Spirit to be among us. And we remember Him. "Do this in remembrance of me." Christ has washed us, so we are clean to eat this holy meal. We receive His righteousness and give Him our thanks. He sends us out with His blessing, and we believe even though we have not seen Him (John 20:29). Because of Him we follow His example. We say and do words and actions of service that prepare others so they too are ready to meet God. Joined into one body, the church, we are His holy people forever and ever.

What Is There to Say?

GOOD FRIDAY
JOHN 19:17-30

Kenneth Rogahn

Funeral parlors and cemeteries foster strange conversation. In the presence of death we don't know what to say. It is the living who are doing the talking, yet they aren't comfortable ignoring the deceased. We cannot speak to the dead and expect an answer. It seems that the only way to have a conversation when death is present is by talking about anything but death. And people tend to do just that, to engage in a "conspiracy of silence" even when the evidence of death is close at hand. But not to talk about death, the death of Jesus, would be impossible on Good Friday of all days in the year. And that is our topic of conversation today.

Our situation parallels that of other times when we have been confronted by death. Remember the last time (if ever) that you were with a person when death was inevitable. As death came closer it was probably increasingly difficult to find something to say. Whatever we did say seemed inappropriate. Nothing seemed to help the situation. And yet we talked as death approached and arrived. People always seem to do that.

The death of Jesus did not take place in comfortable or controlled circumstances. He hung on a cross, out in the open, exposed to public view. With his two companions, obvious criminals, he spent his final hours at the Place of the Skull, Golgotha. But before death came, *Jesus gave us something to talk about after He died. What He said and did there corrects all the things that people say and do in ignorance when death approaches.*

I. Ignorance and Evil

At Jesus' death people spoke ignorantly and did evil. Consider the individuals who were intimately involved in the death of Jesus and are quoted in the Gospel. They demonstrate how easy and normal it is to say and do the wrong thing when someone is dying. The words preserved by St. John are familiar in their meaning and natural in their intent, but they are not very helpful to others.

Chief Priests Argued

The chief priests argued. When Jesus was crucified, a title was hung on the cross with Him: "Jesus of Nazareth, the King of the

Jews." Pilate put it there, as he had the right and power to do. The chief priests objected to its presence and its message. Their bickering sounds like the sort of family arguments and petty quarrels that often break out when someone dies. Because death is so shocking, nerves are tense and feelings are exposed. It doesn't take much to create controversy.

Some view the body and object to its appearance. Whoever made the decisions about the arrangements had better be prepared for objections. "He shouldn't have been fixed that way." "She should be wearing something different." Minor items, perhaps, except to those who are most deeply upset by the death. The complaints easily increase in scope and intensity. One remembers something about the deceased. Someone else remembers it otherwise. Opinions differ. Tempers flare. Feelings erupt. A lot of things are said that don't do anyone any good.

The chief priests fit into this category. Jesus seemed to be getting too much favorable publicity. It seemed as though He was achieving in death what they denied Him in His lifetime. They objected to the recognition the words on the title gave Him. As furious as Herod was when he was confronted with the report of the birth of the King of the Jews (Matt. 2:2), the priests exploded when the official notice of His death used the same language. But for all their arguing, they were unable to change a thing.

We, too, may say much about the dead. We may react positively or negatively to what other people say about the departed one. We may object to the claims, the reports, the recollections. But all our talk doesn't change a thing. What is true during a lifetime is sealed at death, and then it is impossible to change the record. People can say what they want about the dead, but it doesn't change what they were and are. Only God has the power to do that.

Pilate Repeated Himself

Some people have more control over the circumstances that prevail at death. For example, when the chief priests objected to the words on the title, their protest was directed to the power that had put them there. It was Pilate, the Roman governor, who had taken the liberty of composing the words. When he was challenged, he refused to change what he had said earlier.

Again, the expression sounds familiar. Pilate said, "What I have written, I have written." It was stated once and for all. It was final, his final word at this man's death. Pilate would not change. He was not open to argument or persuasion. He would not listen to protest or petition. His attitude was the typical one: "My mind's made up. Don't confuse me with facts."

Death forces people to take a position, to adopt a stance, to maintain a conviction. Such an attitude is no surprise, because everyone implicitly recognizes how much is at stake. The writer to the Hebrews says it this way, "After death, the judgment" (9:27). One cannot afford to be ambiguous or irresolute in the face of death, otherwise others might recognize how uncertain and fearful we are. Pilate certainly gave evidence earlier in the trial of how vacillating he was, but when death approached he blustered and presented a false bravado.

People today reflect the same hardness and unchangeability when death is near. No compromise is permitted, no withdrawal from a previously stated position. At the end of life we mask our uncertainty with a display of conviction. Our dogmatic assertions are empty and unconvincing, but they seem necessary. Some people cannot say anything good about the dead, contrary to popular convention. They stand firm with, "I never did like him." "I didn't understand her. "She always seemed to me—" "He never —" People may seem to be unmoved by the radical change that death brings about. They maintain their previous position, no matter what. Don't try to argue with them. Arguments only make them defensive and more assertive. Only God could budge them.

Soldiers Grabbed for Gain

We hear a third important sentiment voiced at the cross. Four soldiers were there to guard the site. They had no direct interest in what was happening or what it meant. But they did have a chance to realize some personal gain from being there. They weren't interested in arguing for or against Jesus. They didn't want to discuss the merits of His character. They had neither knowledge nor authority to bolster their claims. But they wanted to get something. So the soldiers said, as they inspected Jesus' tunic in the process of dividing up His clothing, "Let's not tear it. Let's decide by lot who will get it."

Now isn't the division of property a familiar topic of conversation on the occasion of a death? Who is going to get what? How will the estate be divided? What will I get? How can its value be preserved? How quickly family members turn their attention to what is left behind when someone dies. What squabbles and contests occur because of their competing claims. "She wanted me to have this." "He said I was to have that." "No, that's for me." "I should get this."

It seems that the real value of a person is to be determined by the amount of the inheritance. Even before the body is cold, survivors start to fight and pick over what is left behind. Everyone wonders how much there will be *for me.*

Feelings and affections are sublimated when there is possible material or financial gain. Like the soldiers, all those who grab for property and possessions after a death give a clear indication of where their interest lies. Likewise, their actions are a mute testimony to the finality of death. The one who died cannot convey or bestow anything in a personal way. Now it is the impersonal, material objects which remain that mean everything.

Of course, the soldiers were carrying out a fulfillment of Scripture. Just as God had foretold, so people did. But the fulfillment of God's Word was hardly the motivation of their possessiveness. Indeed, those who are most concerned with things that one can own and treasure are least likely to be concerned with what God has said. They are too busy shouting for what they want, or at least speaking assertively so that they aren't cheated out of anything.

II. Knowledge and Goodness

Jesus' words and deeds show knowledge and goodness in action. One can imagine that the deceased would like to get into the conversation, too, if not prevented by death. If he were still alive while all those words are being spoken, he would certainly have an opinion to voice. What would a dying man say, if he heard those around him arguing about his character or epitaph or possessions during his final hours? More specifically, what did Jesus say?

According to God's Plan

Jesus spoke according to God's plan. It is significant that He did not use His breath to chastise and correct what others were saying. He did not waste words arguing with people who were too busy talking to listen to anyone else. Jesus had always listened to God. He knew what His Father had said. He had learned the Scriptures. So one of His final words was specifically spoken in order to round out the plan of God.

Jesus said, "I am thirsty." Of course, the physical and psychological pain of His ordeal would make His body cry out for a drink. But there was something more than pain reflected in His words. He spoke acceptance and conviction about God. He deliberately echoed what God had said through His earlier speakers; His words were a conscious fulfillment of Scripture. With the zeal implicit in Psalm 69, he earnestly strove to complete what God had planned in spite of the fact that it was painful for Him. He thirsted to do the will of God. Never mind that the soldiers misunderstood and that neither wine nor vinegar could satisfy this God-inspired thirst. He spoke to God, obediently and gladly, as we are so hesitant to do ourselves. His conversation was in heaven. He spoke to His Father as a dear child, in the same spirit in which God had spoken to Him all His life.

Care for His Own

Jesus cared for His own. The words that others spoke or the silence they endured did not dissuade Jesus from speaking in love to them. He could not be quiet when those He loved needed help. He saw Mary, His mother, and His beloved disciple through eyes dimmed with suffering and threatening to close in death. He gave them to each other in love, and joined them by His word of love even as He was about to withdraw His bodily presence from them. "Care for each other," He said.

Jesus speaks to us and to all the brothers and sisters in the faith today with the same concern and command. We, too, huddle closer to one another for protection and reassurance in the face of death. We also are afraid and alone when our Lord seems to be distant. When we cannot even voice our need, then Jesus hears our silent cry. He joins us with Himself in an unending bond established by His death. When we feel the sadness of parting and the tragedy of loss, He speaks to us about each other. "You are brothers and sisters to one another. You are all one family. You belong together. Love one another and care for each other. I also will always be with you. I give you my Word."

The Work of Salvation Finished

Jesus finished the work of salvation. One final word He speaks, a word to all who fear death. Jesus speaks to the soul that recognizes that it will die for its sins. He has a word for everyone who mumbles and mutters or stumbles and stutters in those deathly conversations we overheard earlier. He anticipates God's Word of approval for all His words and works. He says the one word (in Greek) which removes all our doubts in the face of death.

Jesus said, "It is finished." He had accomplished what He came to do. There is nothing more for us to add; there is no concern that more is needed. He had given Himself to rescue us from sin and death.

There is no longer any reason to fret and fumble as we try to find the right words to say when we are faced with death. Jesus has said it all. His suffering and death have overcome death and relieved suffering. The hushed whispers of mourners have given way to the shout of conquerors. Now the word resounds—"It is finished."

We confess that Jesus who died is risen from the dead. As Death shouted, "I have won," Jesus made Death choke on his words. When enemies claimed, "He is gone," Jesus proclaimed, "I am alive forever." When friends and followers wondered, the risen Christ declared, "I will be with you always." His resurrection means life for all. God has the final word. He rules, when all is said and done.

And everything is said and done for our good through Jesus Christ our Lord.

Conclusion

Jesus need say nothing more. He dies. With His final action He conveys His Spirit to us. He tells us what to say when death threatens. He replaces our selfish and argumentative words with the Spirit's sighing in us (Rom. 8:26), and God answers our prayer. God's Word is all about Jesus, that prophet who speaks words from God. God's word tells us that Jesus is the priest who, with the whole and holy garment of righteousness, was Himself offered to the Father as the final sacrifice for sin. Now He intercedes for us and clothes us with His merit. God's Word proclaims Jesus as King, not only of the Jews but of all. God raised Him to be Lord of all, and He rules with the Father forever.

Such good news is the message we receive from the conversations at the cross. Jesus gives us good news to speak, good news about how He has overcome death and given life. Now we can speak, at funeral homes and cemeteries and wherever death threatens, about the hope and power we have in Jesus. And that's quite a mouthful!

Celebrating an Empty Tomb

THE RESURRECTION OF OUR LORD
EASTER DAY
MATTHEW 28:1-10

Donald L. Deffner

Christ is risen! He is risen indeed!

A joyous, blessed Easter Day to one and all of you!

What are we really celebrating here today? *We are celebrating an empty tomb.*

In *Therefore Stand* Wilbur M. Smith notes that "of the four great religions of the world resting directly upon personalities, rather than upon some philosophical system, the Christian religion is the only one that even talks about an empty tomb in relation to its founder."

Abraham, regarded by Jews as the father of their faith, died some two millenia before Christ, but the Jews have never claimed that he has been resurrected. In fact, his tomb is still carefully preserved in Hebron in southern Palestine. No resurrection is ascribed to Buddah, either. In fact, in the *Mahaparinibbana Sutta* we read that when he died it was "with that utter passing away in which nothing whatever remains behind." Mohammed died at Medina on June 8, 632, and he is buried there.

Thousands of devout Muslims visit his tomb annually. So millions of Jews, Buddhists, and Muslims do not claim resurrection for the founders of their religions. They lie in dust in their tombs.

Even the leader of one of our modern American theosophical cults, who claimed that there was no death, lies buried in a tomb outside Boston, where thousands of her followers visit her grave every year.

But in Christianity we have something else. We have an empty tomb, a broken seal, and the stone rolled away from the grave door. For Christ does not rot in a Palestinian grave. He lives and reigns to all eternity. For "He has risen, just as He said." And because He has risen, we affirm that

1. Christ is the Son of God.
2. His teachings are the truth.
3. God the Father has accepted the sacrifices of His Son for the reconciliation of the world.
4. All believers in Christ shall rise to eternal life.

Now if the Easter bunny led any of you here this morning in the spirit of "everybody goes on Easter," then permit me to disturb you sufficiently to see and believe and live according to what lies behind the real celebration of Easter. Because of the empty tomb, you and I have life today and life forever. We will see Christ again and need to go quickly and tell the Good News to others.

Celebrating an Empty Tomb

What does the empty tomb mean for your life here today?

The Empty Tomb

It is proof that Christ has risen—that God the Father in raising Him from the dead has finished the work of all mankind's redemption.

There is a fast-growing cult in the world today whose members say that Jesus Christ failed in His mission. Had He succeeded in His task, He would not have been rejected by the people; He would not have died on the cross; and He would have settled down, gotten married and raised a family. He "failed" and so their leader today whom they call "The Lord of the Second Advent" has come to finish the work of Christ.

How tragic that today they are missing the true nature of Christ's mission and the true nature of our God. For the point is that God in Christ did finish our redemption in the face of rejection! That's the kind of God we have—not our puny misconception of him, but "God's kind of God"—a God who goes on loving us even when we ignore Him. "This is what love is: it is not that we have loved God, but that he loved us and sent his Son to be the means by which our sins are forgiven" (1 John 4:10 TEV). What a God! What a Savior! What a love!

And that's the kind of a God you have today—one who loves you even in the face of rejection. God loves you, and there's nothing you can do to make Him stop. He loves you and me even when we in effect reject Him by living out our lives unmindful of Him.

Is there a single day this week that you planned without first taking your schedule to the Lord in prayer and asking His guidance and blessing on it? Have you been trying to salvage a crumbling relationship with another person by just human means, or have you depended on Christ the Healer to restore you to each other? Have you agonized in loneliness and despair and wondered why God isn't speaking to you? And yet your Bible has remained closed, your baptism forgotten, and the Eucharist ignored as a living source of God's power by which He wants to feed you, uplift and comfort you.

Truly, when you and I examine our lives we must confess that we often live as if Christ didn't really exist as a personal reality in our lives. For we often live as "practical atheists" even though we call ourselves Christians. We live the "as if" life—as if Christ were still in the tomb—dead—and not alive in our hearts and homes today.

The apostle Paul speaks for all of us when he says, "My own behavior baffles me. For I find myself doing what I really loathe.... it must be sin that has made its home in my nature.... I often find that I have the will to do good, but not the power. That is, I don't accomplish the good I set out to do, and the evil I don't really want to do I find I am always doing.... For left to myself, I serve the Law of God with my mind, but in my unspiritual nature I serve the law of sin. It is an agonizing situation, and who can set me free from the prison of this mortal body? I thank God there is a way out through Jesus Christ our Lord" (Rom. 7:15, 17-19, 22-25 Phillips).

And so you and I need to say this happy Easter morning, "Lord, be merciful to all of us—sinners. And thank You, Lord, that there is a way out of the tomb of self-centeredness we have often gotten ourselves into." It is the Christ who burst forth from the tomb and who now frees us from our old sinful selves who has rescued us.

Our Easter Joy

And therein lies our Easter joy and hope. For we are redeemed and forgiven people. And the Holy Spirit in this text now calls us twice to believe and act in four different ways.

First, the angel told the women that Christ was going before them to Galilee, and "you will *see* him." And later Jesus met them and repeated the assurance "they will *see* me."

And you here today—you will see Christ again in His Real Presence in His body and blood in the joyful Eucharist we are celebrating this morning. You will see him in his body broken and his blood shed for the forgiveness of your sins.

And you will see Him one day face to face when on the Last Day you greet your Easter King—then to be in His presence forever.

Second, the angel, and then also Our Lord, says, "Go—and tell." Celebrating the empty tomb this Easter morn is not just assenting to some facts about Christ's resurrection. "We cannot help *speaking* about what we have seen and heard" (Acts 4:20). We are compelled—with joy—to share the Good News with everyone we meet, that God has reconciled us to Himself through the life, death, resurrection, and ascension of His Son, and so I charge you, "Go—and tell!"

Third, the word "quickly" is used twice. "Go quickly," the angel said. And they went quickly. So you and I need to get moving—with joy—as the disciples did. It's not just "here we stand" but "here we go"—with the Good News of Easter Day.

And fourth, the angel and then Christ himself promise that when you go, and when you go quickly, you *will* see Christ. These are only two of the nearly 9,000 promises of God in the Bible. We have a "God of promises"—and God always keeps his promise to you—now, in this life, and in the life to come.

There was a young secretary in a New York City office building who exemplified what I am talking about. Christ was a personal reality in her life—and she did "go and tell" other people about him. In fact, she made such an impression on a sailor who visited the office building one day that he wrote a letter to her employer. He told her boss that he was a sailor and that he would be sailing in a few hours, but that he had to share something before leaving. He related how he had come into that man's office in the morning, lonely and scared to death about sailing again. He needed to talk to someone. So when the girl at the desk greeted him, he asked her if she had a job for him. She said to wait briefly, so he did. He said that maybe there wouldn't be jobs or anything afterwards, and if only a person had something to count on, worth dying for, things wouldn't be so bad.

Then he related how the young woman smiled, and said that it was easy. "Christ is coming through and He's worth dying for." He said he had just stared at the young woman because she talked as if Christ was alive and was a good pal of hers. In fact, he recalled, he was so struck by her comments that he sort of expected to see Christ walk in the door. It was that real.

He was only in the office ten minutes, but the brief encounter made such an impression on him that it changed him somehow. He was no longer lonely or scared. He wrote, "It was as through she had said, 'I want to make you acquainted with my Friend Jesus. You ought to get to know each other since He'll be going your way.' I'm 19 and I never knew before that there was a God like that who would go along with a fellow."

He said in conclusion that it didn't matter so much to him now if his ship did go down—as long as there was a God like that. He had wanted to thank the girl for her help, but didn't want her to think of him as "flip." So he asked the employer to please pass on his thanks to her.

Listen to his words again—"I never knew before that there was a God like that"! That's the God you and I know—a God who is real and alive—and who moves us to "go and tell" others about Himself, as this young woman did to the sailor.

What a great God we have to worship this joyous Easter morn! Unlike the world religions whose leaders lie as dust in their graves, our Savior's tomb is empty. He is risen, as He said. And because of this we know he completed our redemption, and we—once lost—can now call God "Our Father in heaven."

He wants you to let Him live at the center of your life right now, giving you meaning and healing, peace and power in the face of death and despair.

I know and believe this with all my heart. On this joyous Easter morn, do you? God grant that you may know and believe it until that day when you will see Him—and all your loved ones who (have) died "in the Lord"—face to face and live and reign with Him into all eternity.

Are You a Doubting Thomas?

SECOND SUNDAY OF EASTER
JOHN 20:19-31

Donald L. Deffner

Do you ever have trouble with your faith? Many Christians do. And I suggest that the reason many people have trouble with their faith is not because they have gotten to know life "as it really is," but because they know too little about God. I submit that it is not a different faith such people need. What they need is a larger faith, a greater faith, a stronger faith.

That was the problem of "Doubting Thomas." He had been with the Lord for a long time. He believed in Him. But his faith wavered when the disciples told him "We have seen the Lord"—the resurrected Christ. He wanted some proof that Jesus was not still lying in the tomb. "Unless I see the nail marks in his hands and put my finger where the nails were, and put my hand into his side, I will not believe it," he said. Quite a laundry list for requirements for "faith," isn't it!

But note what happened—eight days later. Our Lord appears to the disciples, Thomas being present now. His first words are words of calm, peace, and comfort—not fear. "Peace be with you!" He says. And then He challenges Thomas to the pragmatic test of actually putting his fingers into the wounds He suffered on the cross for us. And He confronts Thomas with "Stop doubting and believe."

And do you know what happened? Some people may imagine Thomas approaching Christ gingerly, touching a wound here and there, then standing back and making a judgment. "Well, Lord, I guess it really is you after all." But that's not what happened. Thomas simply confessed his faith—and it was immediate. Thomas answered Him, "My Lord and my God!"

And the compassionate Christ responds with words which apply both to Thomas and to you and me here today. Jesus said to him, "Because you have seen me, you have believed; blessed are those who have not seen and yet have believed."

The "Unless" Christian

Listen to that challenge coming down from 2,000 years ago to you and me worshiping the risen Christ in this place right now: "Blessed are those who have not seen and yet have believed."

Thomas said, "*Unless* I see . . . I will not believe."

Do you feel like I sometimes do? "Lord, I am so lonely. *Unless* you make somebody 'reach out and touch someone'—namely, me!—I am going to think no one, especially You, cares for me any more."

Are you like me when you often feel, "Lord, *unless* You show me the answer to my financial problems, my problems at school, the illness which confronts me, the future which threatens me—*unless* You come across, I'm really not going to believe in You as my loving, helping Father any more."

Are you like me when I am tempted to doubt God's desire to be a personal, daily reality in my life? "*Unless* . . . *unless* . . . *unless* . . . I will not believe in you."

But you and I can't make deals with God. Our relationship with Him must be unconditional. He says to us, "Believe in me, and I will show you more than you ever dreamed could happen in your life."

This is not "think positive and you will get ahead in your business or marriage" kind of thinking. Rather, this is Jesus asking us to notice the people in His ministry whose faith released His power—the Roman centurion, the demon-afflicted man, the woman with the hemorrhage, the paralyzed man, and many more. He said, "Your sins are forgiven. Pick up your bed and go home. *Your faith has saved you!*"

So I challenge you in your own personal life. God is a God who doesn't make deals. He will escape you forever until you see Him revealed in Jesus His Son. Why in the world do you insist on knocking yourself out pounding on His almighty front door when it has already been opened through the gift of faith in His Son? That faith brings us into a relationship with Him that lasts forever.

A Christian was talking about the age-old problem of human suffering. "Why does God allow it?" he asked. A friend of his answered "This much I know. I have seen a lieutenant send one of his men, a dear and trusted friend, to certain death because the mission had to be accomplished. And the man spent no time in asking why. He saluted and went. And in my own life sometimes I do not know why, and I am not asking. I am just saluting, if that is my post."

In your own life, are you willing, no matter what confronts you, to say: "God knows. He has a reason for permitting this to happen. I trust Him. That's enough for me"?

The Difficulty of Faith

That is Jesus' challenge and loving call to you and me—as it was to Thomas. "Stop doubting and believe." But it's not easy, is it? For the life of faith produces conflicts for us. To "walk by faith and not by sight" in this day and age is to live a life which confronts real difficulties in our hearts and in the world all around us. Everything we see and read and hear is constantly attacking the "walk of faith."

It's not a new problem. Throughout the New Testament there are repeated failures as far as the matter of faith is concerned. The apostle Paul wrote sadly about one of his temporary co-workers, "Demas, because he loved this world, has deserted me" (2 Tim. 4:10). Demas wasn't the first or last who found the "faith life" to hard to take, too demanding when compared to his own desires and needs.

But that's the challenge of Jesus to Thomas and to you and me. Under the most trying of circumstances, "Do you have faith in Me?"

Some Christians, although they know the true God, are prone to waver and fall when the first winds of adversity strike them. We need to look again and again at the faith of the great reformer Martin Luther. Now there was a man with a larger faith, a stronger faith, a greater faith in a great God. He certainly had his doubts and difficulties. Often he faltered when he came to the point of Scripture that says that God is good, and that He is good to me. But then he would realize the meaning of "the righteousness of God" and how that righteousness is transferred to us when we confess our sin and trust solely in the merits of Christ's death and resurrection—*for us.*

He was wise enough to take God at His Word, and to trust the Holy Spirit to give him the power of faith. He knew it was God who saved him. And that's why he was a giant of faith. In the face of all his foes, he cried out, "Here I stand . . . I cannot recant . . . I can do no other!"

His greatest aid in his struggle was the Holy Scriptures. "The true Christian pilgrimage is not to Rome . . . but to the prophets, the Psalms, and the Gospels," he said. That was his ground for certainty, the source of faith in Christ. There, in the inspired Holy Scriptures, he found "a firm foundation."

"Feelings come and feelings go, and feelings are deceiving, My warrant is the Word of God. Naught else is worth believing." So make sure that you find your strength for this difficult life by faith in the unfailing source, the Holy Scriptures. "For you are all the children of God by faith in Christ Jesus." And in Scripture you will meet Jesus face to face.

Find this faith also in the visible Word, the Blessed Sacrament of the Altar where Christ comes to us in His body and blood. Then our prayer near the end of one of our services is answered: "We beseech Thee that of Thy mercy Thou wouldst strengthen us through the same in faith towards Thee, and in fervent love toward one another."

It's easy to become a doubting Thomas. The life of faith is very difficult. There are so many pressures around us tempting us not to live it. There is also our own laziness and self-centeredness. But Christ says to you and me again today, "Are you—as I challenged Thomas—willing to 'walk by faith and not by sight'? Blessed are those who have not seen and yet have believed."

By the power of the Holy Spirit, let me assure you again today, this faith is a gift from God to you which comes when you repent of your sins, and trust in the healing power of Christ. It saves you from sin and death and makes you a child of God. If you would be and remain one of the children of God, it will mean letting Christ work in you through faith, breaking through your doubts, your self-sufficiency, and your despair, and letting Him say to you, as he did to doubting Thomas, "Blessed are you. You haven't found all the answers to the questions in your life, but you still have believed in me. Blessed are you."

There was a woman in a community who was well known for her simple faith and great calm in the midst of many trials. Another woman who had never met her but had heard of her came to visit one day. "I must find out the secret of her calm, happy life," she thought to herself.

As she met her she said: "So you are the woman with the great faith I've heard so much about."

"No," came the reply. "I am not the woman with the great faith, but I am the woman with the little faith in the great God."

Can you say the same? What will it be for you today—an artificial God to whom you pray, "*Unless* you come through this time, I'm not going to go along with you," or, by the power of the Holy Spirit, a little more faith in the great God revealed in Jesus Christ who challenged Thomas and who confronts you again here today?

Christ can turn your life around. You may not have all the solutions to the problems which confront you, but you know that He is with you every step of the way.

What a great God we have! He was willing to come down from on high and become one of us in His Son, Jesus Christ, just so that we might see what He is really like and learn to know Him! Once you see that, you will feel that nothing—absolutely nothing—is too much to do for him . . . in faith!

Walking with God

THIRD SUNDAY OF EASTER
LUKE 24:13-35

Otto W. Toelke

In 1929 a wealthy New York businessman lost everything in the stock market crash. He became extremely despondent. Some of his friends that had survived the crash offered to loan him money so that he could make a fresh start. He declined their offers. He insisted that he was physically and mentally ill, and therefore not to be trusted with other people's money.

His wife managed to salvage a few funds from the financial collapse, and with them she took him to a quiet lake in Florida. It was not a resort area. They were surrounded by rough and tough Florida "crackers." The husband would sit on the bank of the lake by the hour staring into the placid water. He could not sleep, and he could not eat. He continually repeated that he was a failure and that he had come to the end of his rope.

One day as he was sitting on the bank he saw a big boy beating a smaller lad. He tried to stop the fight and in so doing he pushed the bigger boy into a tree so hard that it cut his face. In rage the bigger boy shook his fist and said that his pa would "get even" in short order. That evening the young ruffian came to the despondent man's cottage and informed him that his pa would come over in the morning, and that he would have his gun and would shoot him.

Our fearful friend lay awake all night. He already had more problems than he could handle. He knew that he could not run away from this without adding to his misery. In fact, the thought ran through his mind that perhaps death by a bullet wouldn't be a bad way of bringing an end to the sorry mess he had made of his life.

He arose at 4:00 a.m. and started for the house of his would-be assailant. He decided he would walk straight into the jaws of death and die facing his enemy. However, as he walked along the road on his grim errand, he was no longer afraid. God suddenly seemed friendly and close and real to him. Even the sunrise looked beautiful as it appeared over the Everglades. He knocked on the door and was confronted by the bad man himself, rifle in hand. He was smiling and unafraid. "I am not armed," he said. "You can go ahead and shoot me, but first I would like to have a little talk with you." "I can't shoot an unarmed man on my doorstep, and especially not a brave man like you," was the reply.

When our friend returned to his cottage, his wife was waiting with tears in her eyes and outstretched arms. She said, "I knew you had to go, and all the while you were gone I prayed. Soon a great peace enveloped me and I knew that you had found yourself again."

This is a true story with a happy ending. It tells how a man rose from the depths of despair to peace and tranquility. The change came about when suddenly he felt he was walking with God.

That is what we want to discuss today, namely, what can happen in one's life when he is

Walking with God

The portion of Holy Scripture that we consider tells a similar but more beautiful and inspiring story about two disciples—not apostles—of the Lord Jesus who were walking to a village located seven or eight miles from the city of Jerusalem. The village was Emmaus. The one disciple was Cleopas. We do not know the name of the other.

I. A Time to Share Our Concerns

We may well assume that Cleopas and his friend decided they would take the rather long walk to Emmaus because they "just had to get away" and find some peace and quiet where they could talk. The events of the last four days (Maundy Thursday, Good Friday, Holy Saturday, and Easter) had really shaken them. Everything happened so fast. They were confused. They were filled with sorrow, tension, and anxiety.

Sorrow filled their hearts, and perhaps tears even filled their eyes when they thought about the great prophet from Nazareth that they had come to love so much. They confessed that they had come to the point where they thought that He, indeed, should be the Savior of Israel. Then the events of Maundy Thursday and Good Friday caused their hopes and dreams to collapse like a house of cards. They thought of the manner in which the captors had tortured and humiliated their Master and the agony that He suffered on the cross, and their sorrow turned to almost uncontrollable grief.

Then on top of all this, information came to them that very morning that the body of their Master was no longer in the tomb. They recalled that He had said something about rising on the third day. If this really happened, they reasoned, then where was the body? They talked and reasoned with each other endlessly, but just couldn't put the pieces together.

Before we criticize or censure the disciples for lack of faith, or for not having listened more carefully to Jesus when He was telling them what would happen, let us look at the good and wholesome thing they were doing. They were sharing. They were opening their hearts and their minds to each other, and although they did not know it, they were sharing their concerns with their beloved Master. The risen Savior had joined them as they walked along, but the Scripture says, they "were kept from recognizing Him."

We live in a society and a culture where people, even in the Christian family, seldom share their innermost thoughts and concerns. In times of grief and sorrow we are quite stoic. Pride prevents us from sharing our sorrows and defeats. In times of joy we wear a sort of blasé facade. Selfishness prevents us from sharing our joys.

As we find ourselves in the afterlight of Holy Week and the great Easter victory, would it not be a good time to openly discuss the postresurrection appearances of Christ in our own lives. After all, during the 40-day period that intervened between Easter and the Ascension, during which Christ appeared approximately a dozen times, that is all that the apostles and disciples talked about. We are not advocating Pentecostal curbstone confession and testimonials, in which some people take great pleasure, but we are saying that Easter must have more than emotional appeal if it is to be the lasting blessing in our lives that God intended.

It was excruciating agony and horrible death that Christ suffered because of sin. It was a glorious, incredible, eternal victory that He won at the empty tomb. The sin was our sin, not His, and the victory that He won is ours also. Can a person rise from the depths of condemnation to the heights of sonship with God and only feel it and not think about it? If we think about it, then let's talk about it, always bearing in mind that the risen Christ hears our conversation. We know this because the eyes of our faith are not kept from recognizing Him.

II. A Time to Listen

Scripture tells us that after the two disciples expressed their concerns to their new walking companion, whom they did not recognize as Jesus, He took over the conversation. First, He reprimanded them for their weak faith and dull understanding. Then began for them, we may be assured, the finest and most unforgettable instruction they had ever received. The Master Teacher was at work. He was thorough. He started with Moses and then explained all those parts of Scripture that related to Him.

It is noteworthy that Scripture does not record even a hint of an interruption during the time that Jesus was talking with them. They listened. For some, listening is as difficult as sharing. Yet with listening, especially to the Savior, come many blessings.

As we walk with Jesus, in these post-Easter days, let's listen to Him as He speaks to us in His Word, in the sacraments, and in our worship. The argument could certainly be made that when Jesus spoke to those walking disciples He was with them in person—visibly. However, there are two things to bear in mind. First, at this point they did not recognize Him as Jesus, but they listened just the same. Second, Jesus is with all His children at all times and in all places. He promised us, "I will be with you always, to the very end of the age."

If we listen to Him in His Word, we do not have to be satisfied with one postresurrection appearance. We can enjoy all of them. Because we live in the twentieth century and not the first, we can see and study the founding, the unfolding, and the flourishing of Christ's church here on earth. Those two disciples did not have that advantage. If we listen to history, be it Biblical or secular, we can see that He is the greatest influence the world has ever known, and that now all history revolves about Him. In fact, He has become the pivotal point in history, and that is why we refer to events in history as being either B.C. (before Christ) or A.D. (*Anno Domini*—in the year of the Lord). The two disciples did not have that advantage.

He speaks to us in the sacraments, if only we will listen. As usual, the Lord is not in the earthquake, or the blazing fire, or the roaring wind. In a still, small intimate, personal voice and tone so pregnant and heavy with blessing He says that if we believe in the cleansing water of Holy Baptism and remain true to Him, then He will claim us as His own to all eternity, and no man shall ever pluck us out of His hand.

In the Sacrament of the Altar, in a most confidential manner, He tells us to take His body and His blood as proof and assurance that when we come to Him asking for the forgiveness of sins, then as sure as God's Word is true, those sins are forgiven.

In our worship there is much listening that should take place. If it is not so, then perhaps, like so many, we have become like robots or automatons in our worship. We go through the motions. Our voice, lips, and ears are in one place, but our mind is far removed. The hymns are not simply hymns. Let us think of them as prayers uttered in song or in a musical setting. The Scripture readings are not simply readings. They are God speaking to us through His holy Word. The liturgy is not simply a statement voiced by one, followed with a response by another. Let us think of it as an exchange of blessings, a confession to God and each other of what we believe, and, most of all, a means of helping us choose the right words and phrases as we draw nigh to the presence of God.

The most learned of men are not always the most articulate speakers. We learn by listening, not by speaking.

III. Close Communion with Him

The walk comes to an end. Emmaus has been reached. The Lord Jesus makes as though He would have gone further. Jesus was not pretending. Jesus never pretends. He would have gone on if He had not been asked by the disciples to "stay with us." Jesus comes to all people, but He stays only with those who really desire His presence.

Now comes the climax of the walk, the sharing, and listening. They sit down at dinner together. It matters not whether it was the home of one of the disciples, or an inn, or the home of some hospitable person. The manner in which Jesus suddenly becomes the Host, the way in which He asks the blessing, and the way in which He breaks the bread, reminds them of so many previous occasions. This was not necessarily a reminder of the institution of the Lord's Supper. After all, these two disciples were not present when the Lord shared that meal. It was simply the reenactment of many previous pleasant occasions. Suddenly their eyes were opened. They recognized Him for what He truly was and is—the risen Savior.

At that moment the visible presence of the Savior vanished. Then they spoke those memorable words which we hope all of us have spoken at some time or other when Christ entered our lives in a most intimate way—"Were not our hearts burning within us."

Notice what now happens in their lives. The walking disciples become the running disciples. The doubting disciples become the devoted disciples. The reasoning disciples become the resolute disciples. Within the hour they began the journey back to Jerusalem, and when they arrived, they were filled with joy and victory and confidence. We may well assume that they were so excited they had real difficulty in relating to the disciples all the details about their walk with Jesus.

How is it with you? Did the victorious Easter festival lift you to new and higher plains of spiritual experience? Did it give you a feeling of reckless abandon so that the things that constantly occupy your mind and heart no longer seem so important because Christ really is in charge? After all, he defeated death and brought life and immortality to light. Most of all, did the inspiring festival give you the quiet assurance that He is, indeed, a living Savior, that He stands ready to abide with you now and forever in all circumstances, favorable or unfavorable? Did it give you a confident feeling of bravado that "if God is for us, who can be against us?"

I am sure that for many of you Easter did just that. It should do that. It was meant to do that. However, we cannot live on the Mount of Transfiguration forever. There came a time when even Jesus, Peter, James, and John came down from the mountain.

Do not feel guilty that the emotional crescendo of Easter may have somewhat diminished. Because we are sinners and human beings, our spiritual life as well as our emotional life is made up of peaks and valleys. Very often the height of the wave determines the depth of the trough. The important thing is that we always remember that we have a living Savior, that we can always walk with Him because He has promised to abide with us, and that while walking we can share with Him and we can listen to Him. The result may not be the "high" of Easter, but it can be the quiet assurance that He who created you, redeemed you, and loves you will be with you always, even to that day when you will join the throngs of angels at His right hand.

Pictures in a Parable

FOURTH SUNDAY OF EASTER
JOHN 10:1-10

Otto W. Toelke

The Gospel for today is not one that easily and readily unfolds before our gaze. It is one of those passages that has so many spiritual treasures condensed into a few words that we hardly know how to approach it lest we miss something. We could fragmentize it and consider only a small portion, but that would be like settling for dollars when we could have diamonds. Add to this fact that we are dealing with a parable or allegory, and we have before us an edifying challenge. The church fathers of ancient times had a rather profound saying: "Squeeze parables too far, and you will draw blood from them and not milk." So if there are some minor details that go unexplained, it is simply because we want to draw milk and not blood.

Our passage is inseparably associated with the entire ninth chapter of St. John's gospel. To pass by this relation would be to mutilate. The ninth chapter tells how Jesus one day miraculously restored sight to a man who had been blind from birth. The fact that he performed the miracle on the Sabbath Day caused the Jewish religious leaders to overlook the miracle entirely. Furthermore, they challenged Jesus and accused Him of being a false teacher, while declaring themselves to be the true teachers, the followers of Moses.

It was in response to this arrogance and ignorance that Jesus spoke the words of our text. If there is such a thing as justified anger, then we could say that Jesus was angry. He chose to respond with a parable or allegory. It has in it all sorts of beautiful picture language. The Lord Jesus was a master in the use of picture language. We want to discuss three

Pictures in a Parable

I. A Picture of False Teachers

We come upon the words "I tell you the truth" 24 times in John's Gospel. They always preface a statement of more than ordinary importance. A picture of false teachers is about to be drawn. The Lord begins with a scathing denunciation. A false teacher is "the man who does not enter the sheep pen by the gate, but climbs in by some other way." He is "a thief and a robber." That is powerful language. Again, Jesus was angry; He did not mince words. He was speaking to and referring directly to the Jewish religious leaders.

We must bear in mind that this picture is being drawn for us in the context and in the language of Palestine. Keeping sheep is not a familiar experience for most of us in the United States in the twentieth century. Sheep pens, gates, shepherds, thieves climbing over some other way would all be familiar to Jews. The sheep pen consisted of four high walls surmounted by sharp objects along the top so as to keep out the thief and the robber who might climb up some other way. In one of the walls there was a space a little wider than a man's body. The shepherd stood in that gap facing outward. As the sheep approached to enter the pen, the shepherd, when he was satisfied that all was well, turned his body sideways so that the sheep could move past him into the pen. He literally became the gate.

When Jesus here uses the expression "gate," He is referring to more than proper ordination and calling. The Jewish teachers, generally speaking, were not deficient in this aspect.

Later the Lord interprets the "gate" to mean Himself. The thought is simply that the touchstone of every true minister is Christ. The true shepherd of souls is that man who enters the ministry with a single eye to Christ, desiring to glorify Christ, doing all in the strength of Christ, preaching Christ's doctrine, walking in Christ's steps, and laboring to bring men and women to Christ.

St. Augustine said, "Whoso would enter the fold, let him enter in by the door; let him preach very Christ. Let him not only preach very Christ, but seek Christ's glory, not his own." He says, again, "I, seeking to enter into your hearts, preach Christ; if I preach other than that, I shall be striving to climb in some other way. Christ is my door; through Christ I win your hearts."

We are prone to think that the age in which we live is the most complex age the world has ever known. We must ask whether there was ever a time when Christians had to exercise more care about false teachers than in the latter half of the twentieth century. The great cry is for practical and relevant religion. Some ministers, in attempting to respond to that cry, have, often unknowingly, dethroned Christ and elevated the social gospel, economic ecclesiology, and sacred science to a position totally unwarranted. The latest phenomenon is the electronic church. It vacillates all the way from good, Christ-centered preaching to religious extravaganza. Very often it takes a discerning Christian to mark the difference. The bottom line is, however, "the false teacher is the dry rot of the church."

II. A Picture of True Christians

The next picture that the Savior draws for us is the picture of true Christians. This is a most unusual picture, to say the least. The true Christians are those who hear the voice of a true shepherd, and know his voice! They are sheep; "who will never follow a stranger; in fact, they will run away from him because they do not recognize a stranger's voice."

What Jesus is saying here is that Christians have a kind of spiritual instinct. "You have an anointing from the Holy One, and all of you know the truth" (1 Jn. 2:20). In other words, they have a sort of sixth sense that tells them when they are listening to a false teacher.

We will never cease to be amazed at the extraordinary knowledge that the lamb has of his own mother's bleat among a thousand others. The lamb somehow hears its own mother above a whole cacophany of bleats. In the same sense, Christians, whether they realize it or not, have been given a sense of spiritual taste and discernment.

The story is told of a pastor who had just recently arrived at his new parish. Above all, he wanted to be exciting and relevant in his preaching. He managed to keep abreast of current events, and he carefully prepared his sermons. After some weeks he came to the conclusion that the people were not responding in the manner that he had expected. He discussed the matter with the elders of the congregation, but not much light was thrown on the subject. Then one Sunday morning as he entered his pulpit and opened the Bible to read the text, he noticed a slip of paper that had been inserted. On the slip of paper was a single Bible passage, "Sir, we would see Jesus" (John 12:21 KJV). Apparently one of the elders in response to the discussion had placed the slip of paper in the Bible. From that time on he preached Christ incarnate, Christ crucified, Christ risen, and Christ at the right hand of God the Father. The result was a loving relationship between the pastor and the members.

III. A Picture of Christ

The last picture that Jesus draws for us in our text is a picture of Himself. He takes His word-brush and with one sweep gives us an utterance of gold that ought to be dear to the heart of every Christian. "I am the gate; whoever enters through me will be saved. He will come in and go out, and find pasture."

We all know about the Berlin wall. It stands as an insurmountable barrier between East and West that has torn apart families and separated loved ones. In much the same way sin has separated us from God and stands as a great barrier between us and our Maker.

When we sense His holiness and perfection, He becomes unapproachable. When we sense and recognize our own guilt, both by commission and omission, we become afraid of Him. The great question of life for every person is, "How do I approach God and draw near to Him? How can I get around, or over, or through this barrier or wall of sin that separates me from God?"

The only one that can provide answers to those questions is God Himself. He did just that through His Son Jesus Christ. Jesus says—and we are now paraphrasing the words of the text—"I am the door through which you can pass and get on the other side of the wall and very close to God. There is no other way, no matter what men say. Every single sheep must enter through Me, if he would join God's flock. Every teacher who wishes to be a shepherd over God's flock, must enter this office looking at me." The cost at which Jesus provided the passageway through the barrier or wall is something beyond our comprehension. He didn't raise an army and with a mighty charge breach the wall. He didn't do it with gold or silver. He did it by giving Himself in death on Calvary's cross. When we pass through that door, knowing and believing what He did, we leave all our sins behind and are free to go directly to God without fear.

In John's gospel the Lord presents Himself and His office with many beautiful figures. The Bread, the Living Water, the Light of the world, the Door, and the Shepherd are all in five chapters of this gospel. We cannot help but notice that frequently the symbol of a door is used to describe our relationship to Christ. In Rev. 3:20 we read, "Here I am! I stand at the door and knock." In John 10:9 He says, "I am the Door" (KJV). In Matt. 6:6 he tells us that when we pray to Him we should go into our room, and "close the door."

Have you ever noticed how some doors are constructed? Very often we see a door made up of four panels, two small upper panels, and two larger lower panels, which form in relief the sign of the cross. In the Middle Ages the Carpenter's Guild selected the cross as their symbol and the verse "I am the Door" as their motto. Then they deliberately built the cross into every door that they constructed. That particular pattern of the door seemed best for both hand and eye. It meets both the practical demand and the desire for lovely things. It was intended to turn men's thoughts Godward, to point to the door which Jesus had opened.

Let us accept the invitation extended by Christ and not, like so many, stand paralyzed in sin merely looking at the door. The door is free and open. When we enter by the door we will be saved and we can "come in and go out." "Come in and go out" is a Hebraism that indicates a sense of "feeling at home," of being at liberty. When we want to convey a sense of familiarity and freedom we often say, "I can come and go as I please."

In other words, if you do enter the fold through Christ the door, contrary to popular opinion, you will not be losing anything, except your sin. Jesus isn't here inviting you merely to a different existence. He wants you to have a full life in every sense of the word. He said it beautifully in these words, "I have come that they may have life, and have it to the full."

May God, through His Holy Spirit, grant that we accept His gracious invitation.

Jesus Speaks to Troubled Hearts

FIFTH SUNDAY OF EASTER
JOHN 14:1-12

T. Richard Marcis Sr.

Concern about the future and what it holds in store for us is healthy, good, God-pleasing, and as it ought to be. When God breathed into the nostrils of our first parents the breath of life, they were endowed with qualities, characteristics, and traits which enabled them to communicate. As living personalities, therefore, it was part of their natural makeup to look ahead and be concerned about future events.

This posed no problem for Adam and Eve when their relationship with God was healthy and sinless. But the moment they, in the exercise of their will as free moral agents, opted to challenge the good and gracious will of God, they had problems. No longer were they able to put things in their proper persepctive; no longer were they able to look into the future without having their hearts filled with anxiety and concern; no longer were they free from fear. True, God gave them the promise that He would personally right their wrong and patch things up in due course. Yet in spite of this, their hearts fluttered with fear.

As it was with our first parents, so it is with us now on this side of Christmas, this side of the cross, this side of Jesus' resurrection. We too often find ourselves with hearts that are filled with fear and uncertainty concerning the future. It is to such hearts that Jesus speaks in the Gospel for today.

It should be noted at the outset that these words from St. John's inspired gospel account came from the lips of our Lord Himself on the night before His crucifixion. Further, it should be kept in mind that, while they were spoken directly to the disciples, they are just as applicable, timely, and important for us today in the latter half of the twentieth century.

Heaven Is a Reality

For many in Jesus' day heaven and everlasting communion with God were denied and rejected as realities. The Sadducees, a religious sect among the Jews, openly held this position (Matt. 22:23; Mark 12:18; Acts 23:8; Luke 20:27). As far as they were concerned, heaven was nothing more than a figment of man's imagination, a dreamer's wish, something that had no substance in truth or fact. It was therefore ruled out and eliminated from their teaching and preaching. For those who did acknowledge the existence of heaven, such as the Pharisees (Acts 23:8), another religious sect among the Jews, it was something that was earned or acquired by men through their own effort. For still others, heaven was looked upon as nothing more than a state of mind, a view held by a contemorary cult known as Christian Scientists.

In spite of the conclusions drawn by men, the Bible tells us that Christ, on that memorable evening before his crucifixion when the Last Supper was shared, turned to His disciples and said, "Do not let your hearts be troubled . . . I am going there to prepare a place for you."

With these words our Lord wished to make clear that heaven is a reality. It is a place where our love-relationship with God, which begins here on earth the moment one comes to faith in Christ as Lord and Savior, will continue in perfection. There, we are told, we will be free from sorrow, pain, death, and tears (Rev. 21:4). The expression "In My Father's house are many rooms" clearly indicates that heaven is a reality where people of faith who accept Jesus Christ as their personal Lord and Savior will spend eternity in the presence of God.

He Can Be Trusted

But our Lord didn't stop with merely making clear that there is more to life than the here and now. At the same time, He wished to make clear that his parting should not concern them to the point of despair. After having said, "Do not let your hearts be troubled," He went on to identify Himself as worthy of their trust. He wanted them to realize that everything He told them about heaven could be relied upon without question.

He did it by presenting to them His credentials in the form of a statement about Himself: "I am the way and the truth and the life." With this statement the disciples were given a guarantee that embracing Him would assure them, not only of everlasting life, but also of glory, honor, majesty, and might.

Since Christ's primary objective was to remove the anxiety and fear that troubled the hearts of these disciples, He had to give them something of substance on which to rely. That's why He pointed to Himself. That was adequate, for throughout His public ministry He had demonstrated that He was God incarnate, that is, God who took the form of a living human being. Christ's message to them was, essentially, "I would like you to accept My claim concerning Myself simply on My word. But if you have difficulty doing that, just stay by My side and learn from Me. If that is done, your questions concerning my credibility will not only be removed, but you, at the same time, will become like Me. The result will be that others will come to trust in Me because they have seen you."

Some time ago, an article appeared in the *Christian Herald* about a senior executive of one of the largest banks in New York City. In that article he told how he had risen to a place of prominence and influence. At first he served as an office boy. Then one day the president of the company called him aside and said, "I want you to come into my office and be with me each day."

The young man replied, "But what could I do to help you, sir? I don't know anything about finances."

"Never mind that," the president said. "You will learn what I want to teach you a lot faster if you just stay by my side and keep your eyes and ears open."

"That was the most significant experience of my life," said the banker. "Being with that wise man made me just like him. I began to do things the way he did, and that accounts for what I am today."

The Answer for Troubled Hearts

The last point Christ wished to put across in this discourse with His disciples was "I am the answer for troubled hearts!" Life situations have a way of catching up with us emotionally, and they can take their toll on us spiritually. Sickness, the death of a loved one, a broken home, unemployment, loneliness, the betrayal of a friend and a whole host of other things can often leave their mark on most of us. When such times come, God's loving concern and capacity to do something constructive about them are often called into question. Why did this have to happen to me? What did I ever do to deserve this? Where did I go wrong? Is God blind or ignorant of my situation? These are questions common to troubled hearts.

The mere thought that Jesus would be leaving soon was more than the disciples felt they could handle. As a result, their hearts were filled with anxiety, frustration, and fear. Realizing this, Jesus turned to them with the comforting words: "Do not let your heart be troubled." Then pointing to Himself He said in essence, "The reason why you need not fear is that I am the answer for troubled hearts. That's why I came to this world in the first place, to help you look up ahead with hope, confidence, and trust." Christ knew that this was something easier said than done. So in answer to Phillip's request, "Show us the Father," He said, "Anyone who has seen me has seen the Father." He came to reveal Him who brought this world and universe into being. There should be no reason to question His capacity to remove all fear from us.

The concern of Christ in the Gospel for the Fifth Sunday of Easter is to provide every true, sincere child of God with confidence, courage, joy, gladness, and hope as he looks at life whether it be past, present, or future. His desire is that we who know and love the Lord may be hopeful and expectant, especially during times of sorrow and separation. Our Lord does not chide us for being sorrowful. He simply states, "There is no need for despair, for I have made all things right!" Those, therefore, who accept, acknowledge and embrace Jesus Christ for who He is in truth and fact, namely, as Lord and Savior, equal with the Father and Holy Spirit in power, glory, honor, majesty, and might, experience sorrow and sadness from time to time when separated from family, friends, and loved ones, but never to the point of despair. Even as this knowledge gave comfort and assurance to the disciples then, so it can do the same for us today. We too can look forward with confidence and trust that the same Christ who saw the first disciples through their days of despair will see us through ours.

When God Seems Far Away

SIXTH SUNDAY OF EASTER
JOHN 14:15-21

Dirk van der Linde

"If you love me," Jesus said, "you will obey what I command." That's what Jesus of Nazareth said. "If you love me, you will obey what I command."

Although that's how our text starts, that's probably not where we would like to start. We are, after all, twentieth-century people, and we don't talk much about commands, laws, orders, or authority anymore. We do things *if* we want to—*if* it helps us make the grade, *if* it makes a profit, *if* it helps our children. Why, it's almost bred into our bones that laws are made by majority vote, that our rulers rule only by the consent of the ruled. We belong to a nation that has gotten rid of slavery, demanded equal rights, and toppled presidents. We are members of a race that showed the world there is no master race, and when we speak of freedom, of liberty, of our right to happiness, we sound almost religious.

The Spirit of Independence

And we are a confident people—most of the time. Self-made, independent, we like to do our own thing and think in our own way. Perhaps there's a bit of rebel in all of us and a native skepticism towards anyone who's over us. That's not all bad. It has paid off splendidly. We have been mightily successful, mightily wealthy, and mightily envied by a world full of folks who can only dream about what we've already got.

So this spirit of independence is not all bad. But it's pushing common sense (and the plain facts of history) too far to make believe that this independent spirit is all good. Many idealistic folks around would tell us that democracy and self-rule of the people is the only way to go *because* people are basically sensible, wise, and good. But most of our "founding fathers" would have had a big chuckle over that one. Democracy, they'd smile, may be the only way to go, *not* because humans are basically good but because humans are basically *evil.* Rule-of-the-people was invented not because we live in a good world that is getting better but because we live in a fallen world, and democracy is the best way we know of protecting ourselves from each other. We have learned what evil men can do with too much power, so it pays to hold power back—check it, balance it, divide it up. We have experienced what governments or mobs can do if they're not bridled by fair laws, so it pays to demand protection and equal rights. We've seen, at least on TV, what happens when a nation of people can no longer think or worship as they wish, so it pays to be suspicious and do our own thinking. It's not all bad, but let's not pretend that it's all good either.

To be a bit suspicious, a bit of a rebel, watchful of folks who might not have our good in mind is all part of an attitude we must have to survive. But the bad thing is how quickly we have carried this same attitude into our relationship with our God. The American colonists finally had enough and declared their independence from King George the Third across the sea. Could it be that we have done the same with King Jesus—Emperor of the universe and Son of the Creator of all?

Perhaps you do not think so, but the parallels haunt me. Maybe we, too, think our King's laws unfair, that He's too far away to know our problems, but still expects us to obey. "Obey what I command," He says. It's not without sympathy that I say that I know more than one Christian who chafes at that. Do I dare mention what so many folks secretly think? "How can I obey a God, when I'm not at all sure I love Him—or that He's got my good in mind?"

How do we crank ourselves up to love God, if this is how we feel? I imagine we all would *like* to love Him. I'm sure that most of us at least give it a good try. But what must go on in so many minds is the struggle to love someone we can't see or hear, touch or talk with face to face. The struggle only worsens if we read through the Old Testament and are brought up short by some of the folks who walk through those pages, like David, King of Israel. Here is a man who, as a rough shepherd boy, had a flair for the harp and slingshot, but who no more had met God face to face than we have. Yet this primitive man could write poetic psalms, describing God's laws as "more precious than gold," something "sweeter than honey" (Ps. 19:10). Then take a look at our children when we teach them the Ten Commandments. Why, they look like they're eating dill pickles, not sweet honey! Did David of old know something about God that we don't know? Was he thinking of something different than we do when we hear the word "law"? Did his relationship with God make the difference?

Here was a man, a powerful, semibarbaric man, a tribal chieftain who could wield a sword with the best of them and slay enemies without guilt, but who cried like a baby if he felt his God was far away. You realize, of course, that it was first David, not Jesus, who cried, "My God, my God, why have you forsaken me?" (Ps. 22:1) as though he would just wither up and die in agony if his God were not nearby.

We read that Psalm and it haunts us, troubles us, disturbs us. "What's wrong with us?" Why is it that I (or you, for that matter), rather educated, somewhat cultured—and much more civilized than this ancient king—chafe under the very laws of God which David cries he couldn't live without?

Of course, there is a reason. We don't like to admit it, but it's there. We *know* what God wants. We know, too, that somewhere along the line, we are even to *want* what God wants. We're supposed to be able to pray Jesus' garden prayer, "Father, not as I will, but as you will." If we've convinced ourselves ahead of time that God's will already goes along with ours, no problem. But what if God's will does not? What if His will goes against our grain? How can we pray that prayer to a God who wants something we oppose? A woman who was going through a terrible divorce broke down and finally told her pastor, "I will not pray God's will be done. I just can't! Suppose He wants me to go back to that monster husband of mine? What am I going to do?"

But Jesus still said, "If you love me, you will obey what I command."

Well, that is the test. If it does nothing else, it shows what a sham our love for Jesus often is. In one breath Jesus blows away our smoke screens and excuses. He knows us. He sees how much of our democratic spirit is really open rebellion against Him. He knows how often in the name of "doing our own thing" we have declared civil war against our King. He sees that if we avoid His Word it's not really because "we don't get anything out of it," although that's the common line. It is because we're afraid of it, afraid His Word will nail us. He may be calling for changes we don't want to make, bidding us go to places we don't want to go, commanding us to do what may never profit us but profits only someone else He loves. "If you love Me," Jesus said, "you will do My bidding."

Fear of God

If God seems far away, quite remote, hardly real, could it be that somewhere, at the bottom of it all, we are wondering about His motives, doubtful about His promises, not quite certain that He's got good in mind for us?

Every one of us has grown up with our parents telling us that they're doing such-and-such a thing "for your own good." Dad clears his throat, says, "Son, right now you don't understand, but one day you'll see that I'm doing this for your own good." Then, the very next thing that happens to us doesn't feel so good. We get grounded. We get spanked. We get sent to apologize to old, grouchy Widow Perkins who's window was (again!) right in the wrong place when our softball came through. We've heard that "for-your-own-good" routine once too often to take much stock in it now.

Is that perhaps what's at the bottom of the problem between ourselves and God, that what He thinks is "our own good" doesn't agree with what we think? I ask because I keep running into folks who, when they let it slip out and confess that they're afraid God is out to punish them, they sigh, sob, and sadly say, "Maybe, Pastor, it's for my own good." But they're crying when they say it.

Have you ever met someone who, when something good comes along, starts wondering when God's going to take it back? Our pagan ancestors in Germany and Holland used to think that way. If Johann met Hans in the forest and said, "Hey, Hans! I got that horse I wanted—good price, too!" then in a second both men would gasp, and Johann would run to the nearest tree and start pounding on it. Those Druid ancestors of ours believed that the gods lived in trees, and if the gods heard about any human happiness, they'd become angrily jealous; they'd cause mischief. So Johann, realizing his mistake in the listening forest, would rap on trees to drive the gods away. "Knock on wood!" Quite a custom, don't you think?

Is that our custom with God? It's either "Thy will be done," or else it's "Knock on wood." It's either that God is out for our good, or we must be out for our own, on our own. There is a community of folks around us who are afraid of losing jobs and afraid that it's God's way of punishing them. I know young mothers, afraid that if they ever slip in life, God will teach them a lesson and take their child away. I know teens, so afraid because they did make a terrible mistake; they didn't mean to do it, but their passion got the best of them. Now they're waiting for God to lower the boom, like a man on death row awaiting execution, afraid the Divine Henchman is coming around. No wonder it haunts so many when they feel they don't love God. Who can love if a God like that comes around?

A God for Us

But let's suppose He does. With the moods we sometimes get into, He'd have to come in disguise. We've built up so many arguments against Him, plotted so many strategies to ignore Him, developed so many prejudices to dismiss Him, and gathered a bagfull of excuses to disobey Him, that He could hardly come to us and tell us who He is. No, He'd have to come among us without our noticing it. Once here, He'd have to do an almost impossible job. He'd have to convince us to believe what we might be afraid to believe: God is *for* us!

Could He carry it off? Could He live and visit us? Could He persuade us that He's more fun than Disneyland, more rewarding than the prizes we seek? Could He bring it off if He told us that He's the King who cares about His folk, that He's not far off across the sea, but so near that no one hurts more than He hurts when we hurt ourselves?

Yes, it's asking a lot of God; it's so outrageous a request that we'd never dare to ask. But, for goodness sake, let us try:

"God? If You really love us, could You show it? Come down from Your far-off throne, join us here? It's so easy to pass down commands if You've got no notion how it is down here. So, could we challenge You to come for a visit?

"Try being a teenager; face their fights as one of them—and still love God at the same time!

"Or, for that matter, try growing up into adulthood. Would You dare join us if You really knew what kind of folks we are? We compromise, we juggle books, we step on or get stepped upon. Would You still come to our house if You knew what went on there? Would You come to our work, our school—as One with us—and face what we must, and still be so in love with God? If You knew firsthand what decisions we must make to survive it all, would You still be so ready with Your talk of love and forgiveness towards folks who've done You wrong? It's easy to forgive when You're so high above it all You can't get hurt!

"Would you still love folks who laughed behind Your back, or spat in Your fce? Please, be honest; could You love someone who holds no love for You? You surely expect a lot when You say, 'If you love me, you will obey what I command.' But, if You loved us, could You?"

And as though it was the only answer He could give us, Jesus stretched His arms out this wide, and said, "This is how much I love you." This is how He answers. The God we complained against has come for us. The God we rebelled against has, silently, joined our side. We thought He was on our case; instead He takes up our case. He doesn't condemn us before His Father's throne; instead, He pleads, "Father, forgive them, for they do not know what they are doing."

And suddenly, the Divine Henchman vanishes. In his place comes the God who turns out to be our Friend. Whatever punishment comes, He steps up to meet it on a cross. He takes it. I'm free. I'm even free to go, if I so choose. But now, after all this, can I? Or, for that matter, can you?

"I will not leave you alone," He says. "You are no longer orphans." But if we ever feel alone, as though God is far away, He just wants to tell us, "I send you a Comforter; you don't even have to ask. I just send. He will be with you, speaking whispered reminders about Me. He will see you through it all and, little one, soon, very soon, I shall see you face to face."

Were we expecting something more—a sign, a miracle, something which would stun and amaze us about God? Well, hasn't He already shown us? The sign of Jonah, the Son, buried three days, now alive!

Were we hoping to know ahead of time what is going to happen, wishing that this Spirit was a fortune-teller? Suppose, instead, He does not tell us *what* will happen to us, only *Who* will go through it with us?

Were we hoping for some warm, glowing feeling inside? What if that's not given? Suppose, instead, the Spirit gives assurance, a conviction, tempered like fine steel, helping us stay strong when feelings let us down.

It seems that God's not so far away, after all! Perhaps we've only looked in the wrong places. We've looked for God's grandeur, and overlooked the common Carpenter. We've looked for inner feelings, and missed, perhaps, the Brother who comforts us no matter how we feel? We've looked for proofs but received a promise—"I will never leave you." That says it all. Although we may not always be so sure how much we love God, God is quite sure how much He loves us.

Now More Than Ever

THE ASCENSION OF OUR LORD
LUKE 24:44-53

Joel D. Heck

If we ran a survey, designed to discover the passage of Scripture considered to be most comforting, I wonder which passage would be selected. No doubt the 23rd Psalm would rank quite high. Perhaps Isaiah's words would be cited by many, "Fear thou not, for I am with thee; be not dismayed, for I am thy God. I will strengthen thee; Yea, I will help thee; yea, I will uphold thee with the right hand of my righteousness" (Is. 41:10 KJV). Others would select Jesus' words, "Come unto me, all ye that labor and are heavy laden, and I will give you rest" (Matt. 11:28 KJV).

There is, however, one passage of Scripture that ought to rank right up there with the rest of them—"And, lo, I am with you alway, even unto the end of the world" (Matt. 28:20 KJV). These words assure us that even though our Lord has ascended into heaven, He is still by our side. The ascension of Jesus does not mean that He is no longer with us; it means that He is no longer with us in the same way that He was with His disciples. On the contrary, now more than ever Jesus is with us, even though we cannot see Him.

The reaction of the disciples to the ascension of Jesus and the corresponding physical absence of their Savior indicates that this was a part of God's plan.

> When he had led them out to the vicinity of Bethany, he lifted up his hands and blessed them. While he was blessing them, he left them and was taken up into heaven. Then they worshiped him and returned to Jerusalem with great joy. And they stayed continually at the temple, praising God (Luke 24:50-53).

Sometimes we get discouraged because God seems so far away. Sometimes we forget that Jesus has promised to be with us. Sometimes we think that only those things are real which we can touch, and none of us have ever touched God. However, the disciples were not sad and discouraged. They were filled with joy. They realized that now more than ever Jesus was with them.

We can arrive at the same point in our faith by the grace of God. We can realize that now, after the Ascension, more than ever, Jesus is with us. He is with us more than ever, first of all, because of His person; secondly, because of His prescription; and thirdly, because of His promise.

I. Because of His Person

No Mere Human

First of all, Jesus is with us more than ever because of His person. Because of who He is, Jesus can leave us and yet stay with us at the same time. No one else that I know can be in two places at one time, though we might often wish that we could. For Jesus to be with us always, as He has promised, He must be God. Only God is capable of being everywhere at once, as He said through the prophet Jeremiah, "Do not I fill heaven and earth?" (Jer. 23:24).

Now more than ever, because Jesus is God, He can be present with us and with all Christians everywhere through the Holy Spirit. We sometimes think that Jesus is not near to us. "Out of sight, out of mind," the saying goes. We have a tendency to think only of those things we can see and to forget the things we don't see. That's why I have to remember to write myself notes about important items, and that's why most of us have to have a calendar or appointment book.

When Jesus tells His disciples, "This is what I told you while I was still with you" (Luke 24:44), He means something very special. Why does He say "while I was still with you," if He is actually with them when He says it? What Jesus means is that His former way of associating with the disciples through His physical presence is now ending and will not be resumed. From this time on, "the Counselor, the Holy Spirit, whom the Father will send in my name, will teach you all things and remind you of everything I have said to you" (John 14:26). "He will testify about me" (John 15:26). Jesus will be present through the Holy Spirit.

The Promised Messiah

That Jesus is able to keep His promise to be with us always is also shown by His fulfillment of Old Testament prophecies. If Jesus was able to keep all of God's promises of a Messiah, a Savior, then Jesus will also keep the promise of His continued presence.

> "This is what I told you while I was still with you: Everything must be fulfilled that is written about me in the Law of Moses, the Prophets and the Psalms."
>
> Then he opened their minds so they could understand the Scriptures. He told then, "This is what is written: The Christ will suffer and rise from the dead on the third day" (Luke 24:44-46).

Mary Baker Eddy was the founder of the movement known today as Christian Science. It has been said of Christian Science that it is neither Christian nor scientific, and that is true. This religion led many people away from Jesus Christ. One of the books that Mrs. Eddy wrote was entitled *Science and Health with Key to the Scriptures*. The key to the Scriptures was her own particular interpretation without which, she claimed, no one could truly understand the Bible.

Other religious movements have also claimed to have the key to understanding the Bible, but here Jesus offers Himself as that key. Another time He said as much when He stated, "I am the way and the truth and the life" (John 14:6).

It is in believing that Christ suffered on the cross for our sins and rose again from the dead for us that we find the Scriptures an open book, their message made clear, and the door to heaven unlocked by the forgiveness of sins.

Now more than ever Jesus is with us, because of His person, because of who He is—our God and our Savior.

II. Because of His Prescription

To Preach Repentance and Forgiveness

Secondly, after His ascension into heaven, Jesus is with us now more than ever because of His prescription. His prescription recorded by Matthew is called the Great Commission. Jesus said just before His ascension, "Go and make disciples of all nations" (Matt. 28:19). Here we have Luke's version of that prescription, or commission. He writes, "Repentance and forgiveness of sins will be preached in his name to all nations, beginning at Jerusalem" (Luke 24:47).

Repentance and forgiveness is the message of the Gospel which makes disciples of people. It involves true sorrow for sins that have been committed, the belief that Christ has paid for those sins by His suffering and death, and the desire to turn away from those sins. It recognizes that the achievement of eternal life is taken out of our hands entirely and placed into the nail-scarred hands of Jesus.

There has been a rumor abroad in the human race for centuries that entrance into heaven could be obtained by presenting a satisfactory work record on earth. That is similar to a rumor that spread in the United States in 1947 that

> the Ford Motor Company would give a Ford in exchange for every copper penny dated 1943. The rumor spread so fast that Ford office throughout the country were jammed with requests for information, and in spite of a telephone strike, thousands of inquiries came in by telelphone as well as by telegram and mail. . . . It all turned out to be a joke. The statistics of the mint show that in 1943 there was no copper available for coinage and that 1,093,838,670 pennies were minted of steel-zinc, but that the number made of copper was exactly zero.

(Donald Grey Barnhouse, *Let Me Illustrate* [Westwood, NJ: Fleming H. Revell Company, 1967], p. 356)

Rumors so often prove to be to be wrong. Forgiveness of sins is not received in exchange for the proper amount of good works that are performed here on earth, no matter how sincerely they are done. Forgiveness comes to the sinner who repents, that is, who admits his guilt before God, despairs of his own ability to merit forgiveness, and trusts only in the merits of Jesus Christ and His death on the cross.

In this message of repentance and forgiveness we can be sure that Jesus is present. The message conveys Christ Himself, and for the person who believes that message, Christ is present by faith in his heart.

To All Nations

Christ is also present with us as we take that message to all nations. It is not only the final chapters of Matthew and of Mark that tell us to take the gospel to the whole world. Here in the closing chapter of Luke we are told by Christ that this message of "repentance and forgiveness of sins will be preached in his name *to all nations*" (v. 47).

Throughout the Gospel of Luke we read of the universality of this message. In the song of John the Baptist's father Zechariah we read that John was to bring a message "to shine on those living in darkness and in the shadow of death" (Luke 1:79). In the next chapter we learn from Simeon that Jesus is God's salvation, "prepared in the sight of all people, a light for revelation to the Gentiles and for glory to your people Israel" (Luke 2:31-32). Later the Baptist preaches, "All mankind will see God's salvation" (Luke 3:6). Many other passages in Luke tell us the same thing.

Yes, now more than ever Jesus is with us, because of His prescription, which sends us to the whole world with Christ by our side.

III. Because of His Promise

The Promise of the Father

Thirdly, after His ascension Jesus is with us now more than ever because of His promise. It is because of the Father's promise that we know Jesus is with us. Jesus said in our text, "I am going to send you what my Father has promised." What is it that His Father promised? Just this, in the words of Jesus Himself,

> I will ask the Father, and he will give you another Counselor to be with you forever—the Spirit of truth. . . . the Counselor, the Holy Spirit, whom the Father will send in my name, will teach you all

> things and will remind you of everything I have said to you (John 14:16, 26).

The promise of the Father is the Holy Spirit. He is called the Counselor, the Spirit of truth. It is said that the Spirit will teach us and will remind us of what Jesus taught us. He will be with us forever, just like Jesus! Notice that the Holy Spirit will be doing the same things for us that Jesus did for His disciples.

And Jesus tells elsewhere, "It is for your good that I am going away. Unless I go away, the Counselor will not come to you; but if I go, I will send him to you" (John 16:7). The promise of the Father could not be kept until Jesus has ascended into heaven. The keeping of that promise would mean that Jesus would be able to be with all believers everywhere at the same time, whereas prior to His ascension He was able to be with only a few believers in one place.

The Power of That Promise

There is more. The promised Holy Spirit would not only be with us forever. He would not only teach us all things as well as the things Jesus had taught on earth. He would also fill us with power to be witnesses for Jesus. "Stay in the city until you have been clothed with power from on high," Jesus says in our text (Luke 24:49).

Jesus said in another place, "But you will receive power when the Holy Spirit comes on you; and you will be my witnesses" (Acts 1:8). The Holy Spirit not only brings us to faith in Jesus Christ; He also gives us the power to live for Christ and to testify to Christ. As a matter of fact, the Holy Spirit simply gives us power to do what He does—to testify of Jesus. "When the Counselor comes," Jesus says, "he will testify about me" (John 15:26).

> There are all sorts of power. Without gas, our cars are not empowered to run. Without Lake Mead, Hoover Dam could not provide electrical power through its turbines for Arizona, Nevada, and California. Without the pellets of fissionable material that make up the bundles used in atomic plants there would not be power to make power. So too, the church is powerless without the Spirit; but with the Spirit it is empowered to do great and wonderful things when it claims the promises of God (Richard Anderson and Donald L. Deffner, *For Example: Illustrations for Contemporary Preaching* [St. Louis: Concordia Publishing House, 1977], p. 163).

One of our greatest sins as individuals and as a church is to try to do things for God by our own strength with our own power. Worse yet, we fail to even attempt things for God because we do not trust His promise to give us the power to do them.

The disciples of Jesus Christ were Christians before Pentecost, but they were still powerless to serve Him until they were "clothed with power from on high." However, after they were filled with the

Holy Spirit, the world was turned upside down within a few short decades. Have you asked God to fill you with His Spirit, and have you then stepped out, trusting in that power to enable you to do great things for God?

May God forgive us, when we doubt Him. May God forgive us for thinking ourselves incapable of service to Him, even with the Spirit's power, or for thinking of Him as powerless to change things in our lives and in our world.

Yes, since Jesus has ascended into heaven, He is with us always, now more than ever. He is present because of His person, because of His prescription, and because of His promise. His person is God and Savior. His prescription is to make disciples, and He is present through His Word and in our hearts as we seek to carry out that task. His promise is the Holy Spirit and, along with the Spirit, the power and presence of God.

After Jesus had gone up into the clouds, "they worshiped him and returned to Jerusalem with great joy. And they stayed continually at the temple, praising God." They had that kind of joy because they knew that Jesus was still with them.

And so the Book of Luke ends with the same joy as at the beginning. The shepherds experienced "good new of great joy" at the birth of Jesus. Now the disciples experience "great joy" at His ascension. May that joy be yours in the knowledge that now more than ever Jesus is with us always.

The Glory of the Cross

SEVENTH SUNDAY OF EASTER
JOHN 17:1-11

Joel D. Heck

You will seldom, if ever, find a crucifix—a cross with the suffering Savior hanging on it—in a Lutheran church. Instead, you will most likely find an empty cross. There is a reason for that.

It was once explained to me that the reason Lutherans prefer an empty cross is that we like to stress that the crucifixion was followed by the resurrection. We like to celebrate the victory of Christ over sin and Satan and would remind people that the death of Christ is meaningless if He stayed dead.

All of this, of course, is well and good. No doubt this emphasis is the result, in part, of an overemphasis in some circles on the blood and the sacred heart of Jesus, to the point that the blood or the heart of Jesus are venerated in themselves and become little idols.

Nevertheless, in spite of the excesses of some, we can affirm with confidence that it is legitimate to glory in the cross of Jesus. It is at the cross of Jesus where the great transaction was made that purchased a place for us in heaven.

In His great high priestly prayer Jesus prays to His heavenly Father about the cross that lay ahead of Him, about the disciples who believed in Him, and about the church in ages to come. From these words of Jesus, we learn that the cross brought glory to Jesus, salvation to man, and unity to the church.

I. The Cross Brought Glory to Jesus

The Common Conception of Glory

First of all, the cross brought glory to Jesus. You will notice immediately that I am not using the word "glory" in its usual sense. The world defines glory in terms of success, notoriety, prestige, and accomplishment. Certainly that is a legimitate definition. However, it is not the only one, even if it is the usual one.

Christ's Conception of Glory

The real glory of Jesus was in the cross. What did Jesus mean when He prayed, "Father, the time has come. Glorify your Son, that your Son may glorify you" (John 17:1)? The world laughs at the idea that suffering may actually bring glory to anyone. St. Paul writes, "For the message of the cross is foolishness to those who are perishing" (1 Cor. 1:18).

Jesus had said earlier, " 'The hour has come for the Son of Man to be glorified. I tell you the truth, unless a kernel of wheat falls to the ground and dies, it remains only a single seed. But if it dies, it produces many seeds. . . . But I, when I am lifted up from the earth, will draw all men to myself.' He said this to show the kind of death he was going to die" (John 12:23-24, 32-33). At other times Jesus spoke in the same way. The glorification of the Son took place, not only in His resurrection and ascension, but also and especially in His crucifixion. It is the glory of Jesus that His life was given up on the cross for the salvation of all people, even for those who would reject it.

Many of us will recall the crash of that Air Florida jet into the Potomac River in Washington, D.C., on Jan. 13, 1982. It resulted in the death of 74 of the 79 passengers aboard the flight. Most of us have heard of the self-sacrifice of an Atlanta man who passed the life preserver three times to other people as the rescue helicopter hovered overhead. When the helicopter came back a fourth time to save the man, he had gone under. The glory of that man was in his self-sacrificing death, and an entire nation was momentarily inspired by his heroic actions. His death meant that three others lived.

The death of Jesus Christ means that *many* others live. It, too, was a self-sacrificing death, because He took the wrath of God, which we deserved, upon Himself. Jesus has passed the eternal life preserver to all mankind, and in so doing He has inspired hundreds of millions of people for a lifetime. Most of all, when He could have chosen to save Himself, He chose to give Himself up in death so that He could save others. That is the glory of Jesus Christ. The suffering and selfless service of Jesus brought glory to His name. "For even the Son of Man did not come to be served, but to serve, and to give his life as a ransom for many" (Mark 10:45). The resurrection of Christ has no meaning without the crucifixion. His exaltation to the right hand of the Father has no meaning without His voluntary humbling of Himself to die on a cross. Yes, the cross brought glory to Jesus.

II. The Cross Brings Salvation to Man

The Disciples Understood Jesus' Mission

We have already seen in part that the glory of the cross of Christ is inseparably bound to the salvation of men. Therefore, we can say that the cross which brought glory to Jesus has also brought salvation to man. That is the thrust of John 17:6-10. There Jesus prays for His disciples who have come to believe in Him.

Jesus is grateful that the disciples had come to understand that He was the Messiah sent from God. "Now they know that everything you have given me comes from you," He prays to the Father. "For I gave them the words you gave me and they accepted them. They knew with certainty that I came from you, and they believed that you sent me" (vv. 7-8).

The apostles were familiar with the Old Testament promises of a Savior. Although many of their fellow citizens denied that Jesus was that Savior, they did not. They had been convinced by the teachings of Jesus. "For I gave them the words you gave me and they accepted them." They had confessed on another occasion, "You have the words of eternal life. We believe and know that you are the Holy One of God" (John 6:68-69). They knew that through believing in Him they had the sure hope of heaven.

That doesn't mean that they always understood how Jesus was going to go about securing eternal life for them. At one point in His ministry we read that He

> began to explain to his disciples that he must go to Jerusalem and suffer many things at the hands of the elders, chief priests and teachers of the law, and that he must be killed and on the third day be raised to life.

> Peter took him aside and began to rebuke him. "Never, Lord!" he said. "This shall never happen to you."

Jesus had to put Peter in his place with the words, "Out of my sight, Satan! You are a stumbling block to me; you do not have in mind the things of God, but the things of men" (Matt. 16:21-23).

They didn't always understand the way in which Jesus would accomplish His goal of man's salvation, but eventually they fully understood and believed and saw their lives transformed. Sometimes, I'm afraid, we fail to understand the connection between the way in which Christ died and our sin. Too often we only accept the crucifixion of Christ intellectually and do not understand that it was our sins that nailed Him there, our sins that were paid for there, and our sins that are now forgiven.

The Disciples Brought Glory to Jesus

The disciples believed. They believed in Jesus, and they believed in the truth of everything He said. Jesus said, "I gave them the words you gave me and they accepted them" (John 17:8). As a result of their having believed, Jesus was glorified, for He said, "Glory has come to me through them" (v. 10). The disciples brought glory to Jesus because the teaching and preaching and healing which He did brought forth the fruit of faith for their lives.

It is the glory of the teacher that his students go on to live productive lives as a result of his teaching. It is the glory of the parent that the child grows up to treasure the same values, the same principles of truth, the same morals and beliefs. Likewise, it is the glory of Jesus that the disciples did what Jesus had preached from the beginning, "Repent and believe the good news!" (Mark 1:15). They had grieved deeply over their sins. They had despaired of finding anything good in themselves. They had come to believe that Jesus' death and resurrection removed their sin and ushered them into the kingdom of God.

Today also the disciples of Jesus are the glory of Jesus. Why is it that the Scripture says, ". . . there is more rejoicing in heaven over one sinner who repents than over ninety-nine righteous persons who do not need to repent" (Luke 15:7)? It is because every sinner who repents brings glory to Jesus, from the time of Adam until today. Jesus is glorified when you are sorry for your sins and believe that by His death on the cross He has washed them away.

III. The Cross Brings Unity to the Church

It Creates a Common Faith

Having seen how the cross is really the glory of Jesus Christ and how the message of the cross brings salvation to us individually, we can see how that same message of the cross brings unity to the church. It does so by creating a common faith among Christians of widely varying nations and languages, cultures and races.

It's true in the business world. The common belief of a particular company that people need their product creates a measure of unity within that company, whether the product be carpet, chocolate, or pharmaceuticals.

The same is true in the church. The message of eternal life through faith in Jesus Christ, who died for our sins on the cross, creates a common faith among all Christians. That common faith is in Jesus as Savior. It produces a unity of heart, mind, and will, regardless of other differences between people. That's what Jesus is speaking about when He says, "Holy Father, protect them by the power of your name . . . so that they may be one as we are one" (John 17:11). Here Jesus is not speaking of an outward unity of organization, but an inward unity of common faith.

The Scripture tells us that there is but "one Lord, one faith, one baptism; one God and Father of all" (Eph. 4:5-6). This unity the disciples had at the time of Jesus' prayer. Disciples of Jesus today throughout the world have this same unity, regardless of denominational labels. Jesus is praying that His disciples may continue to be one. He is not praying that they become one, because they already are.

The late Dr. Donald G. Barnhouse of Philadelphia was preaching in a church where the pastor's wife was scheduled to have a baby. One evening the service started without the pastor. Dr. Barnhouse assumed he was at the hospital.

Midway into Dr. Barnhouse's sermon, the pastor entered behind the pulpit. Dr. Barnhouse and the congregation smiled at him, thinking everything was going well. But the pastor did not smile back.

When Dr. Barnhouse concluded, the pastor asked to talk to him. They went to a quiet place, and the pastor blurted out, "My wife has given birth to a mongoloid child. She doesn't know yet, and I don't know how to tell her."

Dr. Barnhouse talked with the grieving pastor for several minutes, then said, "God has a purpose for you and your wife in this. He has given you this child to love. Tell her, 'God has blessed us with a mongoloid child,' and assure her of God's love."

The pastor hurried back to the hospital and talked with his wife. It was hard for both to understand and accept, but they managed. They did not know that the switchboard operator was listening. She was a skeptical person, frankly critical of Christianity. The faith of the pastor's wife astounded her. The following Sunday the switchboard operator and 70 nurses attended the minister's church.

That same Sunday more than two dozen of the nurses indicated their desire to become members of that Christian congregation. The message of the cross, which brought meaning and purpose to the life of this pastor and his wife, created a common faith in the lives of those nurses. It united them spiritually with one another, even though they came from widely differing backgrounds. That's part of the glory brought to Christ because of the cross.

It Unites Believers Under One Head

The message of the cross creates a common faith, and it unites believers under One head, Jesus Christ. "He is the head of the body, the church," Paul writes; "He is the beginning and the firstborn from among the dead, so that in everything he might have the supremacy" (Col. 1:18).

It is this Head who leads and guides us through His words. It is this Head who prays for us, as Jesus did for His disciples. It is this Head who preserves us in our faith. He prays, "Holy Father, protect them by the power of your name." That's actually one of the purposes of the church—to create the strength of a unified body of believers so that an environment exists where Christians can grow spiritually and be sustained in their faith.

The glory of the cross is the glory of Jesus. Now it is our glory, because it has saved us and brought us together as one in Christ's church.

Our *Spirit*ual Advantage

THE DAY OF PENTECOST
JOHN 16:5-11

Edwin Dubberke

Every sports enthusiast knows the importance of "home field" advantage in an athletic contest. When a team or individual plays in a familiar area surrounded by partisan, cheering fans, they have a definite advantage over their "visiting" opponent. Not only in sports but in most other spheres of life, being in a familiar place with familiar, supportive people is a definite psychological plus. In fact, most of us avoid getting into places, situations, or company that are not familiar and secure.

Among other things, the exciting Pentecost event that we are celebrating today offers a "home field" advantage to every disciple of Jesus Christ in the struggle to live for the Lord. The presence and power of the Holy Spirit demonstrated in and through Christ's followers on that first Pentecost Day and promised to all His people gives us assurance of

Our *Spirit*ual Advantage

This is in perfect fulfillment of the promise of Jesus to His disciples in today's Gospel reading.

I. For Our Personal Life—the Spirit's Presence

An Absent Lord?

It was the night before Calvary. Gathered with His followers in the Upper Room, Jesus was speaking at length about leaving them. Even as He was bidding them a farewell, the Lord spoke some precious and essential promises to the disciples. But they heard little of the promises. Their Master was leaving them alone. The very thought of it left them bewildered and grief-stricken. For three years they had been following Him, quenching their thirsty souls with this Water of Life. More than once He had rescued them from physical or spiritual danger. What would happen to them when they could no longer see and talk to him? How could a leader who is not around be of much help?

The disciples of Jesus were so self-absorbed that they never asked the Lord a sympathetic question like, "Where are You going?" Perhaps it never crossed their minds to consider what was going to happen to their beloved Teacher. That is the way self-pity blinds people to what is happening to those close to them. How often haven't we failed to minister to the deeper needs or hurts of another person because we were too concerned about our own welfare or success? It is this same ego-centered kind of thinking that hinders our spiritual vision and keeps us from seeing the good things of God's will for our lives. Our problems are so real and personal, but the Lord seems remote--even perhaps uncaring. If only we could see Jesus, hear His kind yet authoritative voice and feel His healing touch!

Profitable Sorrow

It was the loss of Jesus' visible presence that grieved His disciples. He understood their pain, but He also knew the necessity of it. "I tell you the truth: It is for your good that I am going away. Unless I go away, the Counselor will not come to you; but if I go, I will send him to you" (v. 7). It is typical of children (God's children, too) to prefer something good right now to something better that is promised for the future. The Lord was telling His disciples that it would be most advantageous for them to lose His bodily presence, which they prized so highly, in order to have the greater presence of the Holy Spirit. In His physical presence Jesus ordinarily limited Himself by time and space as all men are limited by their very nature. There are no such limitations to the Spirit's presence.

Just as our baby teeth had to be lost before the better permanent teeth could come in, so the coming of the Counselor which Jesus promised required His sorrowful departure from His disciples. The Spirit could not be given until Jesus was glorified (John 7:39). First Christ had to walk the agonizing road to the cross where He paid the final installment on the debt of our sin. He had to leave His grave in glorious and victorious resurrection. He had to ascend into heaven and enter His place at the Father's right hand and be given dominion over all things in heaven and earth. Only then could Jesus pour out His Holy Spirit on His people. Just how profitable Jesus' going away proved to be for the disciples is demonstrated in the night He was seized by His enemies. They fled in fear, but only a few weeks later, after the coming of the Spirit, "they were all filled with the Holy Spirit and spoke the work of God boldly" (Acts 4:31).

Completing His Presence

Just think what all this means for us! We, the disciples of 1984, have not been shortchanged by our Lord because we have not known His visible presence. It really is to our advantage to have the Counselor whom Jesus continues to send to His people. The Holy Spirit is not merely some sort of substitute for Christ in our lives; the Spirit completes His presence. That is the significance of the title Jesus used for the Spirit: "the Counselor." Quite literally the word means someone "called to one's side" indicating a person who will stand by to give his help. When Jesus referred to the Spirit as "another Counselor" (John 14:16), He meant to assure His disciples and us that the Spirit would be supplying the same help for our lives as He Himself would.

How vital the ministry of the Counselor is in every believer's life! He makes it possible for us to put our trust in Jesus as our Lord (1 Cor. 12:3). He guides us into the truth about Christ as our Lord and Savior (John 16:13-15). This same Spirit enables us to have contact with our Lord in prayer, even praying for us when we cannot (Rom. 8:26). When we live in the Spirit, He produces His fruit in us and enables us to die to our sinful flesh and its evil works (Gal. 5:16-25). The activity of the Spirit is both vast and greatly varied. But one thing is abundantly clear: His presence in our lives is the grand assurance from our Savior that we never have to face the trials and struggles of life alone.

II. For Our Witness Life—the Spirit's Power

We *Are* Witnesses

By the same token we shall never have to witness alone either. The Lord has left little doubt that He expects His disciples then and now to witness about Him to others. A few verses before our text He is quoted as saying, "When the Counselor comes, whom I will send to you from the Father...he will testify about me; but you also must testify" (John 15:26-27). The connection between the coming of the Holy Spirit and witnessing is even more obvious in the Lord's assignment to the disciples in Acts. "You will receive power when the Holy Spirit comes on you; and you will be my witnesses" (1:8). And how they did witness on that tremendous day when the Spirit was poured out on them. In the power and languages the Spirit gave they were excitedly "declaring the wonders of God" (2:11). Jesus knew the obstacles His disciples would face in trying to witness to Him, but no matter what the opposition, they would still have the advantage of the very Spirit of God at work in them.

Jesus knows the obstacles we face in being witnesses to Him. While they are not very often violent, they are real obstacles. One in particular makes the average Christian today fearful about trying to share his or her Lord with others. It is the prevailing spiritual atmosphere in daily life around us. Almost everyone will say, "I believe in God," but the majority are not actively involved in either a church or personal worship life. Their "faith" is often little more than their own subjective conclusions, decidedly colored by what they *want* religion to be. Religious beliefs, either positive or negative, are also greatly affected by what people learn from science and philosophy. Then there is the inborn egotism of man's sinful nature which makes individuals very determined to stand by their own conclusions. It is a form of self-defense that makes many simply refuse to listen or get very hostile. Christians generally respond in one of two ways to such resistance: either they militantly attack and try to overwhelm the person with "Jesus facts" and condemnation, or they simply "clam up" because they do not feel they have what it takes to out argue anyone. Doesn't that sound familiar? But Christian witnessing is always a two person activity. The advantage is ours because of the power of the Counselor in us and in our witnessing.

Convincing and Convicting

No one who believes in Christ and takes the New Testament seriously can claim exemption from the command of our Lord to be witnesses to His truth. Nor could such a person ever think that the task of convincing an unbeliever to accept Christ is up to him. Jesus said of the Spirit, "When he comes, he will convict the world of guilt in regard to sin and righteousness and judgment." By the word that He used Jesus was describing the work of a prosecutor. This prosecutor's task is not only to *convince* someone that a given fact is true but also to *convict* the person that it is true of him. Without the convincing and convicting work of the Spirit no one in his natural, sinful condition can truly come to repentance and faith. These deal with spiritual matters, and natural man just cannot make any sense out of them by himself; they are foolishness to him (1 Cor. 2:14).

See how this takes the monkey off our back in terms of witnessing? We can tell others what the messages of Law and Gospel are, but we can only reach their ears. It is the Spirit alone who can go right into a sin-darkened heart, expose it for what it is, and then turn on the light of understanding and faith in the Savior. If we just do our job faithfully, the Counselor will powerfully do His.

Sin, Righteousness, Judgment

Jesus focused the convincing, convicting work of His Spirit in three specific areas. "He will convict the world...in regard to sin, because men do not believe in me." Someone has suggested that we need a "Missing Word Bureau" so that people might rediscover the word *sin*. People speak of their faults and mistakes but refuse to acknowledge personal sin. *Sin* is when you do something *real* bad, whatever that means. The word for sin in the New Testament means simply "to miss the mark" of holiness that God demands. Obviously no man or woman of the world will be drawn from sin to the Savior unless deeply convicted regarding the reality and seriousness of sin. The law of God certainly does the exposing. Calvary—the fact that it took the death of God's own Son to finish off the condemning power of sin—demands that our sin be taken seriously. And while it is easy to point out the many, many ways people fail to be or do what God demands, Jesus says that the basic sin is "men do not believe in me." Despite all that God has done for the salvation of the world, people do not turn to Jesus and receive Him by faith. The Holy Spirit must, in effect, seize an individual by the collar and make him or her realistically face total, personal failure to be holy. This is the first, essential step toward new life in Christ.

Furthermore, the Spirit "will convict the world . . . in regard to righteousness, because I am going to the Father, where you can see me no longer," says Jesus. While He was still visibly present in the world, Christ plainly and bluntly exposed the emptiness of all righteousness that people display before God by their own efforts. In fact, many people today are still counting on the value of their own accomplishments to make them right and acceptable before their Maker. They are like the little boy who, when told to clean his room, went out to play instead. Later, when he returned home, he thought he could divert his mother's anger by quickly doing his work. He only made matters worse, because his dirty hands and muddy shoes soiled everything he touched. Because people are convinced that God will surely accept their currency of good deeds, they fail to see cleansing and forgiveness in Christ as the only way of being right with the heavenly Father. Only the Counselor sent by Jesus can show up man's self-righteousness for the hollow, worthless thing it is and point sinners to the righteousness that is by faith alone.

Finally, the Spirit's task is to "convict the world . . . in regard to judgment, because the prince of this world now stands condemned." It is very typical of people to be so consumed by the desire to get the most out of life that they refuse to reckon with the moment of accountability before God. They continue to go their way, sinning freely and neglecting God, and generally no evil consequences ever happen. They seem to be getting away with their sin. But just as Satan, "the prince of this world," was judged and condemned, and his power over sinful man broken by Christ's victorious death and resurrection, so all the sin of the world must eventually get its due--judgment! Actually, "whoever does not believe [in Jesus as Savior] stands condemned already" according to Jesus' own words (John 3:18). However, those who do believe in Christ already have eternal life (John 6:47). The personal conviction of these truths can only come to a person by the powerful and precious working of the Holy Spirit.

Take Advantage

Having the advantage and using it can be two very different things. Having the presence and power of the Counselor whom Jesus sends on His people is a fact based on His promise. The gift of the Spirit and His activity in our personal life as well as in our witness life are there for the real spiritual advantage of every believer in Christ. I urge you in the name of our Lord: Use the advantage that is yours!

What's So Great About God?

THE HOLY TRINITY
FIRST SUNDAY AFTER PENTECOST
MATTHEW 28:16-20

Edwin Dubberke

Once in London during the Second World War J.B. Phillips, a well-known churchman, asked a group of young people if they would answer a question quickly without thought. "OK," they said. "The question," he said, "is this: Do you think God understands radar?" They all said "No," but then began to laugh as they realized how ridiculous their answer was. Later Phillips observed, "The snap answer showed me what I suspected—that at the back of their minds there was an idea of God as an old gentleman who lived in the past and was rather bewildered by modern progess."

If that kind of understanding of God existed 35 years ago, it is no doubt even more prevalent today. For many, the tremendous advantages in human technology of recent years has made the idea of God outdated and unnecessary. The modern "miracles" worked in the areas of medicine and computer sciences alone simply bewilder our minds. For example, it is expected that before long a computer will be developed that will actually surpass human beings not only in speed of computation but in intelligence. From the wonders of space exploration to the fantastic world of the micro-sciences it appears to some that mankind has moved far beyond any need for a God such as is described in the Bible. People don't hesitate to ask,

"What's So Great About God?"

This day is celebrated throughout most of Christendom as Trinity Sunday; it is a day of remembering who God is and what He has done to deserve the worship and allegiance of all people. It is most fitting that we address ourselves to all that we do know about the greatness of our God. Is He outmoded by modern advancement? Is He impotent before the powers men now control? Does He have anything to offer to "have-everything" people like us? Let's allow His word to speak to us now about just such things.

I. Unique in His Being

The Three-in-One God

What's so great about God? Well, His very person is such that He is far beyond our ability to comprehend. In the Gospel we heard Jesus give the name of God as Father, Son, and Holy Spirit. That is pretty amazing in view of the fact that the Bible insists over and over that "the Lord our God...is *one*" (Deut. 6:4). There are not thousands upon thousands of gods as some oriental peoples believe; neither is there one supreme god with inferior gods under him as some so-called religious groups in our own land claim. As God reveals Himself to us in His inspired word, He is one God in three persons. Of course, the statement is illogical and contradictory to our minds, but what else might we expect of *God*! People have tried to find ways of illustrating what our three-in-one God is like. He is like steam, water, and ice, each so different, and yet all three are one thing: H_2O. Someone has suggested that God is like a clock with three faces and only one set of works to keep time. Here's another illustration: I am pastor to many people, father to a few, and husband to another; yet I am just one man. All of these illustrations fall short, however, of perfectly and fully expressing what we know God to be. We must simply bow in humble adoration before Him whom we have come to identify as the triune God.

Glorious Mystery

At the same time we dare not shrug off the mystery of the Trinity, as if it really does not make any difference what God is like, as long as we believe in a supreme being or at least some sort of a God-in-general as many people do. Centuries ago the Christian church expressed its conviction that only God as He has revealed Himself in the Scriptures can be our God and receive our worship. Otherwise we in reality have *no* god. This was stated in the Athanasian Creed. Although found in our Lutheran hymnals, it is unfamiliar to most Christians. Nevertheless it clearly states: "The [universal Christian] faith is this, that we worship one God in three persons and three persons in one God...one person of the Father, another of the Son, and another of the Holy Spirit...all one: the glory equal, the majesty coeternal." With the psalmist we stand in awe of Him and proclaim, "Great is the Lord and most worthy of praise; his greatness no one can fathom" (Ps. 145:3). We must join the seraphim of heaven in their song: "Holy, holy, holy is the Lord Almighty; the whole earth is full of his glory" (Is. 6:3). We must worship Him with the apostle: "Now to the King eternal, immortal, invisible, the only God, be honor and glory for ever and ever" (1 Tim. 1:17).

Holy, holy, holy, Lord God Almighty!
Early in the morning our song shall rise to thee.
Holy, holy, holy, merciful and mighty!
God in three Persons, blessed Trinity!

II. Unmatched in His Works

More Than Discovery

What's so great about God? Well, He is not only far above us and our understanding in what He *is*, but what He has *done* and still *does* is beyond our comprehension also. The amazing accomplishments of man must always involve discovering what is here in our world and then putting it to use in His service. For instance, science discovered the presence of nuclear energy and then worked until they were able to release it to generate power. They discovered the power of concentrated light and were able to build the laser. They have discovered the helping, healing effects of drugs and chemicals and prescribe them to aid us in recovering from illnesses. We are told that there is practically no end to what man will finally be able to do, but he must forever be only a discoverer and user—God alone is the Creator. "In the beginning God created the heavens and the earth" (Gen. 1:1). Despite all that is said and written about where the world came from, the best explanation still is the simple fact that God made all that exists and so "by faith we understand that the universe was formed at God's command, so that what is seen was not made out of what is visible" (Heb. 11:3). If people are to be praised for their accomplishments, how much more must we join the psalmist in saying, "How many are your works, O Lord! In wisdom you made them all" (Psalm 104:24)?

In Him We Live

So while people sail along through life (the life God gave them) and take pride in what they have gained or accomplished, the fact is that we exist and have such abundant blessings only because our good and gracious God keeps us. We have life and being only because He maintains it. We have what is necessary for life, and our efforts are rewarded with success only because He makes it possible. We can do all the planning in the world, but it is finally our God who decides what shall be and when. Thus we must agree with Paul who said, "In him we live and move and have our being" (Acts 17:28). Without Him we are literally nothing.

III. Supreme in His Love

The Real God

What's so great about God? We have considered who God is, what He has done and still keeps on doing. That is enough to overwhelm us with His greatness. But as we learn to know Him from that holy Word He gave us, we quickly realize that the greatest, most amazing thing of all about God is the love He has shown us in Jesus Christ. Of all the wondrous things that we might seek to know about our great God, we do not really know Him until we have come face to face with the simple truth that above all "God is love" (1 John 4:16). Love is not merely a characteristic of God; it is His very nature!

Many people will categorically reject any statement about the love of God. They point to all the evil, pain, and death in the world and say, "If God is love, how can He allow these things to happen?" Very honestly, we don't fully understand just why God does what He does or allows what He allows, and we might as well admit it. But this much we do know: God has demonstrated His love for us in a way that simply overrides any questions to the contrary. He Himself died for us to deliver us from the worst, most destructive problem of all—our sin. That is the message and meaning of all that Jesus Christ was and did.

Love Is a Person

To understand what God has done, try to picture it like this: Out there in the eternity of His existence God decided what He would do about the sin and disobedience of mankind that threatened to stand forever as a wall between the gracious Creator and the most special of His creatures. It was finally decided that the Son would be sent on the rescue mission. Because He was and always would be "very God of very God," the Son would have full authority to do whatever was needed to accomplish the deliverance of man from the eternally fatal infection of sin. That is why Jesus could say, "All authority in heaven and on earth has been given to me." Thus "when the time had fully come, God sent his Son, born of woman, born under law, to redeem those under law [and, we might add, condemned by it], that we might receive the full rights of sons" (Gal. 4:4-5).

Just think of the love power that was in action in Jesus! God Himself was entering His creation to become a creature. In His mission on our planet He had two objectives: First, He was to live a truly human life as the representative of all people who would ever live, to face every temptation, to bear every burden, and yet to remain totally sinless before the grinding demands of the law of God. Second, God's Son was to sacrifice His sinless life in death, suffering the wages of sin as if He were guilty of every sin imaginable because the iniquity of every one of us was laid on Him (Is. 53:6). The New Testament, especially in the four gospels, tells how our Lord fully and completely carried out His assignment from His lowly birth in a stable to His agonizing death on a cross and burial in a tomb. Then, as a stamp of approval and acceptance on all that Jesus had accomplished, God raised Him from the dead in the glorious victory of Easter. Forty days later the Son returned to His

Father's right hand and the divine glory that had been His from eternity—He ascended to heaven.

Outreach of Love

But there is still one more step in the amazing grace of our God. All those for whom Christ had lived and died had to hear about what he had accomplished so that believing in Him with trusting hearts they might receive the gift of forgiveness of sins and a new and eternal life with the Father. Thus, just before His grand return to heaven, Jesus gathered His disciples around Him and gave them the tremendous assignment to "go and make disciples of all nations" and the authority to baptize and to teach in the name of God Himself so that people called to faith would be sealed in their salvation and grow in faith and Christian life. Making disciples is still the number one challenge confronting Christ's church, a challenge that demands and deserves an all-consuming effort from every one of us.

What's so great about God? To this very day He is continuing His promise given first to those disciples: "I will be with you always, to the very end of the age." By the powerful working of the Holy Spirit, which He has bestowed on His people, the Lord continues to have His word of life and salvation proclaimed; He continues to touch hearts and bring men, women, and children to faith; He continues to make them God's very own by adoption; and finally He continues work in them a life of service and love to the glory of the Father. Pray God He has worked all of this in us and will keep on rescuing people from their sins until this world ends.

What's so great about God? Now you know!

Wolves and Sandcastles

SECOND SUNDAY AFTER PENTECOST
MATTHEW 7:(15—20)21-29

Rex D. Spicer

Jesus concludes His Sermon on the Mount with a warning. "Watch out," he says. "Beware!" Something, or rather, someone is lurking about ready to do you in. In these closing words Jesus expresses a deep concern for His disciples, cautioning them lest they be snared by a double trap. The first such trap is the fatal seduction of false prophets. The second is to think we can build a life apart from the Word of God. In order to bring home His warning Jesus uses the picture of wolves and sandcastles.

A key theme that runs throughout today's Gospel is *deception.* It is often used in Scripture but probably not given enough serious attention. It means to be tricked or to trick oneself. It involves accepting as true or valid what is false or invalid. Because of a lack of training and knowledge, far too many people are more confident than they should be that they could never be enticed away from Christ and His Word. Former members of sects and cults have expressed with lament and surprise how easily they were misled from the truth.

I. Where the Wolves Are

Wolves in sheep's clothing, while sounding like Christians, are in fact leading people away from Christ. They speak in half-truths, using familiar terms but distorting what God has to say in His Word. The "sheep's clothing" is their appearance as lovers of Christ and defenders of the faith. Their wolflike behavior is not always evident in what they say and do. There is another intent than that of bringing people to faith in Christ. In fact, the spirits that drive them are not always holy. By contrast, they reflect greed, self-glorification, and power. So Jesus declares, "Watch out." These wolves seek to tear apart what the Word proclaims as good and true. Jesus says, "By their fruits you will recognize them."

Throughout the Scripture Jesus is willing to hold Himself to the same test. He wants us to know the truth and experience the grace of the heavenly Father. He is the One who came not for His own good, but for ours; not to bring glory to Himself, but to God; not to start a cult, but to bring the kingdom of heaven. In Him is the power to move beyond deceit and to know the good. Into the arena of our apathy, ignorance, and despair comes Emmanuel to be the door to life with God, the life that finds its direction apart from the pretenses and deceptions of this world.

Now in His light, guided by His Word, enlightened in His truth, seeing Him as the standard who passes the test of the good fruit, we can by the vision He grants, by the new life He instills, and by the power of the Spirit He gives begin to check out what people are saying about God and truth and the Christian life. We can compare their statements with the revelation shown us in this Christ and with His Word. But we must note that right at this point lies a most tragic dilemma. Think on this: to know what is *not* true, we must know what *is* true. The sad fact that confronts the church today is that far too many of its people do not understand its message, do not know its doctrines, and are more often than not unaware of its Lord in their lives.

Is this true for us? Have we allowed ourselves to become a Biblically ignorant people? Is the Bible for us more of an heirloom than a handbook for life? Are we playing in the sand enjoying momentary distractions and failing thereby to build a life on the Rock which is Christ and His Word? If this is the case, we are ripe for deception. For then we cannot tell the good fruit from the bad. Rather our judgments will be made on the basis of personality, good deeds, and fine voices putting forth what sounds good to us and tickles our fancy. Such a way of judging allows us to be deceived and to come up empty, deprived, and diminished.

If we are to deal with error and confront untruth then, as people standing in the light of Christ, we must first overcome the idea that to speak up against what is wrong is somehow un-American and un-Christian. We have become too afraid of the words "prejudice" and "discrimination." In some areas of life they are wrong, but what is wrong with being prejudiced against evil and able to discriminate between right and wrong, truth and error? Why not expose would-be deceivers who are not of the Lord? What is wrong with siding with those who favor good over evil?

If we are to deal with error and confront untruth, then, as people enlightened by Christ, we must learn that we cannot handle false teachers with only an early Sunday school training. Often we are confronted by clever and knowledgeable people who use a variety of tactics to intimidate and seduce. It's like going up against a hungry lion with a popgun. That's not only stupid; it's dangerous! My prayer for all of us is that God will help us put aside those things that hold us back from the study and learning of His most precious, life-giving, corrective, guiding, and sustaining Word. Of all the things of which we might be ashamed, let the Gospel not be one! Jesus in this text exhibits His abiding concern for His people lest we be deceived by those who would lead us from Him for their own purposes. He is the Good Shepherd who encourages us to be prepared through the study of His Word to walk with Him in life. We should be willing and able to make the distinction between good and bad fruit.

Some things are not what they seem. Butterball turkeys contain no butter. Listerine does not cure sore throats. Rev. Moon and others of his kind are not of God. Christ alone is what He claims to be. As the prophet says, "nor was any deceit in his mouth" (Is. 53:9).

II. Where the Delusions Lie

Now having warned us about false teachers, Jesus turns to the more subtle temptation to deceive ourselves by building sand-castles. This deception begins when we are quite young. We are taught to build a life on being both nice and successful. Our culture programs us to rely on our own strength of mind and body, on financial resources, on family and social connections. This training seeks to convince us that this is the life—that this way of life will make us happy and bring us wholeness. Be well fed, have a good job and fine friends, and maybe add a little religion and nothing can go wrong. Right? Fools building castles in the sand with their very own lives! It is foolish because it is a deception.

> If I know all baseball stats
> and know not Christ,
> I am a fool
> left with trivia.
> And if I can repeat the names of football stars,
> and can quote each Soap's disasters,
> but have not Christ,
> I am a fool
> most shallow.
> And if I am well liked,
> and feel good about myself,
> but cannot think a beatitude,
> nor know my destiny,
> I am of all fools
> most deceived.

The ultimate question life asks of us is not can we play bridge or basketball or the stock market, but how well have we built our life. To whom do we belong, the master of the shadows, or the Light of the World? If we would build on the Rock and be wise, it is important to know in whose name we are making a life. A mother raises her children with love and sacrifice. She sees to it that they are well clothed and fed. She goes to their many school activities and stands by them in difficult times. Yet she never tells them of Jesus. With one hand she gives them all things, and with the other she deprives them of eternal life. Practicing the greatest deception of all, this mother (as well as any of us) holds out to the children through the things of this world a promise which the world can never fulfill.

The deception continues when people believe that if a child has a bright mind, that is all that is needed for the good life. It has not occurred to many that what counts is which light makes this brightness—the light of God's eternity, or the sulfurous light of Satan. The wise person of which Jesus speaks is alive to the truth that one's job, house, fun, spouse, and children were not made to do with as one pleases. They were made to fit into God's plan. This plan has to do with the Man who is here speaking to His disciples and to us. If we are not to be the fool, then Jesus points to "these words of mine" as the sure and only foundation upon which to build an unshakable faith, an unyielding hope, and a secure life. The Man who can so address us has become the Rock on which God has established His church and provided us with a foundation stone for this life.

Once you were a people led by deception; now you are children of the truth, letting others see the good works that proceed from your faith that they might glorify God themselves rather than be misled into darkness. All this because, as St. Peter so well says, Christ "bore our sins in his body on the tree, so that we might die to sins and live for righteousness; by his wounds you have been healed" (1 Peter 2:24). Because He died in our place, we can now live in His. These are not the words and deeds of a crackpot, but of Him who molds all life and gives it its breath and hope.

On the basis of what Christ has done for us, He now encourages His people to put His Word into practice. In His Spirit you can live this Word, believe it, and let it be the guide for life and the way to heaven. In Christ we discover this to be a Word good for all seasons and all stages of life from the cradle to the grave. When wedding bells ring; when sorrow begets brokenness, and brokenness returns the favor; when dreams dissolve and friends are gone; when life seems devoid of any reason to go on, this Word is still there. In the hour of guilt it judges, and then turns to grant forgiveness. In the time of storm it gives solitude; in time of grief it provides comfort. When all else passes away, it continues to shine as the star of hope. Everything will burn out, but not this Word.

This Word which we hear and do leads us to know that we are in the hands of Someone who has the final say about it all, who can and does transform burdens and cares into pure blessings. If we build on anything less than this Word, we have wasted the time of our life. If we hear and do His Word, we can know that we are safe for eternity and that the Eternal will keep us safe in time. This is the Word of the God who works all things for good to those that love Him. What Christ builds, the waves of time cannot destroy.

Therefore, let yourself not be deceived by false prophets nor by the wisdom of this world. Learn the Word and let it shape your life. Let it be the foundation on which you build and the blueprint by which you plan and live. In so trusting your life to Christ and His Word, you too will discover that He indeed knows what He is talking about. Your life can sustain whatever comes your way. The wolves and sandcastles may have their day but soon fade away, dissolving into what they always were—the dust of earth, not the Rock.

Maybe It's Better to Be Sick

THIRD SUNDAY AFTER PENTECOST
MATTHEW 9:9-13

Rex D. Spicer

Maybe it's better to be sick. That's a strange statement, isn't it? We are living in a time when people are quite aware of good health and treasure it highly. Yet Jesus in our text suggests that the healthy and the strong can fail to recognize an illness which in reality afflicts us all. We have to ask what that could be and what Jesus means, or we are going to be confused and find ourselves turned off by this One who always seems to be at odds with what most people believe.

A Surprising Choice

Jesus had just surprised a lot of people, including a tax collector named Matthew. To be a tax collector, or customs official, required that a man work with the enemy Roman invader against his own people, the Jews. Such a person was neither respected nor trusted by those for whom he worked nor those from whom he collected. The Jews most certainly looked with disfavor on one who could so betray their race, their culture, and their religion. Now Jesus enters the scene and calls this man Matthew to be a disciple—to follow in the steps of the One claiming to be the "Son of Man." To say the least, Jesus' other disciples must have wondered what their Master was doing. Matthew also must have wondered. Is this Jesus some kind of nut? Doesn't He know who and what I am? Is He not aware of the distaste that people have for me? You are a Jew, Jesus. What have you to do with one who abuses the traditions as well as the rights of the people?

Perhaps in some ways we can identify with Matthew at this point as we think of the ways we have betrayed what we were baptized into and how we have often exchanged commitment to Christ for what is expedient. Whatever the case may be, Jesus calls the sinner Matthew to be a disciple.

Having been called by Jesus, Matthew now serves dinner to the Lord and His disciples. As a person responds positively to the call of Jesus, something begins to change in the life, heart, and mind of that individual. So it is with Matthew as he invites Jesus into his home and life and invites his friends to meet the Master. Money, ripping people off, not caring, living only for one's self—all of our modern maladies are found in Matthew. But now we see these symptoms of illness giving way to signs of health evident in concern and fellowship.

As usual there are people who are not happy having sinners or Jesus in the neighborhood. And so the Pharisees, who seem to have a tendency to follow Jesus wherever He goes, show up at the house of Matthew. They are men of strict obedience to the Law and religious leaders of the community. Their picture of what is of God, what is good and proper, what is righteous, and what is acceptable is often contrasted with the position of Jesus. Here again we find them clashing.

The Pharisees corner some of the disciples and question them on the behaviour of Jesus. "Why does your teacher eat with tax collectors and sinners?" they inquire. Doesn't He know any better? Is He insane, sick, so irreligious that He abuses all the traditions and customs? What manner of man is this that associates with outcasts and rejects? These religious men are serious in their questioning and honestly perplexed by this Man who claims to be the One hoped for, but who seems so disrespectful of His heritage.

Jesus as usual is tuned in and hears the remarks of His challengers. In His response He confronts their position and offers them a way to understand what He is teaching and doing so that they too may know the kingdom of God has come. He encourages them to go back to the Old Testament that they so fervently defend and learn again what it means to be merciful. If they would do this, they would have a different view of who is sick (sinner) and who is healthy (righteous), and a different attitude toward those who are less righteous at this point than themselves.

Health and Sickness

Jesus thus instructs them and us on what it means to be healthy and sick. He says it is not the healthy who need a doctor, but the sick. In saying these things He is facing the reality before Him. He is acknowledging that the Pharisees are healthy, and the sinners are sick. Jesus never backed off from calling a sinner a sinner. He knows all the psychological and social problems that beset people, but that does not undercut His courage to call wrong wrong. So in our text Matthew calls himself and the others with him sinners, and Jesus accepts the label without question.

The same is true of the righteous. They are seriously called righteous. In a strange twist, however, Jesus condemns this righteousness and allies Himself with the sinners. It is strange because it seems to go against what we normally hold religion and worldly wisdom to teach. Wouldn't it seem to you that Jesus should favor the good guys? Perhaps the reason He doesn't is that these men are not really righteous.

Let's look again at the Pharisees. The righteousness of these men came with much self-control, hard discipline, and continuous self-observation. They were pious leaders and morally zealous. In their day they were guardians of the law of God. It would be more than accurate to compare them to those within the church today who are active members, have a well-established morality, and do charitable works. Such people are, by all normal criteria, righteous. So what is wrong? We must note that it is not in the keeping of the Law that Jesus condemns the Pharisees; it is in their lack of love. Jesus once said to another Pharisee that sinners have greater love than the righteous because more has been forgiven them. Repentant sinners are aware of failure, of the lack of love and goodness that has characterized their life. They are acutely aware that they lack the moral and spiritual strength to change the direction and pattern of their living unless they have help beyond themselves.

The Healing Call

It's at this point that Jesus is so vital. He lays claim to being the great Physician who has come to bring life to sinners and sufferers. He is the One who restores the despairing. He does this by drawing them into fellowship with Himself and thereby granting them fellowship with God. In this communion they begin to see that the root of their sin and plight is separation from God. This is their sickness. This is why Jesus Christ is the Savior. The healthy or the strong can make nothing of Him. They are not aware of their sickness. As the great Physician Jesus took our infirmities and bore our diseases (Is. 53:4). He is the Servant of the Lord, that Servant who goes the downward way of a quiet and selfless ministry for the broken and despairing. He gives Himself into an atoning death for the sins of many. Thus His calling of Matthew and eating with the tax collectors and sinners is not a violation of God's righteousness, but a reflection of God's compassionate forgiveness and grace. This is what He wanted the Pharisees to understand as He called them to mercy.

The Pharisees are offended because Jesus has definitely shown a difference which can only cause division and which will demand decision. What Jesus is and brings differs from people's ideas of piety and of the way to God. His picture will not be trimmed to fit into the existing frames of man's making. He comes as the fulfillment of God's promise, not as a mere addition to the accumulated piety of man. He seeks the sinner and forgives him. He separates Himself from the righteous because they would use their righteousness to assert themselves and oppose the highest righteousness of love, the divine compassion which is at work in what Jesus is doing and saying.

The cross of Christ proclaims that the grace of God is available to all—Jew or Greek, righteous or unrighteous—who respond to the call of the great Physician. The sin-sick, those sick in sin and those sick over their sin, have One who stands in their corner, who comes not to condemn but to save and restore them to God and to the wholeness of a truly righteous life. He comes for us, not because of what we are what we have done or failed to do, but because of who and what He is.

A Healing Relationship

People who have suffered the pain of self-accusation, self-rejection, and self-punishment in order to deal with their guilt happily discover in the new relationship with God through Christ that God's forgiveness is independent of anything we do. God does not demand that we feel good because we first make ourselves feel bad. He acts in spite of what we do and how we make ourselves feel. The sickness that can kill is a failure to open the heart to the effectual workings of a gracious Savior. When we open up to forgiveness, we open up to health. We have the possibility of learning to love as we let ourselves be loved.

Jesus says you cannot love unless you first experience forgiveness. You cannot love a self you reject, and you cannot love those who reject even if the rejection is done in righteousness. As one experiences the acceptance of Jesus, he finds Jesus already helping him deal with the side effects of sin such as hostility, cynicism, bitterness, and accusations against life itself. Matthew could never have overcome whatever disgust he had aimed at himself without finding this power working through Jesus who called Him and thereby declared "You are forgiven." Though Jesus speaks of the sinners as the sick ones needing a physician, they are also the ones now identified as well, whole, and restored.

The Pharisees, however, possess a fatal flaw. They are righteous, but in their heartlessness they would allow those they consider sick to perish. This reveals the hollowness of their claim. Because they see little need for a Savior, believing they have little to be forgiven, they can love little. This is the reason Jesus must confront them. This is why people turn away from such as the Pharisees. They could not have helped Matthew. They cannot help us, even if we admire them. People turn from the righteous parent, the righteous spouse, the righteous pastor not simply because they wish to escape critical judgment from these people, but because they seek a love rooted in forgiveness, and this the righteous cannot give.

Jesus does not applaud sin in calling Matthew. He does not want people to be unrighteous. But in His accepting of Matthew and the other outcasts, Jesus reveals that true righteousness cannot turn on the very people who are rightly judged unacceptable. Our tasks as the church of Christ is not to be a gathering place of Pharisees, but to call sinners to repentance. And we will certainly become more faithful and loving as we could allow ourselves to see our sickness in the light of God's law, and to find in the Light of God's Son our health. When we turn ourselves over to God and His way, we love more and are better able to resist presenting ourselves as acceptable to God by our own righteousness. May we know with St. Paul that when we are weak, then we are strong. For as we put ourselves into the hands of God, we discover that God's grace (alone) is sufficient for us. Hurray and Amen! In His love and through the faith He bestows I am made whole!

Love's Overspill

FOURTH SUNDAY AFTER PENTECOST
MATTHEW 9:35-10:8

Samuel Boda

When our Lord Christ passed through the world of His day, it may well have seemed to Him to be much like a large hospital with long corridors of sick and needy people on all sides. All were "sin-sick," and this had a variety of manifestations.

As many of these as came to the Lord for relief and help received His compassionate attention. He didn't refuse any of them. He saw them as "harassed and helpless, like sheep without a shepherd" (Matt. 9:36).

Multiple Blessings

Today's Gospel describes the Lord bringing a three-pronged blessing to the people of His day. "Jesus went through all the towns and villages, *teaching* in their synagogues, *preaching* the good news of the kingdom and *healing* every disease and sickness" (Matt. 9:35—emphasis added). Our Lord revealed Himself to the masses as the Good Shepherd who had come to befriend the straying and the lost and to lay down His life for them.

His primary purpose in coming was to bring spiritual enlightenment and spiritual healing. He proclaimed the startling truth that "one greater than the temple is here. . . . one greater than Jonah is here. . . . one greater than Solomon is here" (Matt. 12:6, 41, 42). And indeed, one greater than sin and Satan was there. This was the good news of the Kingdom! The King had entered upon His kingship at a specific time in history. He had come to exercise His power and dominion over the grip in which sin held mankind. He had come to win smashing victories over Satan, death, and hell, as well as over all the oppressive forces of evil arrayed against God's people.

The principal blessings would be spiritual—to effect a heavenly and holy cure, to provide a washing away of sins through the cleansing power of His holy blood which was to be shed innocently and willingly, and to work out a perfect reconciliation between God and us. All this He would make available to us through His astounding grace. We are called to respond in repentance, faith, and the grateful follow-through of an obedient, sanctified life under the direction of the Holy Spirit.

There would also be secondary blessings. The primary spiritual blessings would cause a spilling over of blessings in all aspects of our lives.

The Blessings Multiply

The blessed news of the heavenly King's arrival and presence was to be taken first to "the lost sheep of Israel" (Matt. 10:6). The children were to be fed first. Later, all others would also have access to the Lord's banquet of blessings.

On the cross of Calvary love's overspill would come into its own as the Lord Christ would work out a perfect atonement between God and man not just for Israel nor just for the people of His day. His forgiving love would spill out over all generations of past centuries and over all still to be born until the end of time.

When the Lord sent out the 12 and later the 70 "two by two ahead of him to every town and place where he was about to go" (Luke 10:1)—there was to be still more of love's overspill. Not only was the spiritual side of man to experience Kingdom blessings, but the whole person would also enjoy the benefits of Christ's kindly and compassionate love.

Our Lord "gave them [His disciples] authority to drive out evil spirits and to heal every disease and sickness" (Matt. 10:1). He charged them, "As you go, preach this message: 'The kingdom of heaven is near.' Heal the sick, raise the dead, cleanse those who have leprosy, drive out demons. Freely you have received, freely give" (Matt. 10:7-8).

This was to be no less than the full power of the anointed Christ and of God Himself working in the disciples and accomplishing the very same victorious results which Christ Himself had been achieving! The temptation to take advantage of the situation and to look for personal gain and fame would indeed face the disciples. They were to remember that they were but instruments of Christ's merciful kindness and grace, and all thoughts of self-seeking were to be set aside.

Blessings by Association

The fact that the physical, mental, and emotional facets of man's make-up were also to enjoy the overspill of our Lord Christ's love might be likened to the blessings by association that many had experienced already in Old Testament times.

When God was pleased with Joseph's faithfulness in the house of Potiphar, "the Lord gave him success in everything he did" (Gen. 39:3). But Joseph was not the only one who experienced blessing. Others were also blessed *because of Joseph.* "The Lord blessed the household of the Egyptian because of Joseph. The blessing of the Lord was on everything Potiphar had, both in the house and in the field" (Gen. 39:5). This can be called blessing by association. Even though Potiphar and his household were heathen as far as we can tell, they were also blessed because they were in the same physical and geographical area where God was blessing Joseph. The blessing spilled over also onto them. The sunshine of God's loving blessings fell not only on Joseph but also on those nearby.

Jacob also enjoyed the Lord's blessings for his strenuous labors over many years in the service of his uncle Laban. Those blessings, however, spilled over on undeserving Laban as well. Laban later confessed to Jacob, "The Lord has blessed me because of you" (Gen. 30:27). This is blessing by association, a form of love's overspill.

The house of Obed-Edom was especially blessed when King David housed the ark of the covenant there for three months. "Now King David was told, 'The Lord has blessed the household of Obed-Edom and everything he has , because of the ark of God'" (2 Sam. 6:12). This was blessing by association.

Because of the 100 prophets whom Obadiah hid (1 Kings 18:13), "and who were trampled underfoot by the ungodly and were compelled to go into exile—they were the saviors of the land" (*Luther's Works,* Am. Ed., vol. 8, p. 300). The whole land was spared because of these 100 godly prophets. That's blessing by association, because of somebody else. Luther explains, "The ungodly fare well because of the godly. Evil men enjoy the blessings of the saints, whom they hate, even though all good things fall to their lot because of their association with the godly and as a result of the blessing of the godly" (*Ibid.*).

So in a similar way, because of the spiritual blessings Christ was bringing to the people of his day, there would be physical blessings also, because the body is part of the total person. There would be overspill of blessings on the whole man because of the richness of the spiritual blessings. Christ's love would touch not only the soul of man but also the entire person.

This is not to say that there would be total healing for the body in every case. The body is affected by sin which continues with us throughout our lives. It is hampered by many limitations because of sin; there are many resultant weaknesses. The body is easily exposed to all sorts of infirmities and failings. Nevertheless, because it is associated with the spirit, the body enjoys blessings and help that an unbeliever would not experience under normal circumstances. Secondary blessings result because of the primary spiritual blessings which Christ Jesus brought. All these secondary blessings serve as bonus blessings, proofs of Christ's true kingly authority, now delegated to the 12. They were to demonstrate incontestably that "the kingdom of heaven is near," (Matt. 10:7).

What of Today?

Is there an overspill of our Lord Christ's love also in our day in the form of secondary blessings for the body, mind, and emotions—the whole person—in addition to the most important of all primary spiritual blessings?

This was Dr. Martin Luther's teaching in his exposition of the Sacrament of the Altar in the Large Catechism. There he urges Christ's believers to regard this Sacrament "as a pure, wholesome, soothing *medicine* which aids and quickens us *in both soul and body*. For where the soul is healed, *the body has benefited also* (LC V 68—emphasis added). Later he adds, "For here in the Sacrament you receive from Christ's lips the forgiveness of sins, which contains and conveys God's grace and Spirit with all His gifts, protection, defense, and power against death and the devil and *all evils*" (LC V 70—emphasis added).

The Scriptures also indicate that the more we involve ourselves with God's holy Word, the more blessings there would be not just for our souls but for our bodies as well. "My son, pay attention to what I say; listen closely to my words. Do not let them out of your sight, keep them within your heart; for they are life to those who find them *and health to a man's whole body*" (Prov. 4:20-22—emphasis added).

Our Lord does not want us to bypass the wonderful help that He has given us in the field of medical science and its arts. We should use them! They are God's gifts to us. But there is additional help for us. The primary spiritual blessings produce secondary bodily blessings so that God's people often do bounce back from illness more quickly than medical personnel sometimes expect and often more speedily than those who claim to have no faith whatsoever.

As we taste our Lord's love, whether through His word of pardon spoken in absolution or in the experience of the Holy Supper, we are strengthened and blessed not only spiritually. When we "depart in peace," the mind and emotions and body can also experience rest and blessing.

Here is a case in point: Some who have failed to demonstrate a forgiving spirit toward an individual (or individuals) have sometimes found themselves becoming tied up in nervous knots and have become burdened with all sorts of anxiety. Yet when such unforgiving people have been led to a change of heart and have come to repent through the power of Christ's own forgiving and melting love, they have found that their new attitude and approach of forgiveness toward others brought not only spiritual relief and blessing, but their emotional and physical tensions often left them as well. Their nervous knots were untied. Spiritual blessing brought also secondary physical and emotional and mental relief—by association—through overspill.

Our Lord God encourages us to pray fervently for recovery from our bodily ailments, as well as for spiritual growth to maturity. He is concerned about our bodies as well as our souls. The Spirit has James write, "And the prayer offered in faith will make the sick person well; the Lord will raise him up. If he has sinned, he will be forgiven. Therefore confess your sins to each other and pray for each other so that you may be healed. The prayer of a righteous man is powerful and effective" (James 5:15-16).

The apostle John prays for love's overspill for the recipient of his third letter. "Dear friend, I pray that you may enjoy good health and that all may go well with you, even as your soul is getting along well" (3 John 2).

There is far more blessing available to us in this life than we might imagine. Scripture reminds us that our God "is able to do immeasurably more than all we ask or imagine, according to his power that is at work within us" (Eph. 3:20). Spiritual blessings are meant in this passage, but because our whole person is inseparably linked with the spirit and soul, secondary blessings of an overspill nature result. God be praised for such a generous love that causes our cups to overflow (Ps. 23:5b) in so many ways—all because of our Lord Christ's fully atoning work of reconciliation on our behalf. "To Him be glory in the church and in Christ Jesus throughout all generations, for ever and ever! Amen" (Eph. 3:21).

Divinely Computerized Concern

FIFTH SUNDAY AFTER PENTECOST
MATTHEW 10:24-33

Samuel Boda

There would probably be some shrieking and surely a great deal of strong protest if we heard that the public school teachers in our nation were training our children in the tenets of atheism. Yet this is precisely what is happening in a number of totalitarian countries in eastern Europe today.

Teachers there are hired to teach children from age 4 on up in the fundamentals of atheism and communism. Children are exposed to statements such as these: "Believing in Christ is just an old fairy tale, just for old people. Children should be wiser than all that and should not be influenced to believe in Christ" (Evangelical sources in eastern Europe).

Parents who protest, along with their children, are quickly subjected to persecution of every sort. Christian church leaders as well are experiencing an increase in persecution in non-Christian countries, rather than an easing of it.

In one province of Ethiopia it has been reported that 33 churches and 31 preaching centers have been closed down, as persecution of Christ's people has been stepped up in that country. Similar reports are reaching us from other parts of the world where freedom to worship as one chooses is denied.

Our Lord Christ's words of prophecy continue to see fulfillment in our day: "If the head of the house has been called Beelzebub, how much more the members of his household!" (Matt. 10:25b).

No Exemptions

If Jesus, as God's own Ambassador from heaven, didn't come away unscratched—holy and innocent in every respect though He was and One who taught "the way of God in accordance with the truth" (Matt. 22:16)—we shouldn't expect to come away unscathed either, if we really and consistently live out the Christian faith and life as our Lord Christ expects us to.

St. Paul reminds us, "Everyone who wants to live a godly life in Christ Jesus will be persecuted" (2 Tim. 3:12). St. John uses striking, picturesque language to underscore the same truth in his vision: "The dragon [Satan] was enraged at the woman and went off to make war against the rest of her offspring [the church]—those who obey God's commandments and hold to the testimony of Jesus" (Rev. 12:17).

If we in our nation have been spared the agonizing mental and painful physical persecution going on elsewhere, might there be reasons? One Christian writer hazards the opinion that this might be an embarrassing reflection on our lukewarm witnessing. It might also be the result of some among us accommodating the Gospel to the mood of the world.

It's also true that a goodly number of believers move about, for the most part, in Christian circles and are fairly well insulated from the world's persecution. If they do experience it, it's of a mild and more tolerable form. Those who are more bold in their witnessing, as we all should be, will surely meet and feel an increasing intensity of opposition.

Adopt a Fearless Front!

God does not desert those who rise up to witness for Him. He Himself will have the last word in His dealings with those who persecute His followers. God will one day expose the tactics and inner machinations of those who deride and try to suppress Christ's committed believers. "So do not be afraid of them," encourages our Lord Christ. "There is nothing concealed that will not be disclosed, or hidden that will not be made known" (Matt. 10:26). God will reveal the thoughts and secrets of those who attempt to thwart and frustrate His work, and He will deal justly with them in His time unless there is genuine repentance on their part.

The earth and everything in it serve as Christ's footstool (Acts 7:49). We're to defend courageously His holy causes with God-given courage and not fear the consequences of evil men's wrath. "What I tell you in the dark, speak in the daylight; what is whispered in your ear, proclaim from the housetops" (Matt. 10:27). Be open about your faithfulness to the holy God, for He has placed limitations on the threats and persecutions of men. He reminds us that they can't touch the believer's soul. "Rather be afraid of the one who can destroy both soul and body in hell" (Matt. 10:28b). Even in the face of the possibility of personal injury and death, Christians can show the highest respect for the sovereign God and render Him a fitting, humble obedience. Their dedicated reverence for Him can far outweigh any fears they might have of earthly persecutions.

God "Covers" His Own!

The Lord Christ does not send His own into the world without cover. He "covers" us, as a policeman covers a fellow-officer who goes into a risky and dangerous situation. If God looks out for the common, seemingly insignificant sparrow, which was used by people in New Testament times for food (at "two for a penny"), Jesus assures the 12 and us that He will more surely look out for us. Were these lowly birds really worth the time and concern of a God who fills the galaxies and whom the "heavens, even the highest heavens, cannot contain" (2 Chron. 6:18)? God Himself determined that they were indeed worth His care; they were, after all, His creatures. He keeps track of each of them in His divine "computerized" way. "Not one of them [thousands upon thousands though they be] will fall to the ground apart from the will of your Father" (Matt. 10:29)—so particular is God with what He has placed on earth.

"So don't be afraid; you are worth more than many sparrows," Jesus reassures us (Matt. 10:31). He was on His way to put the highest price tag possible on each of us who possess living souls—that of His holy, priceless, and innocent blood. If persecutions come, they will come only to the degree that God allows.

Talk About Sensitivity!

Our Lord Christ adds another astounding truth for our comfort: "Even the very hairs of your head are all numbered" (v. 30). None of us knows the exact number of hairs on our head, and even if we did, we could not possibly keep track of those we are losing from day to day. Yet our meticulous God does keep track of the exact and changing number. The psalmist says He also counts the number of tears we shed and the tossings we experience during sleepless nights: "Record my lament; list my tears on your scroll—are they not in your record?" (Ps. 56:8).

What a sensitive God we have! He is always fully aware of every movement we make, of every loss we experience, and of every pain we feel. It's as if it were all happening to Him, for "whoever touches you touches the apple of his eye" (Zech. 2:8).

Compensatory Blessings

When our Savior and Lord urges us to take a consistent and firm stand for Him, He also provides solid encouragement for us. There will be compensatory blessings! "Whoever acknowledges me before men, I will also acknowledge him before my Father in heaven" (Matt. 10:32). But the reverse will also hold true: "But whoever disowns me before men, I will disown him before my Father in heaven" (v. 33). The boldness and inner courage which we all need for this task are Christian virtues which Christ's Spirit will increase in us as we continue seeking them through the reservoir of His channels.

Martin Luther writes from much personal experience when he encourages Christians to face persecutions fearlessly. "When the heart is cheerful, everything looks happy, even the cross and persecution.... But the highest joy is to rejoice and be glad in every persecution and upheaval. Let the Christian know that though all else has been taken away, Christ has not been removed from him, and let him spurn everything outside of Christ" (*Luther's Works,* Am. Ed., vol. 17, pp. 258–59). William Barclay describes the patience ascribed to Job as being "that gallant spirit which can breast the tides of doubt and sorrow and disaster and still hold on and come out with faith still stronger on the other side."

Our Lord Christ walked into the teeth of the fiercest of all persecutions when He made His way slowly but determinedly toward the altar of the cross. He tasted the worst of tortures that He might win for us the finest of blessings, including an eternity free from all harmful persecutions and griefs.

It was this moving love of the Lord Christ that gave Maria Durant the inner strength to make of her life an exemplary and inspirational model for all succeeding generations. She took the kind of stand that can be taken in confrontation with persecution, even of the severest sort. She lived in southern France during the 17th century. Described as attractive and intelligent, she was also a deeply spiritual person and did not hesitate to take a public stand for her Savior when the situation called for it.

In her part of France, persecution for one's Christian faith was more stinging than in other areas. She was not intimidated by threats from the authorities even when ordered to be silent. Her open and continued public witnessing to Christ, her Savior, led to her imprisonment. She could have been released had she been willing to compromise her faith and renounce her Lord as her captors were insisting.

But her witnessing remained undiminished and untarnished. Life began to pass her by with its possibilities of the bliss and joy of marriage and a family. For 38 years she refused to budge from her loyal commitment to her blessed Redeemer, Jesus Christ. Throughout all these years she was constantly victimized by her persecutors and subjected to much privation. This drained her strength and eventually took her life. She became a shining example of one of Christ's martyrs who remained faithful to Him even when it called for total sacrifice. Tourists have made trips to pay their respects to her stalwart confessing of Christ as Savior. They have looked with deep regret but also high admiration at a slogan which she purportedly had scratched on the dungeon wall where she had been held. It was the single word of challenge: RESIST!

Our Lord calls on us also to take a stand for Him at every opportunity. He himself will provide the strength to do so by the mighty working of His Spirit within us.

What We May Expect as Christ's Disciples

SIXTH SUNDAY AFTER PENTECOST
MATTHEW 10:34-42

Rudolph F. Norden

Leaders of religious cults tend to paint rosy, unrealistic pictures of their movements when recruiting followers. Aided by the electronic and print media, they often make false promises to those who seek health and wealth for themselves, or who altruistically seek the well-being of others. Bitter disappointment is sure to follow when people have been led to expect too much—when they have been told about the roses but not about the thorns.

Jesus too enlisted followers who were to be spiritual leaders after His departure. But He was very forthright in telling them what lay ahead, both evil and good. In Matt. 10 we read that our Lord called to Him the 12 disciples, giving them instruction before sending them out on their mission. In His teachings the Savior tells us frankly that following Him—and endeavoring to persuade others to do the same—involves losses and gains.

I. Discipleship Involves Losses

Our Savior elsewhere declared that His words would abide, even when heaven and earth had passed away. His teachings are always valid, always in force. Consequently what He told the Twelve then and there He now tells us, His 20th-century disciples.

The Sacrifice of Peaceful Human Relations

"Peace! It's wonderful!" This was the greeting in the Harlem section of New York City a generation ago when the followers of the cult leader, Father Divine, saluted one another. It is true; peace in the proper sense—peace with God through our Lord Jesus Christ—is wonderful. Peace with God is what the Christian religion is all about.

The Son of God came into the world to bring peace. St. Paul writes, "All this is from God, who reconciled us to himself through Christ and gave us the ministry of reconciliation: that God was reconciling the world to himself in Christ, not counting men's sins against them" (2 Cor 5:18-19). This reconciliation Jesus effected at great cost to Himself; His suffering and dying was the price of peace, as the prophet declares, "The punishment that brought us peace was upon him, and by his wounds we are healed" (Is. 53:5). The outcome of Jesus' self-sacrifice on the cross is the blessing of peace for us based on the forgiveness of sins. The apostle affirms, "Therefore, since we have been justified through faith, we have peace with God through our Lord Jesus Christ" (Rom. 5:1).

Peace with God is the basis for peace of conscience, that is, peace with oneself, and for peace with fellow human beings. The Christmas angels sang, "Glory to God in the highest, and on earth peace to men on whom his favor rests" (Luke 2:14). God's peace in Christ has healing power for Christians who are divided by controversy. When the apostolic church was divided over circumcision, St. Paul proclaimed the unity in Christ: "He himself is our peace, who has the two one and has destroyed the barrier, the dividing wall of hostility" (Eph. 2:14).

The blessed truth of our peace with God through the Prince of Peace is firmly established in Holy Scripture, and we know that nothing can ever contradict it. What shall we make then of Jesus' words, "Do not suppose that I have come to bring peace on earth. I have not come to bring peace, but a sword"? How is this saying to be understood?

Our Lord is briefing His disciples as to peoples' reaction when "the gospel of peace" (Eph. 6:15) is proclaimed. The effect it has on some is entirely negative due to the hardness of their hearts. The very means God has ordained to bring peace can touch off such opposition that it becomes the occasion for strife. As the same sun that melts wax hardens clay, so the Good News of Christ, which for some is the power of God unto salvation, becomes for others a stone of stumbling and a rock of offense.

Not only those who *bring* the glad tidings, but also those who *receive* it in their homes are apt to experience hatred, if not persecution. The loss of peace usually occurs in a place where it hurts the most—the family circle. There, on account of Christ, children may rise up against parents, husbands against wives, and vice versa. And the in-laws, too, may get into the act. What poignant words! "A man's enemies will be the members of his own household." That's the way it has been in totalitarian countries where children sometimes report their parents to the authorities for their alleged lack of loyalty to the government. The choice that disciples must make is this: Shall Christ have first place in their hearts, or shall it be son or daughter, father or mother?

Discipleship may also involve the loss of peaceful relations with people in the community, state, and nation. It may mean estrangement of friends, alienation of neighbors, social ostracism, the loss of one's job, or being passed over when business promotions are made. Jesus wants us to be realistic about our discipleship. It may mean the loss of peace with people close to us. Of couse, no one shall go out of his or her way to antagonize people. Over against the mandate of true discipleship, even at the cost of peace, stands this apostolic directive: "If it is possible, as far as it depends upon you, live at peace with everyone" (Rom. 12:18).

The Assumption of One's Cross

In the context of suffering for His name's sake Jesus speaks of another loss—the self-sacrifice involved in taking up the cross and following Him. This phase of discipleship, like other aspects of it, is often misunderstood. An obvious example is the case of a boy who came home from Sunday school and announced that the children had sung about an animal that could not see well. When asked to explain, he said the song was about "the cross-eyed bear." Misunderstanding about crossbearing was common in the Middle Ages when people, many of them soldiers of fortune, signed up for the Crusades and, as the saying went, "took the cross" and appliqued the symbol to their garb. "Taking the cross" meant going on an adventure that had little to do with serving Christ. Further, among Christians today crossbearing is often associated with special burdens, such as sicknesses, which do not result from one's commitment to Christ.

Crossbearing in its proper sense means suffering and denying oneself as a disciple of Jesus. In the New Testament, Stephen the Martyr is an example of those who take up the cross and follow Jesus, even when it leads to death. St. Paul likewise bore the cross when for the sake of Christ he suffered the loss of all things and counted them as refuse, in order, as he declares, "that I may gain Christ" (Phil. 3:8). In 2 Cor. 11:24-28 the apostle enumerates his losses as a crossbearer: beatings, imprisonment, toil and hardship, many a sleepless night, hunger and thirst, cold and exposure.

The Exchange of One Life for Another

Jesus tells us what further losses we may expect when we become His disciples. "Whoever finds his life will lose it, and whoever loses his life for my sake will find it." Here the Savior speaks of life in a twofold sense: (1) physical life in this present world, and (2) life in His kingdom which He blesses with salvation and eternal life. The first life is one that people by nature prize highly, bending every effort to sustain it with food and drink and to enhance it with treasure and pleasure, with prestige and social position. The other life is that of the soul, the life in Christ both here and hereafter. Those whose main interest is to satisfy their "this-worldly" desires will forfeit the greater and more glorious life of serving Christ now and of inheriting life in the world to come.

A loss is involved when we, Christ's disciples, exchange the one life for the other. Lost are ease and convenience, worldly enjoyments and advantages, interests that serve the human ego, and the like. But the exchange is one that Christ's disciples gladly make, for they know the difference between temporal and eternal values. Jim Elliott, one of several Christian missionaries killed by the Auca Indians in Ecuador, said before going on his mission, "He is no fool who gives what he cannot keep, to gain what he cannot lose."

II. Discipleship Involves Great Gains

In preparing His disciples for their work, Jesus told them that they could expect to encounter difficulties, the same difficulties we can expect, for Satan and the world have not changed. The question is, Are we willing—are we worthy—to be Christ's disciples? Before we reply, we want to hear what our Lord has to say about the blessings of discipleship.

Christ's Promises to His Disciples

Christ's instructions to His disciples as emissaries to preach the Gospel, heal the sick, and cast out demons are filled with comforting, strength-affording promises. The disciples were not alone when carrying out their mission. They heard Him say that "the Spirit of your Father" would be with them and would give them the right words to say when hailed before the authorities.

Christ gave them a further promise, the promise of divine protection, reminding them that no sparrow falls to the ground without the heavenly Father knowing about it. He added, "So don't be afraid; you are worth more than many sparrows" (Matt. 10:31). Based on these words is the song that the popular Ethel Waters loved to sing after her conversion. It was no longer "Stormy Weather," for which she had become famous, but "His Eye Is on the Sparrow," a song expressing the conviction "I know He cares for me."

But what effect would the encounter with raw unbelief have on the disciples' faith? Would it endanger their salvation? No, for Jesus assured them, "He who stands firm to the end will be saved" (Matt. 10:22). And Christ Himself would help them to endure, for He was their Aid and Advocate who would acknowledge them before His Father in heaven. These promises reinforce the Savior's references in today's Gospel to the blessings of discipleship.

The Blessing of Speaking for the Receiving Christ

Discipleship brings a blessing to those who speak the Word, and that blessing is Christ Himself, who tells us, "He who receives you receives me, and he who receives me receives the one who sent me."

Christ's spokesmen hold Him in their hearts as their highest Good, their priceless Treasure, their King of kings and Lord of lords. They gain a sense of highest worth when Jesus pronounces them His ambassadors, His representatives. It is a great honor and privilege to be in the vocation of disciple who witnesses to his or her Lord and who presents His cause. Jesus makes this very plain when He says to pastors and lay people alike, "He who listens to you listens to me" (Luke 10:16). Angels well might envy us our assignment, and so also human dignitaries who represent the princes of this world. Wrote Paul Lindemann in his book *Ambassadors of Christ* (St. Louis: Concordia, 1935), "Our ambassadorship was never more necessary and more promising of definite results than it is at the present time."

Christ's messengers have a blessing to share with those who open their hearts and homes to them. That blessing is Christ Himself and the forgiveness and peace with God He offers in the Gospel. This is readily understood by missionaries who were welcomed by Christian hosts—people who let it cost them to extend hospitality to Christ's emissaries so that their families and communities might be blessed through the Word of God.

In Second Kings we read about a pious woman in Shunem who gave the prophet Elisha a standing invitation to take meals in her home whenever he came that way. Further, she told her husband, "I know that this man who often comes our way is a holy man of God. Let's make a small room on the roof and put in it a bed and a table, a chair and a lamp for him. Then he can stay there whenever he comes to us (2 Kings 4:9-10).

This sermonizer, having graduated from the seminary in the depth of the Great Depression in the early 1930s, himself experienced such hospitality when "on a wing and a prayer," that is, on a subsistence salary of 25 dollars a month, he was sent to do mission work in Salida, Canon City, Pueblo, and other cities in Colorado. Christian families in those places, out of the kindness of their hearts, gave the missionary free room and board. Many were poor themselves, as were the Macedonians of whom St. Paul wrote, "Out of the most severe trial, their overflowing joy and their extreme poverty welled up in rich generosity" (2 Cor. 8:2). The missionary was well aware that he himself was not really the object of the people's generosity. He was received with kindness because he represented Christ and the Father who sent him. The hearers of the Word, who were disciples themselves, knew what a blessing it was to have Christ proclaimed in their midst.

The Rewards of Grace

Christ continues the thought about gains and blessings inherent in discipleship by speaking of the rewards in store for those who speak for Him and who receive His Word. The rewards are special—"a prophet's reward" and "a righteous man's reward," that is, returned favors in keeping with the initial favor shown to Christ's honored spokesmen. The Greek noun used here for "reward" is *misthos*, which originally meant an earned wage, a payment for work done. Used in a figurative sense, as in this text, it is rightly translated as a reward. *Misthos* is the term Jesus used in His beatitude for those who on earth are persecuted for righteousness' sake: "Rejoice and be glad, because great is your reward in heaven" (Matt. 5:12).

The Savior goes on to say that the reward applies not only to those who befriend human dignitaries or who "have entertained angels without knowing it" (Heb. 13:2), but also to a disciple who "gives a cup of cold water to one of these little ones." It is a noteworthy act, for what in faith is done to one of the least of the Lord's brothers and sisters is done to Him. The rewards promised for such an act of love will surely be realized one way or another, if not in this life then certainly in the life to come.

We designate these return favors as "rewards of grace," that is, true rewards, not earned by human effort, but given by God in His grace. Rewards of grace are not "credits" by which salvation is earned, for always this is true: "By grace you have been saved, through faith" (Eph. 2:8). The saving faith in Christ's merit, by which alone we are saved, never stands alone but is always accompanied by good works as the fruits or outward evidences of faith. These God has promised to bless in His own special way.

Our Commitment

What do our Lord's words, spoken in another land almost 2,000 years ago, mean to us here and now? We are not just "listening in" as He briefs His 12 disciples on what to expect when carrying out their assignment of proclaiming God's kingdom. His words are spoken also to us who through our baptism and the same Gospel addressed to us were called to be His disciples wherever we live—in our homes, in school, at work, in our communities.

We have heard and have responded to the summons of our Savior to come and to follow Him. It is most helpful to know what losses we may be called on to endure as His devoted disciples—sometimes the loss of peaceful relations, the need to bear our cross after Christ to our distinct disadvantage, and the exchange of a life of ease and self-service for the life in Christ that brings salvation. To be forewarned is to be forearmed.

But in order to be really equipped and properly motivated for our discipleship, we need to take to heart the great gains—Christ's promises of aid and comfort, the blessing of sharing the Good News of Christ, and the guaranteed rewards of grace.

Now what is our commitment? We may well state it in terms of the renewal of our love for Christ, for when we love Him, we will gladly serve Him.

> You will I love, my strength, my tower;
> You will I love, my hope, my joy;
> You will I love with all my power,
> With fervor time cannot destroy.
> You will I love, O Light divine,
> So long as life is mine. (*LW* 375)

Why We Heed the Clarion Call of the Gospel

SEVENTH SUNDAY AFTER PENTECOST
MATTHEW 11:25-30

Rudolph F. Norden

Quite often we receive fantastic offers through the mail. An invitation is extended to spend a free weekend at some resort or retirement village. An unbelievable promise is made with regard to an investment. We are told about a wonderful product that can be had on such and such terms. We have learned, of course, that it is a good policy to investigate before we invest, to ponder before we plunge. There are things we want to know: Who is making this offer? Are the people behind it able to deliver on their promise? What commitment on our part does the invitation call for?

In His mail to us—the writings of the prophets and psalmists, the messages in the four gospels, the letters of the apostles in our Bible— God is making us an astounding offer. He asks us to be His guests; He offers salvation, and it is all free as the prophet said, "Come, all you who are thirsty, come to the waters; and you who have no money, come, buy and eat!" (Is. 55:1). In the New Testament Jesus makes a similar offer: "Whoever drinks the water I give him will never thirst. Indeed, the water I give him will become in him a spring of water welling up to eternal life" (John 4:14). People who first hear this offer of the Gospel would call it fantastic—too good to be true. But it is true, and although it is most amazing, it is worth our serious attention, for we know what the terms of this offer are and who stands behind them.

I. In the Gospel the Father Reveals the Plan of Salvation

One would think that people, lost in sin and subject to death, would welcome the Gospel. But Jesus experienced otherwise. He had encountered unbelief in Chorazin, Bethsaida, and Capernaum, and He deplored it. But impenitence and unbelief, as grievous as they are, take nothing away from the glorious grace God has revealed in the Gospel.

The Revelation

In His prayer of thanksgiving Jesus expresses gratitude—more literally, His joyful assent, His grateful acknowledgment—because the Father has revealed "these things." They pertain to the plan or counsel of salvation which God formulated in eternity to save the fallen human race. Conceived in the mind of God, it was a mystery, unknown to the wisest of people, even to the angels. It would have remained a secret had not God in His mercy revealed it in the Gospel which the prophets of old, then Jesus and the apostles, proclaimed.

The truth revealed is this: "God was reconciling the world to himself in Christ" (2 Cor. 5:19). Again, St. Paul exults, "Beyond all question, the mystery of godliness is great: He appeared in a body, was vindicated by the Spirit, was seen by angels, was preached among the nations, was believed on in the world, was taken up in glory" (1 Tim. 3:16). In a nutshell, the Good News is that the Father so loved the world that He gave His only Son into death to atone for the sins of all, and that He through the Holy Spirit revealed this in the Gospel. The revelation deals with the things that belong to our peace: forgiveness, pardon, salvation.

The Revealer

He who is the Author and Source of the everlasting Gospel that brings salvation, and who stands behind every word of it, is God. Jesus declares, "I praise you, Father . . . because you have . . . revealed . . . ." He speaks of God as Father, His Father, and, thanks to His reconciliation, your Father, "from whom his whole family in heaven and on earth derives its name" (Eph. 3:15). This Father is dear to us, for He has made us His children and the heirs of eternal life. To Him we can pray with all boldness and confidence, calling Him by the endearing name "Abba." In his book *Life with Father* Clarence Day describes his domineering father. While He respected him, he could not really love him. If we were to write on *Life with the Heavenly Father*, we would dwell on His great love. We sing, "The Gospel shows the Father's grace, Who sent his Son to save our race" (*LW* 330:1).

Jesus addresses the Father as "Lord of heaven and earth." As Creator and Ruler of the universe, the Father has the power to fulfill what in love He promises. He is able to back up His words with deeds. Throughout the history of His dealing with the human race

He has revealed Himself as an acting God. As the Almighty He acted to deliver His people from adversity. His mighty works became evident in the great events of salvation that we celebrate at Christmas, Easter, and Pentecost.

When someone who is long on words but short on accomplishments holds out a fantastic proposition, we are apt to say, "Promises! Promises!" implying that, very likely, he is unable to do what he says. A famous sports figure, known not only for his athletic feats but also for his tall claims, defended himself by saying, "It is not boasting if you can do it." As for our heavenly Father, He as the Lord of heaven and earth is well able to fulfill every offer of grace made in the Gospel.

Those Receiving the Revelation

In His prayer to the Father Jesus speaks of two kinds of people who, as far as receiving the revelation is concerned, are at opposite ends of the spectrum—"the wise and learned" and "little children." What is hidden from the former is disclosed to the latter.

The wise and learned in this context, are people who are wise in their own conceits. They may have a great deal of earthly knowledge, but that is not their trouble. The problem is that they let it stand in the way of receiving divine revelation. In Jesus' day they were the scribes and Pharisees, who shut the door of their minds against our Lord's teaching on God's kingdom. They demanded signs and wonders, while the Greeks sought wisdom and philosophy. In both instances, mental prejudice stood in the way of accepting the Gospel of Christ. In our day, too, it is not uncommon for sophisticated people to hold Christianity to be foolishness, and on that account God cannot get through to them. The time may well come when He will stop sending them signals. Then it will be as Jesus said, "You have hidden these things from the wise and learned."

But our Savior rejoices that the Father has revealed His saving love to little children. Sometimes parents at home and teachers in a Christian school are amazed at the faith expressed by tiny tots—a faith God has worked in them Through Baptism and the Word. Apart from young children, there are also adults whom St. Paul calls "infants in Christ." These are people who "receive the kingdom of God like a little child," taking God at His Word. It is a blessed church and church school where children and adults hold a common faith in the Gospel. It is a blessed home where children share their parents' faith, and parents their children's. Charles Dickens shared his faith with his eight children when for their use he wrote *The Life of Our Lord*, stating that he wanted them to know Jesus Christ as he knew Him. He wrote, "You never can think what a good place heaven is without knowing who He was and what He did."

II. The Gospel Message Is Centered in Christ, the Son of God

The question we confront, Why do we heed the clarion call of the Gospel? has to be considered also in light of what Jesus teaches of Himself in His relation to the Father.

The Father Has Entrusted All Things to the Son

The words of Jesus read, "All things have been committed to me by my Father." The "all things" comprehend all aspects of the kingdom of grace. There would not have been the aforementioned "these things" for the Father to reveal had not the Son been put in charge of bringing them to reality.

To the Son—and Jesus Christ is that Son—was committed the great mission and ministry of the reconciliation of the world. The hymn writer Paul Gerhardt put the Father's commissioning of His Son into this dialog: "'Go down, my Son,' the Father said, 'To free my children from their dread of death and condemnation. The wrath and stripes are hard to bear, But in your death they all can share The joy of your salvation!'" And what does the Son reply? "Yes, Father, yes, most willingly, I bear what you command me; My will conforms to your decree, I risk what you have asked me" (*LW* 111:2-3).

This mission accomplished, as the Resurrection attests, the "all things" pertaining to salvation are still in the hands of the Son as Administrator of the kingdom of grace. Ascended into heaven and now sitting at the Father's right hand, Christ is the Head of the church, continuing to send the Spirit to guide and keep it in all truth, adding to it as more and more souls are gained, strengthening it for its mission in the world, supplying it with pastors and teachers to equip the saints for ministry, and preparing it "as a bride beautifully dressed for her husband" (Rev. 21:2) as He envisions the time when the kingdom of grace will become the kingdom of glory at His Second Coming. The last great act is also in the Son's hands, for the Father "has given him authority to judge" (John 5:27).

The Son Is on Equal and Intimate Terms with the Father

The "gospel of the glory of Christ" (2 Cor. 4:4) commends itself to us because He who is the heart and center of it, Jesus Christ, shares the majesty of God. Our Lord declares, "No one knows the Son except the Father, and no one knows the Father except the Son." The word in the Greek text for "know," *epiginoskein*, stresses complete and exact knowing, a knowing through and through, based on a close personal relationship. It is more than having a passing acquaintance, or knowing *about* someone. You may know some things about your neighbor, classmate, or co-worker, enough to say hello. But that is not real knowledge of the person. Jesus knows the Father and is known of Him in a fulsome sense.

Here Jesus, still in the state of humiliation, affirms that He is on equal, intimate terms with the Father. At another time He said, "I and the Father are one" (John 10:30). Again, "Anyone who has seen me has seen the Father" (John 14:9). What terrible blasphemy this would be if Jesus were a mere man! But He speaks the truth, for He is the Son of God, "the glory equal, the majesty coeternal," as the Athanasian Creed declares, with the Father and the Holy Spirit.

When in everyday life we are dealing with an active, bona fide father-and-son firm, we need have no hesitancy to accept an offer from the son, for son and father have such a close relationship that the one knows what the other has in mind and what the other is doing. What the Son of God tells us in the Gospel by way of revealing the Father's heart we can take on its face value, for the Son and the Father are on equal and intimate terms. The Father will stand behind every promise that Jesus has spoken.

Can also *we* know the Father? Indeed so, for Jesus not only declares that the Son knows the Father but also "those to whom the Son chooses to reveal him." To many people God is a hidden God. If they lack the Christian faith, they can at best "feel after Him," as St. Paul expresses it, by observing His works in nature. Yes, some truths about the Creator can be known—His wisdom and might, "his eternal power and divine nature" (Rom. 1:20), and also something about His justice. But they can never know God's love unless they have known Christ who reveals the Father to us so that we, too, know Him. This is true: "No one has ever seen God, but God the only Son, who is at the Father's side, has made him known" (John 1:18).

III. In The Gospel Christ Offers Rest for Our Souls

There is yet another reason for gladly heeding the clarion call of the Gospel. It bespeaks one of the most appealing comforts found anywhere in the Holy Scriptures. It is an invitation that none of us would want to turn down.

Those Invited

The general invitation or offer of the Gospel is addressed to all people. Jesus brings this out in His parables of a marriage feast and of a great supper. The "whoever" in John 3:16—"whoever believes in him shall . . . have eternal life"—invites everyone without distinction. It is said that a boy of Chinese origin named Lo happily told his mother that his name was mentioned in the Bible. When asked where, he quoted the text: "Lo, I am with you always." Good, but he could have done even better by finding himself in the "whoever"! The great Bible translator Richard Baxter once observed that if the name "Richard Baxter" appeared in John 3:16, he might wonder if another man by that name were meant. He said the "whoever" makes it absolutely sure that he was meant. The "whoever" issues an all-inclusive invitation—to the boy Lo, to Richard Baxter, and to all of us.

In our text Jesus invites a special group to come to Him: "all you who are weary and burdened." These are the people who bear life's burdens and are growing weary. They are the sick and aging whose distress is mostly physical. They are also the ones of every age and circumstance who have emotional problems, burdens of the mind and spirit, a sense of guilt. These are the people who can identify with everything mentioned in Charlotte Elliott's hymn "Just as I Am, Without One Plea"—"with many a conflict, many a doubt, Fightings and fears within, without." To them Jesus says, "Come to me"!

What Christ Offers the Weary

"I will give you rest," Jesus promises to all who come to Him with their burdens and who cast all their cares on Him. The Greek word for rest is *anapausis,* in which the English word *pause* is embedded. We may think of the relief Christ will grant as a "pause that refreshes," as a rest stop on life's journey, as respite from whatever is bothering us. In John 14:27 our Lord declares, "Peace I leave with you; my peace I give you. I do not give to you as the world gives." The peace that the world gives is at best a temporary relief afforded by tranquilizers. Jesus gives true peace and rest, the peace that passes all understanding, the peace with God that rests on the forgiveness of sins and our good standing with Him.

Here, as on many other occasions, Jesus reflects what is written in the Old Testament Scripture. Isaiah (28:11-12) wrote, "God will speak to this people, to whom he said, 'This is the resting place, let the weary rest'; and, 'This is the place of repose.'" And Jeremiah (6:16) proclaimed, "This is what the Lord says: 'Stand at the crossroads and look; ask for the ancient paths, ask where the good way is, and walk in it, and you will find rest for your souls.'" When we, weary and heavy laden, hear this promise of Christ, we cannot but join in the refrain of Charlotte Elliott's hymn, "O Lamb of God, I come, I come"!

The Gift Reveals the Giver

People reveal a lot about themselves in the kind of gifts they give. Parents would reveal cruelty if they gave stones to children asking for bread, or serpents instead of fish. On the other hand, in giving good gifts they reveal their goodness. In giving us the gift of rest for our souls, Jesus reveals much about Himself—about the kind of person He is, namely, "gentle and lowly at heart." The King who comes to His people is always humble, compassionate, and concerned about their welfare.

Since Jesus is generous and kind, then the yoke which He asks us to assume and the burden He would be pleased to have us bear after Him are easy and light. If the yoke placed on draft animals was not rightly adjusted to their necks, it would chafe and cause sores. But that would not be the case with properly fitting yokes. So it is with Christ's yoke which we voluntarily take on ourselves. It involves no real hardship, for it reflects the character of the Designer, who is considerate and thoughtful.

"Learn from me," the Savior urges. As He is, so let also His followers be. Let the mind of Christ always be in us as we follow in His footsteps. It means that we, too, will be gentle and lowly in heart as we deal with one another in life.

Conclusion

The words of Jesus in the text motivate us to heed the clarion call of the Gospel, for in it the Father reveals the plan of salvation, its message centers in the Son, who is equal with the Father, and through it Christ gives rest to our souls.

> How blest are they who hear God's Word,
> Who keep in faith what they have heard! (*LW* 222:1)

What Happens When We Speak God's Word?

EIGHTH SUNDAY AFTER PENTECOST
MATTHEW 13:1-9 (18-23)

Mark J. Steege

What do you think of Christ? What does He mean to you? I hope the Gospel lessons we have been considering this year have helped all of you to say to one who asks such a question, "Jesus is my Savior."

Just last Sunday the Gospel brought us Jesus' invitation, "Come to me, all you who are weary and burdened, and I will give you rest" (Matt. 11:28). Think of the precious promise that He would always be with us (Matt. 28:20) and the mercy He showed when He said, "Holy Father, protect them by the power of your name—the name you gave me—so that they may be one as we are one" (John 17:11). What comfort there is in these texts!

Today, however our text is different. It is one of the many parables Jesus began to teach in about the second year of His public ministry. During the first year He had taught very clearly that He was the Savior promised in Old Testament times. During the second year He began to describe in greater detail what it was like to live under Him in His kingdom. He used the picture language of parables to show how He operates in His kingdom, a subject that only Christians would be interested in. In the parable which is the basis of His message today, He wants us to note

What Happens When We Speak God's Word?

I. The Nature of the Word

He does not tell us in the parable what word he is talking about. Parables usually do not give the message. They describe the message which may be learned from clearer passages of Scripture. Our Old Testament Lesson for today brings us this clear word of God: "It [my word] will not return to me empty, but will accomplish what I desire and achieve the purpose for which I sent it" (Is. 55:11).

His Word could, of course, be Law or Gospel. In Isaiah's day God had to speak a lot of Law, because most of the people had forsaken the Lord. They were trampling God's temple courts and lifting up bloody hands in prayer (Is. 1:12, 15), refusing His gracious call.

It was the same in the days of Christ. He came preaching forgiveness of sins to those who would accept Him. But they would not receive Him in spite of the fact that He had so clearly presented Himself as their Savior. At the very beginning of His ministry John the Baptist had spoken of Him as the Lamb of God who takes away the sin of the world (John 1:29). In Jesus' first sermon in Nazareth He told the people with whom He had grown up that He was the Messiah. When they refused to accept Him, He went to Capernaum with His message of saving love and backed up His message with miracles of healing which should have convinced His hearers of His love and care. But they also rejected Him, making it necessary for Him to warn them of the wrath that would come upon them if they did not repent.

You certainly will grant that the message of God's saving love also forms the greater part of the message you hear coming from this pulpit. Why, then, do people refuse to hear this message of love?

II. Why So Many Do Not Hear

Jesus answers that question in the parable before us this morning. He gives us a number of reasons why so many do not listen when God speaks.

Some Do Not Really Hear

The first reason Jesus gives is that some people do not really hear God's Word, even though they are present when it is spoken. The Word falls on their ears as seed falls on a dry path. It does not get through to them.

The sower of seed in Jesus' day would spread the seed by hand, some of it falling on a path that had been made the year before. The sower would come along after he had spread the seed and with a small plow would turn over the soil just enough to cover the seed. But if birds happened to be near, they would pick it up. In like manner, Jesus says, the devil is at work every time the Word of God is preached. If people are not on guard, if their heart is hardened like a path, the devil keeps the word from getting into their hearts.

That may have happened to some of you at one time or another in life. You may have been so convinced that you had to take a course of action that involved you in sinning. No matter how hard people tried to help you see how wrong it would be, your mind was made up. Their warnings fell on deaf ears.

That actually happened to King David when he became guilty of adultery and murder. He was convinced that he had the right to take privileges with his subjects even if it meant robbing them of their honor or even their life. The prophet had to trick him into passing judgment on his action and then show him his own guilt. Thank God, Nathan's words did get through. David confessed his sins, and Nathan was able to assure him of God's forgiveness.

That is what God would do for people today who make the mistake of closing their ears to His words of warning. If they would only admit their sins and confess them to God, they would find Him gracious and forgiving. That is so clearly taught in the Gospel we considered last Sunday, where Jesus said, "Come unto me, all you who are weary and burdened, and I will give you rest" (Matt. 11:28).

Some Have Shallow Faith

Many who hear such words of love do come to Christ through the converting power of God's Word. The Holy Spirit teaches them to know Jesus as their Savior. We then hear them say, "It's wonderful. I now know the love of Jesus. He has completely changed my life." What an inspiration they are to us! They seem so happy in their new-found faith.

But Jesus warns in the parable that some of them may not have gotten to know Him well enough. The Word does not always take root in the hearts of converts. Christ uses the picture of seed cast on stony ground, where the soil is only a few inches deep. The seed germinates quickly, but it withers in the heat of the sun because the roots lack moisture.

People who have just come to faith need a lot of nurture. They need more and more of the Word which the Spirit can use to nourish and strengthen their faith. Without the Word they lose their faith. That is the way God works. He says, "If you hold to my teaching, you are really my disciples. Then you will know the truth, and the truth will set you free" (John 8:31-32). It is distressing to see some of those just brought to Christ leaving the Lord as quickly as they came to Him. Don't let that happen in our congregation. Invite them to join you in Bible study. Be a friend to them. They need your love and concern. They need your encouragement to keep on looking to the Lord as their Savior.

The apostle Paul is a wonderful example in the way he cared for those who had been brought to faith in the Lord. He was not satisfied to pray for them. He kept in touch with them, urging them to continue in the Word, to grow in faith and love through study of the Word. Bible study is what makes for strong, faithful Christians.

Some Have Faith Choked Out

But even strong, faithful Christians can fall from faith. That is another loving reminder given to us by our Lord in the parable He told so many years ago. It is comforting to know that He was thinking of all of us when He told it.

In picture language Jesus is telling us that the faith of some who now feel they love Him could be snuffed out. "How?" you ask. Jesus answers, "By a sudden tragedy too great for you to handle at the moment, or by some great earthly fortune too hard to pass up." Jesus likens these to thorns and thistles, the seeds of which were in the soil at the time the good seed was sown. Once they started to grow, they quickly snuffed out some of the grain. Every gardener knows the weeds will grow faster than the tender plant. The inexperienced gardener is even tempted to let the weeds grow and pull up the little greens that later appear, imagining these to be the weeds. Have you ever done a foolish thing like that?

It really hurts when the picture in the parable becomes the life experience of a faithful member of the church. That faithful member could be an elder or a Sunday school teacher or a leader in one of the societies in the church. You think of this person as one firm in the faith, an example to others in church attendance, in giving, and in every thing else that comes as a fruit of faith in Christ.

By Tragedy

But what if this strong Christian sees a two-year-old son or daughter mowed down by a car with a drunken driver at the wheel? The driver may have lost control of the car and cut down the little child playing in the front yard. What is the reaction of the faithful Christian who witnessed it all? Quickly he bends over and calls the child by name, but there is no answer. The child is dead—killed instantly!

"Oh, God, why? You gave me no chance to protect my loved one. Where were Your guardian angels? Where were You? You said You are with us always. You call Yourself the Good Shepherd. Wasn't this one of Your little lambs? Oh, God, I know all of Your promises. What good are they now? I don't believe You really care. You're not my kind of God."

That not only could happen to a faithful Christian. It has happened so often that Jesus warns us in the parable that it could happen to you or me. God does not drive a person to drink. He does not cause a drunk to lose control. He is not the guilty party if a crime is committed that results in the death of any one of His children. But He wants us to remember that we are living in an evil world where too many people are led by the devil and the demons of hell to crime and vice that may cause His loving children to suffer. If we are really listening to His Word, we will hear Him say that He can turn even the worst of these evils into blessings for us if we look to Him through our tears.

You children know the story of Joseph, who was sold into slavery by his own brothers because they were jealous of him. Then he was thrown into prison by the master whom he had served so faithfully, because his master believed the lies of his unfaithful wife. But finally God stepped in. Joseph was taken from prison and made the second highest ruler in Egypt. He was able to tell his brothers, when they finally recognized him, that they had meant to harm him, but God had meant it all for good.

That story is in our Bible for our learning. When deep tragedy befalls us, we are not to ask why the Lord allows such things to happen. We might not even understand his answers if he gave them at once. Would Joseph have understood if God had said, "Joseph, I'm going to let your brothers sell you into slavery, so that I can make you a ruler in Egypt. You will draft a plan to keep millions of people from starving. Just hang in there. It will all come out right"? So don't just look for answers.

If at first we do not understand God's ways, he wants us to know that all things do work together for good to those who love him. And when God says "all" he means *all*. So look to the Lord in the day of trouble. Do not rely on your own insights (Prov. 3:5). He is still in control. He always will be, even though we may not see it. He just wants us to remember that we are in an evil world. He knows what it is like from experience and is with us all the way.

By Wealth

But what if, instead of suffering, you should suddenly become exceedingly rich or some other good fortune came your way? In our parable Jesus warns that pleasure could just as easily cause our downfall as tragedy might.

What if you were offered a promotion on the condition that you would give up some of your religious principles? What if a group of neighbors came to you just after you had moved into their neighborhood and said, "We like to get together every week and have a good time. We want you to feel welcome. We let down the bars. You will enjoy it."

People like that do not consider the cost, and Christians who join them in their evil way of life certainly do not consider the cost. It could cost them their faith and even heaven itself. Judas bought a place in hell for 30 pieces of silver. He most likely figured Christ would elude his captors, and Judas would have his money. But it did not work that way. It did not work out right for Solomon, the wisest man on earth. He had built the temple. He had been a good king. But because he enjoyed the pleasures of heathen wives and sought to please them, he earned the wrath of God. He lost more than half of his kingdom and may even have lost his faith. Do you see why the Lord warns us not to seek after the pleasures of the world?

III. But Some Do Hear

Thank God, you are now listening to His warnings. In every age some have listened. They have been helped to remain true to the Lord who bought us with his own precious blood. They have given proof of their faith, as we can, with works of love.

The Lord also speaks of these in his parable. He likens the lives of the faithful to the good land that brought forth fruit—some of it 30-fold, some 60-, some even 100-fold. You see, even Christians are not all alike. The greater our faith, the more we rely on God. The greater will be the proofs of our faith in the life each of us will be able to live to the glory of God.

There are so many ways in which we can show love to God. A cup of water given to a thirsty person in Jesus' name is at least a beginning. Jesus told the disciples that He would reward even such a little deed (Mark 9:41). But think also of the description he gives us of the final judgment. The King will say to those on His right hand, "Come, you who are blessed by my Father; take your inheritance, the kingdom prepared for you since the creation of the world. For I was hungry and you gave me something to eat, I was thirsty and you gave me something to drink, I was a stranger and you invited me in, I needed clothes and you clothed me, I was sick and you looked after me, I was in prison and you came to visit me" (Matt. 25:34-36). Jesus explained His words by saying, "Whatever you did to one of the least of these brothers of mine, you did for me" (Matt. 25:40). If works like these, done in Christ's name, are pleasing to Him, is there reason for any of us to say, "I do not have the gifts to serve the Lord"? What He asks is that we use the gifts He has given us.

May you, then, with His help and through the hearing of His Word, abound in faith in Christ. May you also, with His help, give proof of your faith with works of love. May you do it to the glory of the Lord.

The World in Which We Live Is God's World

NINTH SUNDAY AFTER PENTECOST
MATTHEW 13:24-30 (36-43)

Mark J. Steege

Are you surprised that the sermon text for this Sunday is another parable? You are in for an even greater surprise. The Gospel lesson for next Sunday consists of three parables. But all of them are very short and closely related to each other.

Jesus actually taught all of these parables and a few more on a single day—with good reason. They all deal with Christ's kingdom. They show in picture language how Christ operates in His kingdom.

In the parable for today the Lord tells us that we who are the members of His kingdom of grace will be living in the world surrounded by unbelievers, and that we should not seek to drive them out. If He were speaking of the church, He would say we could not allow them to remain if they continue in open unbelief. But He makes very clear in His explanation of the parable that the field is a picture of the world. In the world believers and unbelievers will live side by side to the end of time. But the message that comes through loud and clear in the Scripture is that

The World in Which We Live Is God's World

The World God Made

Note that in the parable a man sowed good seed in *his* field. In explaining the parable Jesus says the field is the world, thus *his* world. Surely you will have no difficulty with that. God made the world and is still preserving it. As we sing in the "Venite," "The sea is his, for he made it, and his hand formed the dry land." What a beautiful world it is! Those who have eyes to see can see God's goodness on every side. See the heavens in their glorious splendor, every star attesting to God's might and power and wisdom. See the fields of golden grain, the fruit trees bending their branches to the earth under the weight of the crop, the berry bushes, the vegetables in millions of gardens. All are the gifts of a loving God. In *his* world, "He causes his sun to rise on the evil and on the good, and sends rain on the righteous and the unrighteous" (Matt. 5:45). The Creator opens his hand and satisfies the desires of every living thing (Ps. 145:16). The world we live in is His world. He created it.

Keep these things in mind. They will help you to remember that you are living in God's world. The devil can never take it away from us. God has placed us in His world to live here, to enjoy His gifts, to live a happy life. Even those whom Jesus calls the sons of the evil one are dependent on our God for food, clothing, and shelter. They are God's creatures, living in God's world.

Evil in the World

However, the sons of the evil one are not looking to God for food, clothing, and shelter. The devil dupes them into believing that they are self-sufficient. He enables them through trickery, deceit, robbery, and plunder to get more than their share of this world's goods. He helps them through evil ways to seize power over others, to make themselves great in the world, and even to persecute the children of God.

Easy to Hate

Yet the Lord tells us in His parable, "Don't try to drive them out of the world." The apostles James and John wanted to do just that. They wanted to call down fire from heaven to destroy the Samaritans who had refused to allow Jesus to remain in their city for the night. "But Jesus turned and rebuked them, and they went to another village" (Luke 9:55). When Peter lashed out at those who were taking Jesus captive, He responded, "Put your sword away! Shall I not drink the cup the Father has given me?" (John 18:11). A few hours before, all of the apostles had heard Christ say, "No servant is greater than his master. If they persecuted me, they will persecute you also" (John 15:20).

Our flesh wants us to resist persecution at all costs. It wants instead to take the life of any who would seek to harm us in any way. I am sure some of you have said in an unguarded moment, "They ought to kill the rapists, the murderers, and the kidnappers when they catch them. They don't deserve to live with decent people. They are beasts. Let them die like beasts." And then you remember that this is the flesh in you, wanting you to use the tactics of the world.

No Reason to Fear

Why would we want to get rid of all evildoers? Are we afraid of them? We need not be. They may, at times, kill the body, but after that there is no more that they can do (Luke 12:5). And if God does not will that His children should die at the hands of evildoers, He is able to save us as he saved David from the lion's mouth, his friends from a fiery furnace, and Jonah from the belly of a fish. Prison doors swung open without the guards even noticing it, releasing the apostle Peter for further service to the Lord. The apostle Paul faced perils in the city and in the wilderness. A night and a day he was adrift at sea (2 Cor. 11:25-27). But he survived, and that not by his own power. The Lord protected him, as He promises to protect us in the day of trouble.

The psalms are full of assurances of His help. Psalm 31 is a prayer for help against the wicked. The Psalmist ends on the positive note: "The Lord preserves the faithful, but the proud he pays back in full. Be strong and take heart, all you who hope in the Lord" (Ps. 31:23-24). Again the Psalmist says, "A thousand may fall at your side, ten thousand at your right hand, but it will not come near you" (Ps. 91:7). So take courage. You are living in God's world. He is preserving it and will preserve you in it.

The Danger of Temptation

We possibly should be less concerned about the suffering the world could cause us and be more concerned with the devil's temptation to rock our faith. He is so cunning at that, as the account of his test of Job's faith bears out.

Doubting God's Goodness

The devil came at Job in such a way that this faithful man of God didn't even realize he was being tempted. He first saw to it that Job lost all of his livestock, his cattle, donkeys, sheep, and camels. Job's comment was that the Lord had given him these possessions and had now allowed them to be taken away. He knew he was in God's world and that God would bless him in due time. But the testing became more severe. Job's sons and daughters were partying in a house. The devil caused a strong wind to rip it apart, and Job's sons and daughters perished. But Job figured God had allowed the wind to strike. He did not ask why. Then the devil caused Job's body to be covered with sores that were so painful and itched so much that Job took a piece of pottery to scrape his flesh. When his wife suggested that he take his life and thus end his suffering, Job's answer was that if we take the blessings God sends, we should be willing to take the sufferings as well.

Finally the devil came with the worst test of all. Job's friends had tried to comfort him in his suffering, but when they saw the extent of those sufferings, they felt God must be punishing Job for some hidden sin. So they started questioning him. And Job began to doubt the goodness of God. Finally, God came to the rescue. Read the story and you will see how Job in his later life was more richly blessed than he had been before the test began. And what faith he showed when he said, "I know that my Redeemer lives" (Job 19:25). He knew, as we know, that the world is God's world. He earned salvation for all.

Doubting Redemption

Learn this lesson well. The devil will try his hardest to get you to doubt that your Redeemer is alive, that you are alive in Him. He will seek to get you to turn away from the Lord. Then remember that you are living in God's world. That is why the devil will test you. He even dared to test Jesus when the Spirit led Him into the wilderness. But Christ stood firm in his obedience to the heavenly Father. He fought off the temptations of the devil with three short words of Scripture: that the Lord looks for obedience, for trust, and for worship of Him alone. Know, therefore, what God expects of you. Trust that He will help you to do it. And show your gratitude for His help. That is using the weapons God Himself gives you. With them you will be able to gain the victory over principalities and powers and the rulers of darkness (Eph. 6:12-18). For the world does not belong to the rulers of darkness. It is God's world. His Word rules.

Facing Evil with the Word

Learn to say with Luther, "Though devils all the world should fill, All eager to devour us, We tremble not, We fear no ill, They shall not overpower us." Why not? Because Christ has already won the victory for us. He gave us the Word that He used so effectively while he lived on earth as our substitute.

That Word is also powerful in our confrontations with the children of this world. We have to live with them; the Lord has made that clear. And all the while they will tempt us to join them in their way of life. But God is on our side. We are living in His world. With His help we can resist them, leaving it to Him to punish them for their evil deeds.

A Word of Warning

In fact, the day is coming when all who refuse to follow Christ, all who continue in unbelief, all who now as dupes of Satan are seeking to rob us of our faith will be thrown into hell. In the parable the servants are given the order to bind the weeds in bundles to be burned. In his explanation Jesus says, "The Son of Man will send out his angels, and they will weed out of his kingdom everything that causes sin and all who do evil. They will throw them into the fiery furnace, where there will be weeping and gnashing of teeth" (Matt. 13:41).

The word *fire* is used repeatedly in the Scriptures to depict the horrors of hell. In the story of the rich man and Lazarus, the rich man, being in torment, asked for just enough water to cool his tongue, "because I am in agony in this fire" (Luke 16:24). In John the Evangelist's vision the devil was thrown into the lake of burning sulfur (Rev. 20:10). An angel told the apostle, "If anyone worships the beast and its image . . . he, too, will drink the wine of Gods' fury, which has been poured full strength into the cup of his wrath. He will be tormented with burning sulfur in the presence of the holy angels and of the Lamb" (Rev. 14:9-10).

We cannot imagine the Lamb, who is Christ our Lord and Savior, saying to people in the judgment, "Depart from me, you who are cursed, into the eternal fire prepared for the devil and his angels" (Matt. 25:41). But we have His word for it; it will happen!

A Call for Rescue

Thank God, there is still time to rescue many from the torment that awaits the unbeliever. That surely must be one of the best reasons the servants were told not to try to dig out the weeds, "because while you are pulling the weeds, you may root up the wheat with them" (Matt. 13:29).

We recalled that the apostles James and John wanted to call fire from heaven to destroy the Samaritans for not welcoming Christ into their city. After His resurrection the evangelist Philip went down to a city of Samaria and proclaimed Christ to them. Luke tells us, "When the crowds heard Philip and saw the miraculous signs he did, they all paid close attention to what he said." (Acts 8:6). Eventually, many were baptized. Do you see the mercy of our God?

Saul of Tarsus was on the road to hell while he was seeking to take captive all who confessed Jesus as their Savior. Then Jesus appeared to him on the Damascus road, and Saul himself was saved. Not only that, he became one of the most ardent missionaries. He so desired to save his fellowmen that he was willing to be sent to hell, if that would help to save others. Of course, he knew it wouldn't. But he did know that the Gospel which tells of Christ and Him crucified is the power of God for salvation. He preached that Gospel wherever he went. He preached it so clearly that the people who heard it could practically see Christ crucified before their very eyes (Gal. 3:1).

We have that Gospel with its power to save, to heal, to strengthen the weak, to keep us all in the faith. Let us preach it, listen to it, live it, and love it, looking to the Lord to make it happen in this wonderful world—God's world.

Something Worth Living For—Something Worth Dying For

TENTH SUNDAY AFTER PENTECOST
MATTHEW 13:44-52

Donald C. Rousu

Few things are more alarming today for regular, church-going parents than to lose a son or daughter to a cult. I heard one parent say bluntly over national TV, "It would have been easier to lose our son in a car accident." Shocking events like the Jonestown Massacre have revealed the demonic control which is frequently exercised over members belonging to such cults. Over and over again we hear the parents of these children, along with the clergy of the church, agonizing aloud, "Why do our children fall for this deception and run to the cults? Why?" I think it is a good question. I think Jesus has the answer.

Not Finding It in the Church

No matter how condemning the answer, we have to face the facts: They went to the cults because they didn't find anything in the church worth living for, or dying for! And that's what people, especially young people, are looking for. We in the church have been so intent on lowering the cost of discipleship to bargain basement prices ("Aw, c'mon, you can be a church usher. Anyone can do it, and it won't take much of your time.") that we have failed to notice two very important things:

1. People want to find something in life that is so wonderful, so meaningful, fulfilling, and satisfying that they can give themselves

to it in total commitment. People are not afraid to suffer and sacrifice, if only they can find something that is truly worth it.

2. Secondly, Jesus says that when a man finds the kingdom of heaven, he will automatically, without any reflection, make that total commitment in order to possess it. "He went away and sold everything he had . . ."

Blinded by Presumption

Do you realize how blinded we are by presumption? We presume that children who have been born to Christian parents and raised on a church pew have already, by osmosis, found the kingdom of heaven. We presume them to be in full possession of the treasure buried in the field. What a deadly mistake to simply presume such things! It was a prominent clergyman interviewed for a national magazine several years ago who said something to this effect, "We have exposed our children to the faith in such small doses that we have only succeeded in making them immune; we have inoculated them against actually catching the disease." Because of that precarious reality, it has been observed by men like Luther that the church is never more than one generation from extinction.

Needed: A Life-changing Discovery

That tremendous, life-changing discovery of the hidden treasure is one which each person must make. Indeed, it is the only discovery that can possibly effect such a change. And Jesus says that a dramatically changed life is the inevitable result of finding the hidden treasure of the kingdom. "He went away and sold everything he had . . ." That's how you can tell when the miracle has transpired. A man's whole life, his whole perspective, his value system—everything is changed! In the kingdom a person finds what everyone seeks: Something worth living for, and something worth dying for.

Needed: A Holy Dissatisfaction

What a pathetic delusion if we sit in church Sunday after Sunday, imagining that we have found the kingdom of heaven, and yet our lives are not revolutionized as Jesus intends. We need, then, to be aroused to a holy dissatisfaction with anything in the church that is "ho-hum." Why? Because it's not Biblical! "Ah, but you overstate the case," I have been told. I wish it were true. I wish we could explain the loss of many church kids, the lack of vitality, and the generally low spiritual temperature in the church as being somehow normal. But no matter how hard we try to make our experience the measuring stick to decide what is true in the teachings of Jesus, we only deceive ourselves.

Jesus Makes His Case

In our text today Jesus uses three different similes to make his point. Each one exposes a unique facet of that mysterious thing called "the kingdom of heaven." He first compares it to a treasure hidden in a field. The emphasis here is on the "hiddenness" of the Kingdom. Even though its reality and nearness surround us on every side, nevertheless, it is not discerned by the unspiritual. It is hidden—hidden from the flesh, hidden from the natural man. Once Jesus prayed, "I praise you, Father, Lord of heaven and earth, because you have hidden these things from the wise and learned, and revealed them to little children." (Luke 10:21).

The second simile compares the Kingdom to a pearl of great price. Here the emphasis is not on the hiddenness, but on the seeking. Because it is hidden, Jesus tells us in Matthew 6 to look for this kingdom. We are to seek it at the expense of everything else. We are to seek it first, to seek it with all our heart, and to seek it with the confidence that we will find it. That is His promise.

The final simile is the most perplexing of all, for it compares the kingdom of heaven to a net that is cast into the sea and gathers every kind of fish. For this one, I ran to every commentary I could find. No two commentaries could agree as to what Jesus meant here. Furthermore, none of the commentaries seemed to have anything significant to say. On the contrary, the conclusions were quite trivial. I thought to myself, "Now isn't that strange. I have never known Jesus to waste his breath saying trivial things. And why would the gospel writer save something trivial and anti-climactic for the punch line?" So I put it away for awhile and asked the Lord to open my eyes to what was really going on here. One night, just before bed, it came to me—the "aha" experience.

The Setup

You see, I had always thought that Jesus was comparing the kingdom of heaven to a fishing operation so that the disciples could understand about the angels separating the evil from the righteous at the close of the age, just like fishermen sorting good and bad fish. Nonsense! They didn't need that explained to them any more than you or I do. What I now saw is that this talk about fisherman and angels was a setup for the last statement about scribes. The whole reason for setting up these two images of throwing away bad fish and throwing out evil people was in order to pose the last question. Jesus said, "Have you understood all this?" They said, "Yes."

The Clincher

Now comes the clincher. He says to them, and this is my own revised version from the Greek,

> Therefore (That is, on the basis of what I have just said to you), every scribe who has been discipled for the kingdom of heaven is like a householder who *throws out* of his treasure what is new and what is old.

The whole nature of a scribe was at stake here, and Jesus describes a behavior which is completely contrary to the nature of a scribe. A scribe was a man who began his training at age seven. If he showed promise by age 14, he received his own private tutor who stayed with him until age 40. At that time he became a full-fledged scribe, an expert in the oral traditions of the elders.

He spent his life memorizing sayings that would bring insight into making moral and legal decisions. He became a walking library. Everything that went in, stayed in. He was trained to be rigidly precise, like a computer. More and more was added to the memory storage banks, but nothing was ever allowed to slip away. Nothing was ever discarded. The stability and continuity of Jewish society was dependent on that. Do you have the picture? A scribe in the day of Jesus did not throw anything away from all that he learned, new or old—ever. It was unthinkable.

A Life Radically Revolutionized!

Jesus, however, says that when a scribe becomes a disciple in the kingdom of heaven, that is precisely what happens. He is like a householder doing spring cleaning. He throws out all kinds of things, both new and old. The Greek word *ekballo* means to forcefully eject, throw away, discard; it does not mean to "bring out so as to use." It was like Saul of Tarsus who counted his Jewish credentials as so much "dung" for the surpassing worth of knowing Christ Jesus, our Lord.

I am sure that the disciples whom Jesus addressed could not conceive of a scribe doing such a thing. If they should ever see a scribe willfully casting off a prestigious life that took 33 years to build, that would be a miracle! Values! That's what it's all about. Something worth living for and dying for! When you find it, everything is dynamically changed, revolutionized. And that's what has been missing for so many for such a long, long time.

What Keeps It From Happening Today?

Why don't we see happening this very thing of which Jesus speaks? Oh, it happens, but why don't we see it everywhere we look? It seems to me that there are three deadly things that keep it from happening:

1. The presumption that we have already found the kingdom when there is no earth-shaking evidence that such is the case.

2. The assumption that "churchiness" and "religion" are the same thing as the kingdom of heaven and therefore something that

just won't appeal to everyone—in other words, the assumption that the kingdom is not worth possessing.

3. The assumption that if the kingdom is as marvelous and desirable as Jesus says it is, then it must be generally beyond possessing, for most of us anyway.

Something Missing

I remember a period in my own life of prolonged emptiness and disillusionment when I began experimenting with alternatives, looking for that indefinable "something." In the church I heard words, preaching upon preaching and teaching upon teaching, but the reality of spiritual things was somehow missing. I myself was a prime candidate for the cults, except that in those days we scarcely knew the word. Nevertheless, God graciously protected me from Satan's counterfeit "discoveries" long enough to find the real thing.

Biblical Journey

Through some spiritually mature friends, I was taken on a Biblical journey to seek and find that "something" worth living for and dying for. As you look through the Scriptures, you will begin to see, over and over again, that the preaching of the kingdom of God is invariably linked with the manifest power of the Holy Spirit. In Luke 11:2-13; Acts 1:6-8; Romans 14:17; 1 Cor. 4:20; and many other places this theme resounds like thunder: "The kingdom of God is not a matter of [mere] talk but of power." The Spirit works through the Word of the Gospel to bring new life into being.

Or Take It from Luther

Luther plainly said the same thing in his explanation to the second petition of the Lord's Prayer. God's kingdom comes "when our heavenly Father gives us His Holy Spirit, so that by His grace we believe His holy Word . . ." Take it from Luther, one whose life was so revolutionized by the Kingdom's coming in power that he himself became a man through whom the Spirit of God altered the course of world history. What he asked, he received. What he sought, he found. And what he found, he was ready to die for, as he nearly did.

Something Worth Living For—
Something Worth Dying For

We need to know ourselves, and (by example) we need to convince our children before it is too late, that this kingdom not only exists, but that it will surely be found by all who seek it, that it is worth possessing above all else, and that is is attainable for any and all who cast themselves utterly on Him who won it for us at the cost of His life. We need to know, in the darkening hours of this tormented world, that there is something worth living for and something worth dying for.

The Overwhelming Evidence: A Living Witness

It is strange and wonderful how God sometimes pulls back the curtain to show us just a little bit of that hidden treasure which we seek in order to spur us on in our quest. For me, it came most recently when I read of a Mrs. Kwang in China. She was being brutally tortured during an interrogation before a tribunal of communist officials. She had become a simple evangelist through whose preaching God had brought many, many thousands to faith in Jesus Christ. Now, as a seasoned victim of prolonged cruelty, she was bound at the wrists and forced to bend from the waist at a 90-degree angle as they asked her questions. Any unwelcome answer was met with kicks and beatings. This went on continuously for three days with no food, water, sleep, or relief of any kind. Yet in spite of her incredible agony, she could only speak of the love of Jesus. She invited her tormentors to believe in this One who loves without condition and forgives without price by the shedding of His own blood.

Amazingly, there were those who began to weep. In her they saw the treasure buried in the field, the pearl of great price, the indwelling Spirit of Jesus, the very kingdom of God. Slowly, one by one, these officials began to speak aloud their acceptance of her invitation. What they saw with their own eyes was the suffering of Christ for lost men. They saw His forgiveness overcome sin, His love overcome hatred, His unspeakable goodness overcome evil. They received Christ and the power to become the children of God and entered into the kingdom themselves.

Because of this unexpected turn of events, the interrogation was ended, and the remaining unbelievers had her thrown into a tiny, dark cell. Eventually, God miraculously released her, but not until the witness of her sufferings had caused many more guards and prisoners to renounce all in order to follow Jesus! Think how costly for them! But that is what happens when people find something worth dying for.

The Unconditional Promise

To find the kingdom is really to find God Himself, intensely personal, unmistakeably real, nearer than my own breath. Mysteriously, amazingly, wondrously—the One who speaks the parable is the object of my quest! He is Jesus, showing me the heart of God my Father by pouring Himself out in love on the cross of Calvary! He is Jesus, who by His blood cleanses away all the devastation of my sin to show me the Father I have always wanted and never had. Wonder of wonders, the One whom I seek has sought me first!

To find the Kingdom is not only to find Jesus, but also to find myself in Him—by water and the Spirit dead to the power of sin, victoriously alive to God, seated with Him in the heavenly places to exercise authority over Satan and all the dominions of darkness. What a find! And it has always been there, promised in black and white, sealed in blood, for all who would seek. In Jer. 29:13 God says, "You will seek me and find me when you seek me with all your heart."

How to Feed a Hungry World

ELEVENTH SUNDAY AFTER PENTECOST
MATTHEW 14:13-21

Donald C. Rousu

The other night I was sitting in front of the TV with my entire family, a somewhat rare occurrence at our house. We had been playing all day and now, popcorn in hand, were determined to settle into some relaxing entertainment. Our oldest child was put in charge of spinning the dial. A game show. "No," we all said at once. Next, a panel of prominent journalists challenging some government bureaucrat. "Forget it," the kids cried. Click. Across the screen were written the words, "Report from East Africa." We watched in heavy silence as we viewed scores of sick and starving men, women, and children lining up for emergency food and medicine. We had watched such programs before and had consequently been moved to both pray and give money. But tonight, having already agreed that we wanted to be "entertained," there came forth some quiet groans. With nothing more definite than that, the channel was turned again. It was something loud and fast-moving. I sat back to watch, but my mind was still on those gaunt, black faces, those frightfully emaciated bodies. "We really don't *want* to look at it, do we?" I thought. "After all, what can I do? So many people—so little food."

When watching such programs on world hunger, I have often thought of the miraculous feeding of the 5,000. "Why can such a miracle not happen today?" I have wondered. But now, after much pondering on this Word of God, I am of a mind that it could most certainly happen, if only we would let it. Most of us have never seen such miracles because we have been unwilling to do what we must in order to make them happen. "What?" you ask. "Do you actually mean that there is something we must do?" Yes, that is precisely what I mean. A great deal depends on us. That is the startling truth that emerges from meditating on this Word.

Too Many People, Not Enough Food

The reactions of the first disciples are much like our own. They see thousands of people at day's end, standing out in the middle of nowhere, tired, hungry, and without food. Conclusion? This enormous need can only be met if the crowd should disperse immediately and go to several different towns to buy food.

Despair Leads to Hardness of Heart

It is obvious from the outset that the disciples despaired of feeding the people themselves. After all, this was one of those situations which any reasonable man could size up and reckon impossible. It's the same reaction we have to those TV documentaries on world hunger. "What can I do, anyway?" we ask, and snap off the set or change channels. But the truth of the matter is this: It doesn't have to be the problems of the whole world that overwhelm us. What if there is an appeal, for example, to help fellow Lutherans in Poland? "All those Lutherans!" we say. "What can I do, anyway?"

Well, just bring it closer to home. Forget about all those Lutherans in Poland. With rising unemployment we find increasing needs coming to our attention right in our own congregation. Then what is the response? "How can I feed them and their five kids when I can hardly feed my own?"

You see, once you despair of being able to meet someone else's need, it doesn't matter whether you're looking at 5,000, 500, 50, or 5. Click. Change channels. Look the other way. Pretend the problem doesn't exist, or reassure yourself that this problem is not your problem. Right? And so that sense of despair leads to a hardness of heart. "Send them away," the disciples demand. Out of sight, out of mind.

Hardness of Heart Rooted in Unbelief

But why do we become so hardened? Have you ever been troubled by your own hardness of heart? I have. I often think of I John 3:17 "If anyone has material possessions and sees his brother in need but has no pity on him, how can the love of God be in him?" Is it really true that we can do *nothing*? That we have *nothing* of the world's goods? Or is it that we look to our brother's need, measure it with the blind eyes of human reason, and conclude that because his need is greater than my resources, someone else will have to help? Click. Change channels.

Is it not a fact that we harden our hearts and turn the other way because we fail to believe, even refuse to believe, that our heavenly Father has inexhaustible resources to meet that brother's need? I don't mean in theory. I mean in practical, everyday life. Just like those twelve disciples, we meet difficult situations as if God did not exist. We have eyes only on ourselves and our own limited resources. We have eyes only for what *we* can do. Under pressure we live our lives like practicing atheists. And it is that deep root of unbelief that precludes the manifestation of miracles in the here-and-now.

The Compassion of Jesus

In sharp contrast to the hard-hearted unbelief of the disciples, we see the compassion of Jesus who trusts the Father for everything. Remember that Jesus and this crowd meet in the wilderness only because of one thing—the shocking death of John the Baptist by beheading. Jesus had left in a boat to be alone, but these stunned and frightened people sought comfort in their grief and pursued Jesus on foot. His immediate response? "He had compassion on them . . ." He is deeply moved to do something.

In spite of His own need for solitude, in spite of the overwhelming number of people, He is not overcome. He is not overcome by grief, or shock, or needs, or circumstances, He just dives in by ministering to their most apparent needs. The text says He healed their sick. Total compassion. He immersed Himself in the needs of others. And it is that life, that life of compassion, that life of His Son, that God wants to manifest in each of us when the Old Man has been put to death!

You Give Them Something to Eat

Now at the end of the day the disciples come to Jesus. It seems from the text that they had not been with Him, that they had come on the scene very late. They size up the situation and then presume to tell the Lord of the universe what to do! "This is a remote place, and it's already getting late. Send the crowds away, so they can go to the villages and buy themselves some food."

But the Compassionate One does not yield to cold reason. And He does not accept the humanistic appraisal of things or the heartless remedy. He counters by saying, "They do not need to go away." Then the most stunning thing of all: "*You* give them something to eat"! How often have you viewed the horror of starvation and thought, or even said, "Why doesn't God do something?" Yes, indeed, why doesn't God do something?

Do you know that in every Biblical account of these miraculous feedings, Jesus always turns it back to us? "*You* feed them. *You* give them something to eat. How much bread do *you* have?" You see, we are God's only instrument in this world. He will not act without us.

He is not content that we merely know His power. He wants us to know "his incomparably great power for us who believe. That power is like the working of his mighty strength" (Eph. 1:19).

"We Have Only . . ."

When He says, "You give them something to eat," the response is predictable. "We have here only five loaves of bread and two fish." Attention is on the insufficient resources of man. We sinful men are so problem-oriented, habitually inclined to impossibility thinking. Jesus tells us to feed the hungry multitudes and we submit a report. "Insufficient resources: Mission Impossible."

Now I want you to listen very carefully. Every miracle begins with an impossible problem! Find one place in the Bible where such is not the case. See your own problems as opportunities. He tells us to rejoice in our problems! For it is in problems that God brings us face to face with all our deficiencies and inadequacies so that we see Him—as our only alternative! He is sufficient, all we need! He is able. He is boundlessly rich. And He is our own Father in Jesus Christ by the blood of the cross, that blood that forgives, redeems, and sanctifies! Is it not an enviable thing to have such a rich Father? And what does He have that He has not already given to you, His child? "All things are yours . . . and you are of Christ, and Christ is of God" (1 Cor. 3:21-23).

"Bring Them to Me"—Total Surrender

When the disciples have taken inventory, Jesus does not say, "Oh, I see! You really don't have much, do you." Instead, He says, "Bring them here to me." Bring what? Bring it all. Bring everything you have. This is crucial, because this is where miracles are either conceived or crushed. Here we come to the crux, that is, to the cross of Jesus Christ. It is here that we are faced with the necessity of living out our baptism and answering the call to take up the cross, deny self, and follow Him. You see, I am all that stands in the way. When I consent to let the cross remove me so that Christ might live, that is the beginning of miracle. The miracle begins when the inner man obeys Jesus and places everything into His hands to do with as He pleases. Why? Because it is His. "The earth is the Lord's, and everything in it" (Ps. 24:1).

It doesn't matter if you have a multimillion dollar fortune or just a loin cloth and a rice bowl. All that matters is that everything be surrendered to Him. And this is the great hurdle. How shall we ever see the birth of miracles when so many of us balk at far less than total surrender, when are so often unable to commit our firstfruits gladly and generously to Him? Do you see what I mean? The matter really does depend on us! Do we really want to give birth to miracles? Then we must do as He says: Bring it all to Him.

The Miracle Unfolds

When He had all human resources in hand, He ordered the crowds to sit down. Now to have more than 5,000 people sit down to eat with only five loaves and two fish in hand is an act of faith! Faith is "acting as if" God will do what He promises to do. They act in faith. They sit down to eat.

Giving Thanks—for What?

When everyone was seated, He took the loaves and fish in hand, looked up into heaven, and gave thanks. For what? Those five loaves and two fish? Hardly! He gave thanks for what He saw when He looked into heaven! He gave thanks when He saw the unlimited resources of His Father, all the riches of the kingdom of heaven. He looked beyond the physical world to see a world infinitely more real. He looked into heaven and saw the sufficiency of God. As St. Paul says, "We fix our eyes not on what is seen, but on what is unseen" (2 Cor. 4:18). O Lord, open our eyes to see what You saw!

The Breaking: Miracle Released!

Having laid hold of the unlimited resources of God in the spiritual realm by giving thanks, He then broke the loaves and gave them to the disciples. There is a whole world of meaning in this breaking action that is easily missed by the modern Western mind. Just stop for a moment to "think Hebrew" with me. What is bread to a Jew, but life itself? Jesus even calls Himself the Bread of Life. And because bread was regarded as having a sacred character, it was never cut with a knife. Strange, isn't it! But to cut bread is to put a knife to a living thing. Instead, they broke it, which signifies sharing—the sharing of life. Thus, Jesus breaks the bread and begins a movement of sharing His own life.

Now get this picture in your mind: Jesus has broken the loaves and given them to the disciples. The disciples could have stood around Jesus, looked at the meager rations in their hands and said to themselves, "Just as we thought—only enough for us!" And they could have gobbled it down, brushed the crumbs from their hands and said, "That wasn't bad, but now what are you going to do with those 5,000 other people out there?" Seems ridiculous, doesn't it! And yet, that's just what we do every day when Jesus gives us our daily bread and then explicitly tells us to invite to our table those very people who cannot pay us back (Luke 14:12-14). We think, "Too bad—only enough for us." Why do you suppose the very growth of the early church itself was a miracle of multiplication? If you read the first six chapters of Acts, you will see these words scrawled in giant letters across every page: "They shared." They had all things in common. No one said anything was his own. No one had need of anything!

But, those 12 disciples didn't stop the sharing cycle. Instead, they saw the powers of the kingdom of God taking over, and they broke to leaders in the multitude. And those leaders broke to others around them, until all had received and shared with others. I can imagine that all these people, as they saw what was happening all around them, began to laugh and rejoice. What a revelation it is when we discover that we can feed others without going hungry ourselves! What a liberating discovery when we find that sharing and giving is the very tap that brings the unlimited resources of God gushing into the reality of our present experience!

Satisfied

Now the text concludes, "They all ate and were satisfied." that not only attests to the magnitude of the miracle, but it also tells us that more than the stuffing of mouths and the filling of bellies took place. Together, they had met God in their need. In the wilderness they had eaten not just bread, but the Bread of Life, with one another. They had found reconciliation and peace with the God who receives sinners and eats with them. And they had opened their hearts to one another—to the glory of God! Now that kind of eating and drinking satisfies, really satisfies. And if only you can experience it once, you will never stop the sharing for the pure joy of recognizing Him in the breaking of the bread!

Twelve Baskets Left Over

Not only do they eat to their satisfaction, but when everyone has had enough, there is much left over—12 baskets full! I think it was Oral Roberts who quipped, "One basket left over for each clergyman present who said it couldn't be done!" But those leftovers are more than an exclamation point on the miracle. Those baskets of leftovers speak of the boundless resource again. That means that our loving and sharing of the Bread of Life never stops producing an overflow. We Western-thinking people say, "Wow, 12 baskets full—that's a lot of garbage!" Listen. They didn't pick up all that food just to throw it away in the garbage. If you're "thinking Hebrew," you don't throw bread in the garbage anymore than you throw life in the garbage. That bread represents more life to be shared. That leftover bread constitutes the resources to start another miracle! And the principle is found in 2 Cor. 9:10: "Now he who supplies seed to the sower and bread for food will also supply and increase your store of seed and will enlarge the harvest of your righteousness." Multiplication of resources—that is the promise of our Father. There is no end to the miracle!

How to Feed a Hungry World

Now let me take you back once more and ask a very important question: Who does the feeding? Jesus? No. We heard Him say to the Twelve and to us, "You do it. You give them something to eat." And who did it? They did. In the power of Christ's Spirit the disciples gave to the crowds, and the people fed each other! If you don't see that, you've missed the whole point. Jesus wants us to see that in Him and through Him we can do the impossible, that this miracle is infinitely repeatable, that we can, in fact, feed a hungry world with bread for the body and Bread for the spirit. Sharing life is our job! We can do all things in Him. We have the unlimited resources of God. Look up into heaven and give thanks!

The Devil's Ballgame

TWELFTH SUNDAY AFTER PENTECOST
MATTHEW 14:22-23

Curtis R. Moermond

Although we have given the title "The Devil's Ballgame," a more complete title may be in place. In fact, we could entitle it "It's the Devil's Ballgame—Well, Not Really," and we could even subtitle it "Three Strikes, He's Out—Or at Least He Should Be!"

I. The Devil's at Bat

When we take a careful look at this text, it doesn't take long to come to the conclusion that the devil must have been putting in extra time in the 12 or so hours this text records. We look, for example, at the first verses of the text. At first they seem to be recording a simple act. Jesus "made the disciples get into the boat." We may ask why the concern? Why the hurry? It's not the picture of a friendly suggestion or a mutually agreed upon plan to get to the other side of the lake.

Then consider that Jesus "dismissed" the crowds. The basis of that word is "to send away." One is getting the picture of an eagerness. And that eagerness becomes more apparent when we find Jesus going to the mountain to pray.

Dare we ask why? It's not too difficult to understand when we read the verses preceding our text. Jesus had just prepared a banquet of bread and fish for 5,000 men, plus a large number of women and children. The disciples had picked up the leftovers, and it was 12 basketsful. (Some might suggest it was a basket for each of the disciples.) Then, like a pebble dropped into a pond with ripples leading out in ever-expanding circles, there was a thought someone dared to think aloud, a hope that became a whisper, and a spur-of-the-moment plan that would probably have reflected the lack of thought that conceived it: they wanted to make Jesus their king!

St. John records the event and tells us that Jesus knew what was going on. He said it this way: "Jesus, knowing that they intended to come and make him king by force, withdrew again into the hills by himself" (John 6:15).

Can we read these words without feeling we've heard all this some place before? Isn't it an echo of what St. Matthew had earlier recorded? "Again, the devil took him to a very high mountain and showed him all the kingdoms of the world and their splendor. 'All this I will give you," he said, "if you will bow down and worship me.'" (Matt. 4:8-9).

Is it any wonder that Jesus was eager to get the disciples into a boat? With their muddled concepts of the Kingdom, they might have been ready to join a cheering section urging Him to accept the offer. As for the crowds, they would not have simply walked away. Far too often they were so tenacious as to leave little opportunity for Jesus to rest. Now it looked as if they had every reason not to let Him go. If He could provide bread and fish, what else did He have to offer? And all the time, there was the devil, maybe even a host of them, urging the disciples to question Jesus' direction, encouraging the crowd to press its advantage, and before Jesus' eyes were "all the kingdoms of the world and their splendor."

Jesus knew how to deal with such temptation. Only the foolish would remain in such a place where not only strangers might tempt you, but even your own friends. Certainly it's the wisdom the Psalmist chose to share as the first thought of what we know as Psalm 1. "Blessed is the man who does not walk in the counsel of the wicked or stand in the way of sinners or sit in the seat of the mockers." A blessed man, a wise man, avoids temptation. Jesus shows us what also should accompany such avoidance: a long and earnest talk with God.

And as for the devil—well, it was strike one!

II. Ready for Another Pitch

But the devil wasn't about to give up. Scene two of the text takes us out in the boat with the disciples. From the other evangelists we find out the boat was about three or four miles out from the land when it was caught by a storm. Whether or not we want to credit (or blame) the devil for the storm (remember it was a storm that took Job's ten children, and we know the devil was behind that one), there is little doubt that he was also in the boat with the disciples.

It's not hard for us to see him feeding the doubts that caused the fear in the minds of the disciples. There were doubts that God would or that God could take care of them, even out there in that boat. It may also have been fear that gave rise to anger, and the anger was intensified when they remembered being sent away by Jesus. On top of all that, when one is tired, everything takes on different proportions. Maybe more than one of the disciples whose backgrounds included the rough and tumble company of fellow sailors was ready to curse the storm that deprived him of the sleep he longed for after serving a dinner for 5,000 plus. No doubt more than one hasty word and angry thought might cause of pang of guilt for a sensitive conscience the next day.

Then there was one more element. Sometime between three and six a.m. the eyes of the disciples caught something they simply could not understand or interpret. They were "terrified." Some have suggested the reason for their fear was they were convinced they had lost the battle with the storm. They were ready to identify this apparition as the Angel of Death, seen only by the one who receives the summons from this life. That might well have been their thought. Can we imagine the Devil sitting back and not saying or doing anything in such a situation? Let the television comedian jest about being "too young to die," but thoughts of leaving this world, at no matter what age, are the devil's playground. The seeds of fear he plants grow quickly into a jungle of darkness which would close out the sun (or should it be spelled "Son"?) for those who are not ready to walk the valley of the shadow of death with their Lord.

But there's not going to be a hit for Satan on this pitch either. Strike two is called with the words: "Take courage! It is I. Don't be afraid."

III. One More Try

As for the third strike, it comes close when Peter asks, "Lord, if it's you, tell me to come to you on the water." It's not for us to question the motivation for Peter's request. Suffice it to say that the Lord honored his request and told him to come to Him. What we do know is that when Peter got out, undoubtedly far enough from the boat so that he couldn't make a dive to get back into it, suddenly he began to get scared. He was doing the impossible. Even the Egyptian hieroglyphics pictured the impossible as a man walking on water. As fear and doubt took the place of faith, Peter began to sink.

What a smile must have crossed the devil's face as he saw the expression of confidence change to horror. That cry, "Lord, save me," must have been filled with panic, a panic bred by the doubt that Jesus would be able to do for Peter what that self-sufficient, burly fisherman couldn't do for himself. But what change must have come over that same devil's face when Jesus reached out His hand and caught Peter. He was forced to watch as the two made their way back to the boat.

Strike three! And it may even have been enough when the devil heard the words of the disciples, "Truly you are the Son of God," to make him leave the plate.

IV. He's Out—Or at Least He Should Be!

But are the devil's strikes always so easily counted? Perhaps the problem we have is they are so cleverly disguised that we don't even recognize them. It seems he makes enough home runs that it's his ballgame. How many times hasn't he scored on us when friends tempt us to do what we know we shouldn't. Yet, because of what others will say about us or because everybody else is doing it, we go along with the crowd. Our language is tinged with the crude, perhaps even the blasphemous. We share our shady stories because we don't want to appear to be different. Our tax returns are influenced by the fact that everybody forgets to add one or two little things that Uncle Sam won't know about anyway. Let the boss be gone for the day, and who's to know that the lunch hour extended to two hours and that the beverage was alcoholic in nature. The devil chalks up another home run!

Talk about tempting pitches! How often aren't we thrown by fear? We are frustrated when we have figured out just how we are going to do something and then it doesn't work out just right. We plan on health; we plan on work and income; we plan on the faithfulness of friends, family, and spouse. Then our plans are dashed by some word or event. The devil makes another home run as we lose sleep, turn to drugs or alcohol, and doubt that God can do anything about our situation.

And imagine the "sinking" feeling that must come to someone who has decided that he has the way of salvation all figured out, when, in fact, all the time he has been trusting his own strength and his own good works. Then something happens and he realizes his own strength isn't sufficient and his own good works aren't good enough. He has to admit that he doesn't have salvation after all. If the devil can plug his ears from hearing the words of the Gospel that assure us our Savior has done all that is necessary for salvation, then no hand is there to lift him up. Certainly then the devil breaks forth in loud and boisterous laughter.

But is it really the Devil's ballgame? We know better, don't we! In fact, the score is already posted. The Victor has been declared. The loser should have retired long ago and for good!

The victory was declared on Easter morning, about the time most people were just beginning to get out of their beds. Then a figure appeared on the very field of the devil and held high the trophy that proved the ballgame was over. The last strike had been called. The devil was out!

The sad part is that far too many people still want to play his game. He's always ready for one more inning, and somehow or other he still gets people on his side—forever.

How about you? The Winner invites you to join his victory banquet. How about practicing the theme song? A good chorus could begin, "Truly you are the Son of God." And as a winner, you can devote and dedicate every day as a celebration with the Victor.

When Faith Is Frustrated

THIRTEENTH SUNDAY AFTER PENTECOST
MATTHEW 15:21-28

Curtis R. Moermond

At that human level at which we all live, one of the comforting truths we find in the gospel is the willingness with which Jesus performed miracles. We see His power in all those frustrations that enter the lives of people. A withered hand, eyes which have never seen light, ears which have never communicated a sound, even a host of demons sufficient to fill a herd of swine and cause them to run over a cliff and drown in the sea—none is enough to stay His healing and restoring hand.

He didn't even have to be physically present. The centurion's servant was healed even though the centurion didn't want Jesus to come under his roof. Of that man Jesus was to say, "I have not found anyone in Israel with such great faith" (Matt. 8:10). Jesus never went out of His way to show off His ability to perform miracles, but He was usually quite ready to answer the sincere requests which were made of Him.

Then comes the Gospel for today. A mother comes on behalf of her daughter, and, much to our surprise, Jesus doesn't have a word to say to her. In addition to His silence, the disciples even try to send her away. If we could have spoken with her, might she not have added faith to the list of frustrations of life. Certainly, in her life at this point she knew the frustration that sometimes comes with faith.

I. When Faith Gets No Response

"Jesus, you've done it before!" Such is the cry that faith often utters. And Scripture is filled with examples which suggest that this can be the ground of the plea made in faith. The angel's word to Mary when she didn't understand how His promise could soon happen to her was "Nothing is impossible with God" (Luke 1:37). Jesus said the same thing when talking with His disciples about salvation: "What is impossible with men is possible with God" (Luke 18:27). And to the man whose son had a dumb spirit, Jesus said, "Everything is possible for him who believes" (Mark 9:23).

When one stops to think about it, isn't that message of vital importance to our faith life? What would be the basis for prayer, if God were limited in His ability to do what we ask? If one is going to make a request in faith, then that faith had best be in One who has the ability to answer that request. If one is going to have faith in God, then one expects that God to be an almighty God.

A woman crying out after Jesus as He walked in the region of Tyre and Sidon, looked at just such a God. He was almighty. And yet, this God seemed to turn a deaf ear. Could there be a greater frustration than having the One who is able to do something not willing even to listen? It's like knowing that there is a great scientist who has discovered a cure for cancer, and then finding he is not willing to share that cure with those who are stricken with this horrible disease.

So, in frustration, what does one do? Well, some would become convinced that it is all a ruse! It's all fake! There is nothing to this thing called faith. It is no comfort. It is not a source of power. And all the joy that is claimed for it simply does not exist! Therefore, they simply forget it. What is the good of having a God who won't do things? If He really was a God who could do things, He would do the things we ask. It's the challenge that Archibald MacLeish puts into his play *J.B.* If God is really going to be God, then He must also be good. If He isn't good, then He must not be God after all. Many feel that a good God would take care of all their problems. If their problems aren't being taken care of, then God must not be able to take care of them. In frustration they may even go seeking another god.

But the frustration of faith is that the evidence is overwhelming! God is God! God is an almight God! That's the God the Canaanite woman appeals to. The very title she uses to address Him makes it clear: "Lord, Son of David." True, "Lord" can be an address of honor, much like the word "sire" is still used in some places of our English-speaking world today, but link it with the rest of the title, "Son of David," and this woman knew to whom she was speaking. Even though she wasn't a Jew, not of the children of Abraham, she had a knowledge of the Savior who was to come into the world. Few were the Jews who were willing to grant such a high designation for

Jesus. In fact, it isn't until Palm Sunday that we hear such a title used commonly, and look where it was all going to lead in the space of a few days.

But here was a faith in the true God, the almighty God, the God who could take care of her problem—if He would. But, oh, the frustration of faith, He didn't seem to listen!

II. When Faith Won't Give Up

Well, if we don't want to give up on an almighty God, and if faith still says He is what He says He is and what the evidence shows Him to be, then where do we turn to find a reason for the silence?

Some would turn away, convinced there was something wrong with their faith, their life, or their plea. They find the cause of the failure in themselves! "I know God can do it, but I'm not good enough. I haven't lived right. Too many times I've skipped opportunities to hear the Gospel or to serve God. Now this is my punishment."

You may have heard such lines. I have. I've heard them in hospitals where suddenly people have been brought flat on their backs (and it just could be that is the only way God can ever get them to look up!). I've heard it when people come into my office to tell me about their wayward children. I've heard it about financial reverses, marital problems, and from mourners. The bottom line always is "I deserve to get a cold shoulder; that's why God doesn't listen." And then quietly add, "That's why I don't pray any more."

When that happens, we've lost sight of the example of this woman. Not only did she know who Jesus was; she also knew who she was. She didn't deserve to come to Jesus. Even He told her as much. His mission was not to heal the diseases of all the world. God had, from before the beginning of time, chosen the children of Abraham to be the people to whom the Savior would come. Certainly, His death would effect the forgiveness of the sins of the whole world. The Gospel message was not only for the Jew, but also for the Gentile; none was excluded.

But the mission, the plan which would work it all out, had its stage in no other place than among the Jews. And because of that plan of God, the Jews were given the first opportunity to know who Jesus was. The fact that they refused to believe and accept Him is quite beside the point. In fact, if they had accepted Him, He probably would not have been in this border region. He was there because so many people had already determined to harm Him. This was a safer place to be, safer not only than Jerusalem, but also Galilee. Still, God's plan was going to be worked out; it hadn't changed because of the Jewish rejection.

The woman was not one of the chosen people. She had no claim, either by birth or by blood. She was a Canaanite, unclean, a descendant of one of those tribes God had originally told the Israelites to clean out of the land. And the name she was called, a dog, that which ran wild and fed off the carrion and scraps, would have dashed any illusions she may have had about a position.

Yet she is not silenced. She is willing to argue with God. She was convinced that he could do what she asked Him to do. She knew she had no right to ask, nor reason to deserve such goodness from God. How then dare she continue her plea?

III. When Faith Conquers Frustration

How then does one dare to approach God? Actually, the answer is quite simple. When we cannot argue on the grounds of what we deserve, we make our plea on the grounds of God's mercy. That was exactly what she did. "Have mercy on me" were her words.

When one comes into the presence of God, one never comes from a position of strength or advantage to make any demands. If we would start with such an attitude, we would soon discover that God has the last word. If we demand justice of God, we must be willing to submit ourselves to His completely impartial and righteous justice. Who could stand or would dare to risk that? But if we are willing to beg for His mercy, then we find God to be a merciful God.

Such is the plea of this woman: Mercy—totally undeserved. Mercy—asking not for riches, but only for crumbs. Mercy—knowing that even crumbs from the Almighty's hand are treasures for those who receive them. And because we know the value of God's mercy, just as she knew it, then we also keep repeating our pleas, even as the Lord waits the right time to answer our request. Hearing the words of Jesus, her faith in an almighty God was confirmed. He indeed does what is best for His children. She was assured that her case was heard. The anxious moments of waiting were past. Her request was granted.

But dare we take her example and make it our own? Here we can answer with a bold affirmative! It's Luther's explanation of the word *Amen.* "*Ja!*"—"It shall be so!" It's St. Paul's assurance to the Romans, "He who did not spare his own Son, but gave him up for us all—how will he not also, along with him, graciously give us all things?" (Rom. 8:32).

If you want to know whether or not God is a merciful God, then look at the measure of grace He offers you on Calvary. There is the measuring stick; let the drops of blood shed there wash away any doubt you may have. A God who is willing to go to such lengths to take care of your spiritual needs is not going to be miserly about your physical needs. Oh, He may at first seem silent, but boldly repeat your request to Him. Bring your needs and your wants to

Him, fervently, frequently, in prayer. And doubt not. If it is for your good, then at the right time He will grant it to you. You know to whom you pray; you know on what grounds you pray; so fail not to pray.

St. James knew he was writing a timeless truth when he said, "You do not have, because you do not ask God" (James 4:2). Far too often we are ready to say, "I have not because I asked once. God was silent; I'll not bother Him again." I wonder how many children would get candy or toys if that was their approach. The truth is that only too often we are too lazy to repeat our requests to God so lose out on the treasures of His mercy. Take the example of one who knew of whom she asked—asked and asked again—and then, at the right time, she received. You, too, have a God who wants to show you His mercy.

I Will Build My Church

FOURTEENTH SUNDAY AFTER PENTECOST
MATTHEW 16:13-20

Erwin J. Kolb

A famous Church Growth leader, pastor of a large church himself, is known for repeating the statement: "The church that wants to grow can grow." There are two qualifications, however, which this leader adds: "If there are unchurched people in the area and if the church is willing to pay the price."

When we observe churches that grow or do not grow, we see this statement is true, at least from a human point of view. In growing churches researchers have been able to consistently observe certain principles at work, some of which are basic sociological or psychological principles about how human beings respond and function. But it is common to observe, we are told, these two ingredients in a growing church—they want to grow, and they are willing to pay the price.

But it is important to remember that these principles do not make the church grow. Only God can change hearts. Only God can create faith which brings people into the church. Scripture reminds us that "no one can say, 'Jesus is Lord,' except by the Holy Spirit" (1 Cor. 12:3), and the Spirit, Jesus said, "blows wherever it pleases" (John 3:8), and we cannot program it.

In the Gospel for today, the Fourteenth Sunday After Pentecost, Jesus told His disciples, and He tells us today loud and clear, "I will build my church." That is the theme for our sermon today. We will consider each word in the three parts of our sermon—*I, My church,* and *will build.*

I. "I"—The Builder Is the Messiah

"I will build my church." Who is the "I"? The text indicates that He was three things: a man, a great prophet, and the Messiah.

He Was a Man

Jesus took His disciples on a retreat in the northernmost part of Canaan, the region of Caesarea Philippi. He had spent almost three years teaching His 12 chosen disciples, and He knew that His end was near. So He withdrew for a time of prayer and teaching to prepare for the ordeal of His suffering and death. Luke's account says, "Once when Jesus was praying in private and his disciples were with him, he asked them, 'Who do the crowds say I am?'" (Luke 9:18). Matthew words it, "Who do people say the Son of Man is?"

He was a man, a homeless carpenter, who had become a teacher and a rabbi. At this very moment the Jewish leaders were plotting to destroy Him as a dangerous heretic. He stood in this remote region littered with temples of heathen gods and asked His disciples, "Who do people say the Son of Man is?"

Caesarea Philippi was known for its temples of Syrian Baal worship. It was considered the place of origin for the great god of nature, Pan. It boasted a white marble temple built by Herod the Great in honor of the divinity of the Roman Caesar. The region was originally called Paneas, but Philip, the son of Herod the Great, changed it to honor the Roman Caesar and added his own name to call it Caesarea Philippi. It was no doubt for a reason that Jesus chose this place to ask, "Who am I?"

He Was a Great Prophet

The disciples listed four answers which they had heard among the people. First, some believed He was John the Baptist. Herod Antipas had beheaded John but then was haunted by the idea that Jesus of Nazareth was John returned from the dead. Second, some said Elijah, the greatest of the Old Testament prophets. Malachi had said of Elijah, "See, I will send you the prophet Elijah before that great and dreadful day of the Lord comes" (Mal. 4:5). That was why, when Jews observed the annual Passover meal, they left a vacant chair—and still do today—for Elijah. When he comes, the Messiah will not be far behind.

Third, some believed He was Jeremiah. At the time of the exile he was said to have hidden the ark and the altar of incense in the remote region of Mt. Nebo. It was believed he would return before the Messiah comes to bring them back. Fourth, there were some who said He was one of the prophets returned to prepare the way for the Messiah.

So there was a consensus that Jesus was more than an ordinary man. He was a great man, a prophet perhaps, but still a man. Today there are still many, even in the Jewish community, who call Jesus a great teacher, an important leader in history—but just a man. Jesus was not satisfied with the answer, for He was more than a man, more than a prophet. Napoleon once said, "I know men, and Jesus Christ is more than a man."

He Was the Messiah

"Who do you say I am?" Jesus asked. Peter, whom Chrysostom called "the mouth of the apostles, the leader of the apostolic choir," answered for them all, "You are the Christ, the Son of the living God." That was the answer Jesus wanted. He was the Son of God living in human form so that He could be the promised Messiah. The word *Christ* is Greek for the Hebrew word *Messiah*. It means "the anointed one," the one anointed by the Holy Spirit to be God's instrument to save His people. That is why He was "born of a woman, born under the law, to redeem those under law," that thus we too might become children of God (Gal. 4:4-5). So He took the sins of all mankind on Himself, died to pay their punishment, and rose again to demonstrate that sin, death, and hell had been conquered.

Who do you say that I am? is the question Jesus still asks each of us personally. It is not enough to answer, "Some say . . . ." "People say . . ." or "Others say . . . ." When Martin Luther went to Rome as a humble monk, he sought out the stairway which had been brought from Jerusalem as the very one on which Christ walked going to Pilate. Luther on his knees said a prayer on every step, hoping for deliverance from purgatory because of those prayers. That is what "others" said. But when he reached the top, can't you envision Luther standing up and saying, "Who knows whether it is so?" There was no personal conviction. It took years of study of the Scripture before he found that conviction when he discovered the meaning of the words of Romans 1:17, "The righteous will live by faith." The Messiah has finished the work of redemption. He has paid the price. We receive forgiveness and new life by faith in Him—faith alone!

Peter didn't understand all that until later, but he was convinced of the basis for it and gave his answer. "Who do you say I am?" Can you say with the fervor of Peter, "You are the Christ, the Son of the living God"?

II. "My Church"—The Church Is a Building

Jesus answered, "Blessed are you, Simon son of Jonah, for this was not revealed to you by man, but by my Father in heaven. And I tell you that you are Peter, and on this rock I will build my church."

The Church Is People

This is the first time that the word church occurs in the Bible. (It is used only once more in the gospels—Matt. 18:17). The word in Greek is *ecclesia,* literally meaning "called out." It referred to people who were called out to a public gathering like a town assembly. It is the equivalent of the Hebrew word *qahal,* which meant the congregation of Israel or the gathering of the people of the Lord. The word *ecclesia,* church, is used in the rest of the New Testament for the people who come to faith in Jesus Christ and follow His teaching. Everyone who confessed Jesus as Lord was part of a fellowship of believers which was the church. This is the church that Jesus said, "I will build."

The Church Is a Building That Belongs to Jesus

Jesus referred to the church as a building which He would build, and nothing could destroy it. He Himself would be the foundation, as St. Paul later called Him (1 Cor. 3:11), or the chief cornerstone (1 Pet. 2:6), with the apostles and the prophets (Eph. 2:20) as the rest of the foundation and each Christian a living stone in that building (1 Pet. 2:4-8). That is what Jesus meant in his answer to Peter, "You are Peter, and on this rock I will build my church."

Jesus used a play on words. Peter in Greek is a masculine word, *petros.* Rock is a feminine word, *petra.* Jesus did not mean that he would build his church on the person of Peter, although much of the Christian church believes that. Those words are emblazoned in large gold letters around the dome of St. Peter's Basilica in Rome which houses the famous bronze statue of him as the first pope. We believe this passage means that Jesus will build His church on the rock (*petra*) which is the truth that He is "the Christ, the Son of the living God" the confession which Peter had just made.

Jesus said this is "my" church. It will be built on Him, on the forgiveness of sins which He has earned, on the peace with God that He achieved. It will be His church because He will build it.

III. "I Will Build"—Jesus Builds the Church

The Spirit Is the Instrument

Some years ago as part of a nationwide campaign to raise funds to build churches, a construction company unloaded its equipment on a vacant lot one morning in Santa Rose, California, and by nightfall moved it away. They had completed a new church building in a single day.

The church of Jesus Christ is not always built that fast. It did begin with 3,000 baptized on one day, the day of Pentecost when Peter preached his first sermon, and it grew by great leaps and bounds in those early years. It is still growing today in our world, although where we live and work we may not always see it grow. In fact we may wonder why it doesn't grow when we witness to someone for weeks and months, and maybe years, and see no results. The results, the conversions, the growth we leave to Jesus. "I will build my church." His agent to accomplish that growth is the Holy Spirit whom He sent to "glorify" Himself after He returned to heaven. Just as Jesus told Peter, "This was not revealed to you by man, but by my Father in heaven," so no person comes into the church except by the work of God Himself or, as Jesus put it another time, "unless the Father who sent me draws him" (John 6:44). In His time and place, and in His way, He does "build" the church.

The Church Is Built to Last

And as Jesus builds His church, He gives us the assurance that nothing can destroy it. He told His disciples, "the gates of Hades will not overcome it." That is NIV language. The King James has the familiar translation, "The gates of hell shall not prevail against it." The Greek word used here is *hades* which meant the place of the dead, rather than the word *gehenna,* which meant torment and is also translated hell. The "gate" was the place in eastern cities where justice was administered. Jesus was saying that all the powers of evil and death itself cannot prevail against my church. I build it. I keep and preserve it. It will last forever, for those who are in the church on earth—"church militant" we call it—will also be the church in heaven, the "church triumphant."

The Church Is Built by People

"I will build my church." How will He build it? Through people who use the building equipment which He gives them. The image used in the text by Jesus is the "keys of the kingdom of heaven." Keys were a common figure among the Jews. The rabbis had a saying: "The keys of birth, of the rain, and of the resurrection of the dead belong to God." They were saying, "Only God has power to create life, to send rain, and to raise the dead."

Jesus said, "I will give you the keys of the kingdom"—to you Peter, to all you apostles, and to all you Christians. The key which has the power to open and close the doors of the kingdom of heaven is the forgiveness of sins. That is how the church is built. People receive the forgiveness, and they become members of the church.

They live in forgiveness, nourished in faith by the Word and Sacrament, and they remain in the church and grow in faith and love.

Pastor Hamil from Phoenix, Arizona, tells of canvassing an area to start a new mission. On each call he began by introducing himself and then saying, "We plan to start a new Lutheran church in this area. Are you interested?" One old grouchy man responded to that question by asking "Lutherans? What are they against?" That so shook Pastor Hamil that he vowed always to be ready to tell what Lutherans were *for* rather than merely *against:*

Lutherans are for Jesus Christ, the Messiah, the Son of the living God.

Lutherans are for the church that Jesus Christ builds.

Lutherans are for the forgiveness of sins.

Lutherans are eager to offer that forgiveness of sins as the key to the kingdom of heaven and thus be Jesus' instruments to build His church.

Dare to Be a Disciple

FIFTEENTH SUNDAY AFTER PENTECOST
MATTHEW 16:21-26

Erwin J. Kolb

In the book *Future Shock* Alvin Toffler describes a taxicab driver who has become a fan of rodeo riding—in fact, such a fan that it becomes his reason for living. Toffler says it "not only engages the cab driver's passion; it consumes his time and money. It affects his family, his friends, his ideas. It provides a set of standards against which he measures himself. In short, it rewards him with something that many of us have difficulty finding—an identity."

In our text, which is the Gospel for today, the Fifteenth Sunday After Pentecost, our Lord suggests another way to find an identity, another reason for living, another way to set our standards and to measure ourselves. That is to identify with Him by being His disciples. As we study that text, we choose as our theme

Dare to Be a Disciple

The text follows the great confession of Peter—the Gospel for last Sunday—in which Peter, speaking for all the disciples, boldly asserted, "You are the Christ, the Son of the living God" (Matt. 16:16). Now Jesus seeks to prepare His disciples for what is going to happen to Him when he goes to Jerusalem. There He would "suffer many things at the hands of the elders, chief priests and teachers of the law, and . . . be killed and on the third day be raised to life." Peter immediately rebukes his Master, "Never, Lord! This shall never happen to you." He is ready to draw his sword, as he did later in the Garden of Gethsemane at Jesus' arrest. But Jesus turns to him with the stinging words, "Out of my sight, Satan! You are a stumbling block to me; you do not have in mind the things of God, but the things of men."

Jesus knew what He had to do. He "must go" to Jerusalem to suffer and die. His father would place on Him the sin of the world. He must pay that penalty in order to redeem and reconcile the world to God. That was the reason He left heaven to come to earth. No one could distract Him from that mission.

Any person who wanted to be a follower of Jesus, to be His disciple and learn to be like Him, would need to understand the cost of that discipleship. Yes, there was a new way of life, a life of faith and contentment, a life of peace and love, a life of service and joy in being a disciple. So Jesus challenged His followers, "If anyone would come after me, he must deny himself and take up his cross and follow me." We will examine the meaning of each of those three requirements under our theme, "Dare to Be a Disciple."

I. A Disciple Denies Himself

He Gives Up His Life As Jesus Did

The first requirement is to deny self. That means the disciple is willing to give up his life, as Jesus did. To give up one's life, however, is more than a decision of the human will. It is an act of faith, a faith which is created by the Spirit of God. "Flesh gives birth to flesh, but the Spirit gives birth to spirit" (John 3:6). It is at the cross and open tomb that faith is born. We see Jesus, the Son of God, dying for our sins, paying the penalty of death and hell, and rising victorious. He has reconciled us with God so that when we, too, die—because our old nature has been crucified with Christ or, as St. Paul says in Rom. 6, buried with Christ in Baptism—we will rise to a new life, a new creation of God. It is then that the Spirit motivates us to "come after" Him, to be His disciples and to deny ourselves.

St. Augustine was accosted on the street by a former mistress shortly after his conversion. He saw her and turned to walk in the opposite direction. Surprised, the woman cried out, "Augustine, it is I." But continuing on his way Augustine cried back, "Yes, but it is not I."

He Says No to Self and Yes to Jesus

A disciple gives up his life. He becomes a different person. He learns to say no to self and yes to Jesus. C. S. Lewis in *Beyond Personality* (New York: The Macmillan Co., 1945, p. 40) describes the Christian way as one in which Christ says, "Give me *all*. I don't want so much of your time and so much of your money and so much of your work: I want *you*. I have not come to torment your natural self, but to kill it. No half-measures are any good." Jesus asks for our whole natural self. He gives us a new self instead. In fact, He has given us Himself. His own will becomes ours.

Even when we want to give ourselves wholly to Jesus and make His will our will, we may misdirect our zeal. That's what happened to Peter. In his limited understanding of what it meant that Jesus was the Messiah, the Son of God, he could not understand how suffering and death would fit the picture. So he was ready to stop it from happening. "Out of my sight, Satan!" Jesus had to say. Satan means an adversary. Peter was being a hindrance to the will of God through the faulty understanding in his own mind. The words Jesus spoke are similar to what He told the real Satan in the temptations in the wilderness, "Away from me, Satan," (Matt. 4:10). But here Jesus was also telling Peter, "Don't try to be up front to lead me. Get behind; be a follower. Say no to yourself and yes to me." That is the lesson that we need to learn over and over—say no to self, to our desires, to our sinful nature and learn how as God's new creation to humbly say yes to God.

Alexander the Great as a young man conquered the world of his day as the head of the Greek Empire—and then he wept because there were no more worlds to conquer. He forgot one world that needed conquering, that of his own passions, and they conquered him. He died a victim of his own drunken passion. Dare to be a disciple—a disciple who denies himself, gives up his life, says no to self and yes to God.

II. A Disciple Takes Up His Cross

He Takes the Cross Voluntarily

The second thing Jesus required of a disciple is that he must "take up his cross." He gives us the example. He said he "must go to Jerusalem." He went, as the Scriptures say, like a lamb to slaughter. He Himself said, "I lay down my life . . . . No one takes it from me" (John 10:17-18). So Jesus says the disciple must take his cross voluntarily.

What does He mean by the cross? For Jesus it was more than the piece of wood that He tried to drag out of Jerusalem to Calvary where they nailed Him to it. It meant all of His agony as He suffered the penalty for sin, even complete separation from His Father, the agony of hell. For us the cross is not ordinary trouble or poverty, sickness or hardship that comes to every other human being. The cross is what we carry as a result of following Christ. It is the resentment, the ridicule, the rejection that we receive when we confess Christ before the world. And Luke, in his account of this story, adds that we must take up that cross "daily".

His Life Becomes a Witness

As we take up our cross daily and carry it patiently without complaint, our lives become a witness for Jesus, our Master. In the Middle Ages it was common for Irish monks, in order to further their own spiritual and eternal well-being, to go into seclusion in a remote area and live a life of austerity under a strict routine of worship, work, and study. As they lived this life of piety, self-denial, and love toward others, it was such a contrast to the idolatry, savagery, and immorality about them that people were attracted and impressed. They often asked for instruction, and thus the Christian faith spread. In fact, the evangelization of Ireland, Scotland, and northern England, as well as parts of Greece, Switzerland, and Italy was accomplished in this way by Irish missionaries.

A disciple denies himself, takes up his cross, and thus becomes a witness for his Master. Charles Colson recently wrote about the bewildering paradox that one-third of all American adults claim to be born-again (according to a Gallup poll) and yet fail to impact our society. It becomes sicker and more corrupt by the day. There is much talk about religion but morality is down. Christians have become like the world instead of standing against it. Our calling is to witness to the world about God's new life in Christ, not to live as though the world has a better way.

III. A Disciple Follows His Master

He Follows the Example of His Master

The third requirement of a disciple of Jesus Christ is that he follow the Master. "He must deny himself and take up his cross and follow me." It is by losing our life in this way that we really find it, He went on to say.

Did you ever play the game as a child called "Follow the Leader"? Remember how you had to copy the action of the leader precisely? You watched carefully and tried with every bit of ability and energy you could muster to imitate him. That is how the disciple follows his Master. He studies His life in the gospels, the good He did, His kindness, His concern for others, His forgiveness, His love.

Jesus summed it up in that one word. He said, "A new commandment I give you: Love one another. As I have loved you, so you must love one another." And He added that when we love this way—as He did, with a sacrificial kind of love that was willing to give His own life for others—then "all men will know that you are my disciples" (John 13:34-35).

He Becomes Like His Master

But the disciple does more than just try to follow the example of his model. That's what disciples have always done. When Paul was a disciple of the great rabbi Gamaliel, he tried to learn all that Gamaliel could teach him. He tried to imitate his example and be like him—yes, if possible even surpass him and be a greater teacher than he was. So it was among the Greeks and the Hebrews in Jesus' day.

But when Jesus began to gather disciples around Himself, He changed the concept somewhat. First He added the dimension of being chosen, for He said, "You did not choose me, but I chose you" (John 15:16). Then he added the personal relationship, an intimate oneness with the Master, an indwelling of God in man. So the Christian does more than try to follow the model of a good life that Jesus set. He wants to be like Him, yes, but he also wants Jesus to live in him. Paul said, "I have been crucified with Christ and I no longer live, but Christ lives in me" (Gal. 2:20). That's why Luther loved to call Christians "little Christs."

So to be a disciple of Jesus Christ means that my sinful self has died and Christ lives in me. This is not an action that is accomplished once so that I'm fixed for life. I still have my sinful nature, and I must continue to subdue it or, as Luther said in his explanation of the meaning of Baptism, "the old Adam in us should, by daily contrition and repentance, be drowned and die with all sins . . . and . . . a new man daily come forth and arise, who shall live before God in righteousness and purity forever." This is a growing, developing process as I deal with my sinful habits and desires and learn how to control and overcome them. I grow more and more like Jesus Christ. Paul expressed it to the Galatians, "Christ is formed in you" (Gal. 4:19).

Thus life for me is not like that of the taxi driver. Only Jesus Christ can be the consuming passion of my life, set my standards, and give meaning. I achieve my identity by being His disciple. There is no room for compromise. Jesus once told the crowds, "If anyone comes to me and does not hate his father and mother, his wife and children, his brothers and sisters—yes, even his own life—he cannot be my disciple. . . . any of you who does not give up everything he has cannot be my disciple (Luke 14:26,33).

Dare to be a disciple!

A missionary came to a remote village and began to tell the story of Jesus. After he talked for awhile, someone said, "Oh, yes, we knew Him; He used to live here." Surprised, the missionary tried to explain that He lived centuries ago in another land. The natives insisted that they had seen Him. "He lived in this village. We knew Him." Then one of the natives led the missionary to the village cemetery and showed him the grave of a medical missionary who had lived there years before, served the village, and then died there.

Years from now, when you are dead and gone, if someone were hearing the story of Jesus for the first time, could that person make the same mistake about you? "Oh, yes, we knew Him. He used to live here."

They surely could if you are a disciple of Jesus Christ—a disciple who denies himself, takes up his cross, and follows Jesus.

Dare to be a disciple!

Basic Christian Trademark I: Always Seeking to Save Lost Sinners

SIXTEENTH SUNDAY AFTER PENTECOST
MATTHEW 18:15-20

W. Theophil Janzow

Many of our 30-minute evening television programs are complete stories in themselves. But occasionally the producers of the program take us by surprise. They take us to the end of the 30 minutes and then announce "To be continued." So if we want to hear the rest of the story, we have to tune in again a week later.

This sermon and the one next Sunday are like that, except that I'm telling you in advance. Next Sunday's Gospel you will find, is actually a continuation of today's. They could be treated in one sermon, but then the sermon would be too long.

Instead we will have two sermons on one theme: "Basic Christian Trademarks." In today's sermon, based on Matt. 18:15-20, we will consider the fact that one of the basic trademarks of Christian behavior is the effort Christians make to keep people from losing their souls because of unrepented sin. Next Sunday, as we study Matt. 18:21-35, we will see how the practice of Christian forgiveness is another essential trademark of the Christian way of life.

May the Spirit of God direct our minds and strengthen our wills as, today, we ponder the first part of this important subject:

Basic Christian Trademark I: Always Seeking to Save Lost Sinners

I. Sinners Everywhere

Jesus was talking to His disciples about sinners in the church. But basic to this discussion was their understanding of His attitude toward sinners on all levels of the world community and in all stations of human social life. He expected His disciples to understand how He felt about sinners everywhere.

In Jesus' teaching one thing was clear. He viewed the world as a community of lost souls—lost in sin, lost because of their rebellious attitude toward their Creator God.

Jesus' mission in the world, He told His disciples, was to save this lost community, to rescue it from the consequences of its rebellion, to bring it back into the family of God. "For the Son of Man came to seek and to save what was lost," he said (Luke 19:10).

The first thing, then, that the disciples had to learn was that the church of Jesus Christ had an open-door policy. There was no sign on the door saying "Restricted." Nothing in the bylaws said some people are to be invited to join, others not. His invitation "Come to me" was sent to everyone who was loaded down with the burden of sin. And that meant His church was open to all—"For all have sinned" (Rom. 3:23).

Pride runs deep in the human heart. Someone put it like this: "Pride was the first thing that overcame man, and it's the last thing he overcomes."

Pride makes us feel that we and the other people who are like us are better than people who are different from us. And try as we might to avoid it, this kind of pride also tries to poke it's ugly head into the church. We let ourselves fall into the trap of talking, or dressing, or singing, or behaving in a way that causes other people to think, "They don't really try to make me feel that I belong with them, so I suppose they don't really want me in their church."

Jesus kept discovering these feelings all over the place. Church people frowned when He brought a despised tax collector into their group. And they practically had a fit when he pronounced forgiveness on a woman who had been following the wicked ways of harlotry.

But this is precisely what Jesus wanted to put across. The Kingdom that He came to establish was wide open with no membership restrictions. The only restriction, if you want to call it that was that you have to be a sinner. "I have not come to call the righteous, but sinners" (Matt. 9:13). And, of course, that ends up being no restriction at all. As we've pointed out, everyone meets that criterion. Everyone is a sinner.

This is not an easy lesson to learn, because the sinful heart of man seems to be naturally prejudiced, naturally exclusivist, naturally segregationist. Everybody seems to have something inside that finds pleasure in belonging to a group that other people cannot join.

We hear a lot of negative reference to apartheid in South Africa, a society that legally condones first-class and second-class citizenship. We tend to speak in a tone of self-righteousness when we condemn that system, leaving the impression that it's a kind of discrimination that we wouldn't be caught dead tolerating in groups to which we belong.

Perhaps that's true of some of us. On the other hand, it may also be true that most of us have never examined our inner feelings with total honesty. It may be that our external conversation and our deep inner feelings contradict each other without our realizing this is so.

A few decades ago a prominent and respected United States Senator was asked if he was prejudiced. He answered, "Certainly not. I am not prejudiced at all. It's just that I know that the black race is inferior to the white." He apparently was completely unaware of the contradiction in the two parts of his answer.

Believe me, the open-door policy is basic to what the church of Jesus Christ is meant to be today. We don't understand the church unless we understand that its basic and primary task is to go out into the world and seek to save the sinners who we find everywhere we go. We don't understand what it means for each one of us as individuals to be a Christian, to be a Christ-follower, unless we have within us this desire, this yearning, this drive to be about the Father's business in our contacts with other people. We are called to be always seeking to save the sinner who has not yet found his way through the open door into the Savior's church.

II. Sinners in the Church

Having established that Christians would like nothing better than to have all sinners everywhere in the world join them as members of the Christian church, we move now to that group of people who are already in the church, but who are starting to become backsliders and thus are in danger of losing the salvation to which they are called.

What is the proper Christian behavior toward a fellow Christian who is falling back into the ways of unrepented sin, in danger of returning to the ranks of the lost, in effect throwing himself back into the death-dealing waters from which he had been so graciously rescued?

Some people might suggest that the logical response is to let him go. If he doesn't appreciate his deliverance more than that, let him go.

That can sound so reasonable. Maybe you or I have even had such thoughts ourselves; maybe we've even spoken them to a close fellow Christian.

But, says Jesus, that's not the spirit of Christianity. And then He proceeds to make it very plain. Just as we go all-out to win the unbeliever for the Kingdom, so we must also go all-out to save the sinner who has come into the Kingdom but is in danger of falling away.

Let it, of course, be understood that the saving is not something that we do. Saving is God's work. Salvation is what Christ accomplished. Bringing people to faith in Christ is the work of the Holy Spirit.

But let it also be understood that Christians are God's instruments. God uses us to speak His Word of law and grace. God's call to repentance is spoken by God's people, not only to the unbelieving world, but also to each other as we need it.

Here are the steps that we should follow according to Jesus:

1) Go and speak to the sinning brother. He might say, "I'm sorry; please forgive me." Wouldn't that be wonderful? Then, like Nathan to David, you can joyously respond, "The Lord has taken away your sin. You are not going to die" (spiritually, that is).

2) What if he doesn't say he's sorry? Then we must truly be concerned because his status in the Kingdom is in serious jeopardy. So we try it again. But this time we take one or two fellow Christians with us. Hopefully the voice of a group will prevail, where one alone failed. How wonderful that would be! What rejoicing if this small group can hear the repenting word and embrace the sinner who had been saved from the clutches of the Evil One!

3) If success still eludes you, we ask the church as a whole to help. Notice the emphasis is on helping, saving, restoring. Can the sinner resist the pleading of the entire church? Hopefully such loving concern from the entire congregation can loosen the grip of sin that holds the brother in its vise and cause him, as he listens to the congregation, to hear the voice of Jesus calling, "Sinner, come home, come home." What a thrilling sight such a turnaround would be! What a thrilling sound to hear! "I'm sorry; I repent." It would be worth every ounce of loving patience and earnest pleading that finally led to such a happy outcome.

4) It's only when all such efforts to save the sinning brother have failed that the church must reluctantly admit: He has let himself get lost again. But notice that even in this extremity, the Lord doesn't say, "You can stop trying to save him now." Oh, no, basic to the whole attitude of Christians—this Christian trademark

that we're talking about—is that the effort to save never stops. We may have to say, "You have put yourself out of the Kingdom again." But we must follow that by saying, "We hope and pray that it is only for a time. In the meantime, you are still our burden. And we will keep on trying to be God's instruments to bring you back again."

III. The Sinner in Myself

There is a third category for whom this Christian trademark of always seeking to save the sinner is important. That is the sinner in myself.

You see, the sinner in myself is a constant subversive force working from within, trying to destroy my faith and thus disrupt my saving relationship with Christ. The traditional terms for this "sinner in myself" or "sinner in each of us as individuals" are the phrases "old Adam" or "sinful nature."

All of us who by God's grace and the Spirit's converting activity in our lives have come into the saving kingdom of our Savior Jesus Christ have received a new Christian nature. "If anyone is in Christ, he is a new creation" (2 Cor. 5:17). This new man in us is the being that puts the stamp of Christianity on our heart, that imprints us with these basic Christian trademarks that we are discussing in these two sermons.

We Christians, in honesty, must admit that, even while we are bringing the Word of forgiveness to our fellow men, whether outside the church or in, we are also daily sinning much and deserving God's displeasure ourselves. Nevertheless, we are also hearing God's word of forgiveness in Christ. And that same Gospel word which we proclaim to others is also addressed to us. It's a marvelously comforting and cheering fact. The same Word of reconciliation that saves the outsider and brings him into the family of God—and that saves the backsliding Christian and keeps him in the Kingdom— also saves you and also saves me.

No wonder Christians can do about their daily business with buoyant spirit, confident heart, and happy voice. Are they sinners? Yes, indeed. Are they forgiven? Thank God, yes, by the miracle of saving grace. Is their way of life affected? How can it be otherwise? Indeed, their yearning to bring this same salvation to other people becomes their Christian trademark. It gets stamped all over their daily life and conversation. People soon notice that here as a community of followers of Jesus Christ who are continually about the business of saving souls.

What an important lesson! May God help us to carry this trademark with honor and fidelity. May He bring us together again next Sunday to discuss "Basic Christian Trademark II" as our Lord explains it in the next verses of Matt. 18. And may He be with each one of us till we meet again.

Basic Christian Trademark II: Always Ready to Forgive

SEVENTEENTH SUNDAY AFTER PENTECOST
MATTHEW 18:21-35

W. Theophil Janzow

This is the second in a series of two sermons, both of which have the title "Basic Christian Trademarks." The two texts come from the same chapter of Matthew. They follow one another. They are part of a connected sequence of conversations that Jesus had with His disciples. They both deal with a basic aspect of Christian character and behavior—how Christians are to behave toward their sinful fellow human beings.

Last Sunday we heard one of the basic trademarks of Christian living is that we are always seeking to save lost sinners. Today the emphasis is on our own attitude toward these sinful human beings, especially when the sins they commit directly affect us, when we ourselves are the people who have been sinned against.

Human beings are prone to practice a double standard, that is, to make one kind of judgment when the person being hurt is somebody else, but to make a different judgment when we ourselves are the victim of the transgression. "That's different," we are often heard to say when we are the ones getting hurt.

Jesus says, "Let it not be so. We urge others to practice the forgiving spirit. Let's practice it ourselves." And that brings us to

Basic Christian Trademark II: Always Ready to Forgive

I. No Limit to the Frequency or Fullness of Forgiveness

The most obvious lesson that we learn from a thoughtful study of our text is that, for Christians, there is no limit to how often we are willing to forgive someone who sins against us.

Peter had listened closely to the Lord's instruction regarding Christian discipline. He caught the spirit of the message. The goal is not to punish sinners, but to bring them to an appreciation of God's undying love and gracious forgiveness. He suddenly realized that Christians must be forgiving people, if they want others to understand the wonder of God's forgiving love toward them.

Peter's next question shouldn't surprise anyone. It's such a human question. I suspect that every one of us has asked Peter's question in our relations with someone else, perhaps without even realizing that Peter asked it first. We all know that as Christians we should forgive one who sins against us. But what often puzzles us is how often, how many times should we say "I forgive you," when our neighbor just keeps hurting us time and time again?

Peter doesn't only ask the question. He offers what most people would consider not only a reasonable, but in fact a very long-suffering answer. How about seven times? Surely that would be more than enough. That would more than fulfill all our obligations to be patient, tolerant, and forgiving.

We can almost feel ourselves nodding in agreement. Anyone who has been injured, hurt, maligned, mistreated by another person, time and time again, gets to the point of saying, "OK, that's enough. I've given you all these chances. This is the end of the rope. I've had it with you. Forgive you again? Just forget it."

This is why the response of Jesus is so startling, and why we learn so much about the nature of Christianity from it. "I'm telling you seven times is not enough. If you want to practice forgiveness according to My spirit of forgiveness, you must forgive that person 70 times seven times—in other words, without ceasing, without end. A trademark of your being My disciple must be 'Always ready to forgive.'"

It's interesting that human nature, also in the Christian, keeps trying to find ways to get around, to water down, to modify the absoluteness of this principle, especially when we are confronted with applying it to situations in our daily lives. One ploy that we like to use is "OK, I'll forgive you every time; but don't expect me to forget." We allow ourselves the luxury of at least a little grudge. It keeps us from taking the forgiven offender 100 percent back into our good graces. It keeps him hanging, even if ever so slightly, over the ledge of our possible rejection. It's what, as children, we used to call being an "Indian giver." First we give the gift of forgiveness to the transgressor; then we take part of that forgiveness away again.

Jesus' simple comment would be, "That's not enough." This is not a case where half a loaf is better than none. In this case partial forgiveness is like no forgiveness at all. If God did that to us, where would we be? Lost! If we had to sing "I am trusting Thee, Lord Jesus, trusting only Thee, trusting Thee for partial salvation," what a mockery that would be. Only a forgiveness that covers all our sins, fully and forever, can unlock the gates of paradise for us. And only when the forgiveness that we grant to our offending neighbor is total, unrestricted, and without strings attached can we believe that it reflects the pattern of Christ's forgiveness to us.

What a wonderful gift God gives us, when he fills us with such a spirit of forgiveness. It makes us "always ready to forgive," even as God is always ready to forgive us. It does not count the number of offenses. There is to be no limit to the frequency or fullness of forgiveness. How in keeping with this spirit was the apostle Paul's advice to the Ephesians (4:32), a word that has lost none of its timeliness today. "Be kind and compassionate to one another, forgiving each other, just as in Christ God forgave you."

II. The Source of Such a Limitless Forgiving Spirit

A second lesson that this text, by clear implication, teaches us is that the basis and source of a forgiving spirit in human beings is the incredibly kind and gracious forgiving spirit of our God. This alone can also move us to be always ready to forgive.

Christ's famous parable, of course, depicts a man who had never learned this important and wonderful lesson. As a result he plays fast and loose with the idea of forgiveness. He is a blatant double-standard person in the matter of forgiveness. When he can't pay the huge debt he has piled up against his master, he begs for mercy. He realizes that he is liable to be sold, together with his whole family, into slavery. It's an awful prospect, so he pleads for forgiveness. And, wonder of wonders, he gets it! Responding to compassionate instincts, the master just writes off his servant's entire debt, huge as it was, and sets him free. It was a magnanimous gesture of such major proportions that one would expect the servant to say, "I'll never forget this, and I'll certainly be considerate of other people when they are in debt to me."

Yet exactly the opposite happens. When a fellow servant asks for mercy in connection with a much smaller debt, the unmerciful servant refuses and has the debtor thrown in jail until the debt is paid. It's an unbelievably calloused example of double-standard behavior—expecting mercy for himself but refusing it to someone else. When you first hear this story, it sounds unreal. Surely, few people could carry double-standardness to such odious extremes.

Yet anyone who examines human behavior closely soon must become aware that double-standard practices have been around for a long time and are found, unfortunately, even in the church.

We tell our children not to curse; then we do it ourselves. We send our children off to Sunday school; then we sit home and read the paper. We decry the drug abomination in the world; then we proceed to abuse food and liquor. We condemn the politicians who practice graft; then we jump at chances to make a little shady profit ourselves. We denounce people who subtract truth from Scripture; then we proceed to add human notions and traditions, which is just as bad.

Double-standard behavior is reprehensible, no matter in what area of morality it happens. But when it happens in the area of forgiveness, it strikes at the very heart of what Christianity is all about.

Strange to say, not everyone would fault the unmerciful servant for his behavior. Sometimes people think that being forgiving makes a person a softy or a patsy. Some people will extol the virtues of a man who, like steel, refuses to bend and insists on getting his "rights," even when this brings suffering into someone else's life. They say admiringly, "He's a tough administrator."

The unmerciful servant would have been popular with those who feel this way. But he obviously was not popular with our Lord. Our Lord clearly was opposed to both double-standardness and an uncaring spirit. He knew its dreadful consequences.

It is difficult to find a more severe pronouncement than the concluding sentence of the Gospel. The climax of the parable finds the unmerciful servant back before his master who angrily puts him in jail and says, "Don't let him out until he has paid every penny of the debt." Then comes the Lord's evaluation, His application of this story to the lives of his disciples. It's an inescapable lesson that all of us should never forget. He says, "This is how my heavenly Father will treat each of you unless you forgive your brother from your heart" (Matt. 18:35).

Is it possible that this word of our Lord will come across to us as unnecessarily harsh? Yes, it is. We have a way of forgetting how forgiving God is to us. Over and over we sin against Him. Over and over we hurt Him. When He doesn't cater to our every whim and fancy, how easily we desert Him and turn to money, power, or pleasure to get our way. When life's fortunes go against us, how quickly we are ready to accuse and blame God for our misfortunes and even defame His name. When we get obsessed with the cares and pleasures of this world, how frequently we shut our ears to His voice and fail to seek guidance from His Word.

Yet every time we fold our hands to pray, open His word to read, repair to His house to worship, approach His table to eat and drink His sacred food, our hearts cry, "Forgive us our trespasses." And every time—no doubt it's thousands and thousands of times in the average person's lifetime—God always responds positively, always gives us the same comforting, blessed answer, "Yes, I forgive you. I forgive you fully with no strings attached. I do this for Jesus your Savior's sake."

It is impossible to overstate how wonderful this is. The gracious loving, caring, forgiving nature of our God defies adequate expression. We deserve nothing, yet God gives us everything. We are damnable sinners, yet in Christ God declares us to be saints. We break every law in God's book and deserve to be cast into outer darkness. Yet God, through the redemptive and reconciling ministry of His Son, adopts us into His family, showers us with His kindness, writes us into His will, and eventually will give us His home to live in for eternity.

Given the absolute dependability of these Gospel words, how important it is that we don't let them become commonplace, that we never let ourselves start taking God's forgiving love for granted. Because it is only in experiencing daily a profound sense of gratitude over how long-suffering and incredibly kind God is toward us that we can begin to practice such limitless forgiveness also toward our fellow human beings.

What edifying instruction this 18th chapter of Matthew gives us! How clearly it teaches us our basic Christian trademarks: 1) Always seeking to save lost sinners, and 2) Always ready to forgive. May the Holy Spirit bless the imparting of this sacred word and use it to cultivate in us a pattern of behavior that more and more reflects the seeking-to-save and the willing-to-forgive spirit of our Lord.

Grumbling at God's Generosity

EIGHTEENTH SUNDAY AFTER PENTECOST
MATTHEW 20:1-16

Frederick G. Klein

The principle of fairness is one of the standards which people use in their dealings with each other. We want to be treated fairly, and so we do our best to treat others in a fair, evenhanded way.

We expect to be paid for the work we do. We criticize that lazy, good-for-nothing so and so who lies around all day watching the "Soaps" on TV and lives on welfare money. We expect to advance in our business as we gain experience and skill. We don't look kindly on the boss's nephew who is promoted ahead of us because he knows someone of influence in the company.

God's Principle of Fairness Is Different

Since we live with this standard of fairness in everyday life, it is no wonder that we apply that principle of fairness when it comes to our expectation of the way God deals with people. "God helps those who help themselves," we like to quote as a religious excuse for our initiative and drive to succeed. It's easy to regard success and money as a reward which God gives to those who work hard. When it comes to applying this principle of fairness to God, we expect Him to prosper the good and bring disaster on the evil.

The only problem with our principle of fairness is that it doesn't apply at all to the ways of God. You will forgive me for reminding you that the Almighty God, the Lord of the universe, is not an American. He doesn't behave as we expect Him to behave. He doesn't treat people according to our standards of fairness.

Those who by human standards deserve nothing from God, like tax collectors, thieves, and harlots, get it all as they are invited by Jesus to repent and believe. And those who should have cushions on their thrones by our standards, the righteous, law-abiding Pharisees, are rejected from the Kingdom because they turn their backs on the Messiah and His message. The rain falls equally on the field of Christian and the unbeliever. No one has even proven that the faithful live longer, happier, or healthier lives than the faithless.

Jesus Tells a Story About Grumbling at God's Generosity

Matthew brings to our attention a parable Jesus once told about grumbling at God's generosity. The point of the story is that God equally gives His goodness to all people. God's kingdom is open to all who receive His Son, Jesus Christ, as Lord and Savior. God's loving kindness is given in equal measure to all, regardless of how long or how well each Christian has worked for God. The educated and the illiterate, the rich and the poor, the wise and the foolish—each is loved equally by God and invited to inherit eternal life.

Our idea of fairness is based on the work ethic which says, "You get what you deserve." God works on the principle of grace which says, "You get what you do *not* deserve." You have a gift for which you have not worked. It has not been earned or merited in any way. The gift is eternity with God and the peace which comes from knowing you are a forgiven child of the Father through Christ.

Parable Struck Home

The parable which Jesus told of the workers in the vineyard really struck home for the people who first heard the story. This kind of thing was common in Palestine. The grape harvest came quickly in September. The grapes had to be harvested before the rains came. It was a race against time. Either harvest them, or lose them. Anyone who could work did, even if it was only for an hour or two. And so the owner of the vineyard went out hiring workers throughout the day at 9:00, at noon, at 3:00, and again at 5:00.

We can relate to the scene of the men standing around in the town square waiting for work. We know such a thing goes on in today's employment agencies and union halls. Whether or not they got work determined if they and their families would eat that day.

But, as is often the case, this parable is misnamed. It is not so much a story of workers in the vineyard. It is really the story of the generous employer. For when the payroll is given out, each finds, regardless of his hours, the same amount of pay! Those who worked for just one hour before the whistle blew in the relative coolness of the late afternoon, receive as much as those who broke their backs lifting the heavy crates under the blaze of the noonday sun.

Unfair? Perhaps from the point of view of the 12-hour workers. But look again and you will see the owner of the vineyard did nothing wrong. He paid the full-time help what they had agreed on as a fair wage. Was not the money his to use as he wished?

Protest Strike over Generosity

The reason for the protest strike was not that the owner was unfair, but that he was generous. The owner puts his finger on the problem when he asks, "Are you envious because I am generous?" In Greek it is even more clear: "Do you look with an evil eye at my goodness?" The problem is not fair wages, but envy and greed.

A legend tells of two brothers who lived together in perfect harmony for many years without a quarrel or a fight between them. One day a magic genie appeared to them and said, "You two brothers are about to reap your reward." He told them they could ask for anything—absolutely anything—and it would be theirs. Just before he disappeared, he added two conditions. Said the genie, ". . . and the wonderful thing is that although only one brother can make the wish, the other brother will receive twice as much of whatever he asks for." And the offer was only good until sundown that day.

"How wonderful," the brothers agreed! What should they wish for? The sky was the limit! Would it be a million dollars? a whole kingdom? a thousand servants? Then the realization struck the wishing brother. The other brother would get twice as much as he would. Greed and envy began to fill his heart. The sun was now low in the sky and still there was no wish spoken. Finally, the elder brother seized the younger by the throat and screamed into his face, "Wish! Wish, or I'll choke you!" Gasping for air, he blurted out, "I wish . . . I wish . . . I wish to be blind in one eye!"

We Are No Strangers to Jealousy

We sit back in our seats and think, "Oh, how awful! To be that envious and jealous!" Yet jealousy and envy are no strangers to us, are they? Why does mother sometimes wish she had four sets of bone china instead of just one? Because she knows the trouble it will cause among the children when she dies.

Someone receives a generous gift totally unmerited, and the Bible tells us to rejoice with those who rejoice! But our sinful human natures tempt us to belittle their good fortune. A neighbor wins an all-expense-paid-trip for two to Hawaii, while we struggle to rent a broken down cabin in the backwoods for a long weekend. Now we see why Jesus asks in the parable, "Are you envious because I am generous?" By our human nature we are jealous and envious like Cain who killed Abel because God approved of Abel's sacrifice and rejected Cain's.

Only with God Can We Rejoice

Only as we live with the God of grace are we able to rejoice when blessings come to us and to others. Aware of my own unworthiness to receive any of the gifts God has given to me, my heart is flooded with gratitude for these undeserved blessings. Whether it be family or friends, congregation or home, health or work, rest or play, I realize that I am always on the receiving end of God's love. Aware that all of life is a gift freely given to me by my heavenly Father, I am frankly too busy counting my blessings and being thankful for them to look over the fence at what my neighbor has received from the hand of God.

I am a steward of all God's gifts, and I know that one day I must give a report to the Master as to how I used my gifts. With that thought in mind I am convinced that I simply do not have the time to envy my neighbor who may have more than I. I am busy enough investing my time, talents, and money in kingdom work!

I Am Blessed Beyond Measure

No matter how little or much I may have by the standards of the world, as a Christian I know I am blessed and honored beyond anything I could dream or deserve. For me, Jesus Christ became a human being so that He could take my place and suffer death on the cross. Through His generosity I am saved from my sins and now am on the high road to eternal life through faith in Him. My Savior rose from the dead to give life—eternal life—to me and all believers. I didn't deserve it, merit it, buy it, beg or steal it. Eternal life is mine as a gift by grace through faith in Jesus Christ.

Christ has assured me and all believers that whatever my earthly lot may be, I have His companionship and aid. In sickness or health His Sacrament of Holy Communion strengthens me and draws me ever closer to Him. In good times and bad His Word is a constant source of strength and courage in life. In the eyes of people I might seem weak and useless, but through Baptism I am God's child. I am part of the royal priesthood, a member of the holy nation Christ has brought into being through His death and resurrection.

Thank God His Standards Aren't Ours

It is true. God doesn't treat people according to our standards of what is fair and what is not fair. Thank God! The goodness of God is far above and beyond any system we might dream up for parceling out His generosity. His loving kindness is offered freely to everyone. Why grumble at His generosity? Instead, why not accept it with thanksgiving?

Strong Words—Strong Actions

NINETEENTH SUNDAY AFTER PENTECOST
MATTHEW 21:28-32

Frederick G. Klein

"Actions speak louder than words" is an expression we all have heard and know to be true. We are suspicious of the person who says one thing and does quite another. We much prefer people whose words and actions correspond with each other. Their word can be counted on. It is easy to trust a person whose words and actions are consistent.

Jesus tells a story today of two sons who were asked to work in their father's vineyard. One spitefully said he would not and then went. The other gladly said he would go and did not. The point of the parable is that actions speak louder than words when it comes to Christian faith, too. Doing the will of God is far more important than empty promises.

Strong on Words—Weak on Action

Scribes and Pharisees

The second son was much like the religious leaders of Israel. That's why Jesus wanted the scribes and Pharisees to hear His story. They talked correctly about religion. They knew the Law with all its ramifications well. The trouble was that their knowledge of the will of God never worked its way out in doing the will of God. They were strong on words, but weak on deeds. Jesus knew this and confronted them with their hypocrisy.

Jesus often spoke out against the hollow, empty piety of the Jewish religious leaders. He warned His followers of every age,

"Not everyone who says to me, 'Lord, Lord,' will enter the kingdom of heaven, but only he who does the will of my Father who is in heaven" (Matt. 7:21). The Savior's teaching was consistent with all the prophets. Micah reveals the will of God for all people: "He has showed you, O man, what is good. And what does the Lord require of you? To act justly and to love mercy and to walk humbly with your God" (Micah 6:8).

The Pharisees and scribes knew the vocabulary of faith but would not put faith to work in their lives. They were faithful churchmen—regular in temple worship and generous in their offering of tithes. Yet Jesus calls them whitewashed mausoleums. At a distance they look good. But when we get close to them and find out what is motivating them, like an opened tomb the smell is putrid! The truth of the matter was that, wishing to be considered pious, they were tyrants. With their "proper" background, schooling, and friends, they were still phonies!

Some in the Church

Unfortunately, there are some in the church who are also strong on words, but weak on actions. They use the language of Christian faith easily and openly, but their life is a contradiction of their words. They appear to know Scripture and will freely quote from it when they want God's Word to back up their point of view. You will see them at public worship going through the motions of confession, intercession, and praise, but they leave the sanctuary unchanged by the Word. They have resisted the power of the Holy Spirit who works through the Word to bring repentance and faith in Christ. They leave God's house as they came—vengeful, picky, filled with anger or despair.

They may know the catechism and the difference between Law and Gospel, but it is all safely locked up in their heads. Blocking the power of God to change the sinful heart and corrupted will, their life remains a contradiction of their words of faith. The gifts of the Spirit like kindness, patience, and humility are not mirrored in their lives. Instead they choose to live destructively, copying the sinful world around them with its lust, greed, and pride.

Even worse, at times you will find them in positions of leadership in congregations. There they replace peace with tension and destroy harmony with distrust and suspicion. They are quick to throw out the goals of a Christian congregation to be light for the wandering, a haven for the distressed, the lonely, and the penitent. When they have their way in the fellowship of faith, the ship of church stops on its journey to do the will of God on earth as it is done in heaven, and the witness to Christ is weakened.

At Times All of Us

All of us, at one time or another, have been like the second son who was strong on words, but weak on action. Sinful human nature takes over our lives so easily. At times we have been in the sanctuary for worship while our thoughts were far from the Lord. We have gone through the motions while the sustenance was not received.

Satan comes along tempting us to outwardly give God His due, but live our lives as we will. He tempts us to be courteous to others, while hating them in our hearts. We are civil at home, but in spirit we remove ourselves from the family.

When Satan tempts us to be strong on words of faith, but weak on appropriate actions, we need to remember this story of Jesus. Christ teaches today that the outward mask of piety is not enough if our heart is far from Him. Love is the fulfilling of the Law. Polite conversation is no substitute for genuine Christian love in word and deed. Our goal as Christians is to love God in word and deed with all our heart, mind, and soul, and our neighbor as much as we love ourselves.

Weak on Words—Strong in Action

What about the first boy in Jesus' story? He was asked to work in his father's vineyard, but refused. Later, reconsidering the request and who was requesting it, he changed his mind. He quietly did what his father requested. Of the two responses, Jesus seems to prefer this son over the other.

We have encountered people like him at one time or another. We have been like him ourselves, saying no and then in the end doing what we were asked. Such people can seem tough and callous outwardly, but once in a while they will show a spark of generosity and kindness which contradicts their rough exterior.

As admirable as their sporadic outbursts of love may be, Christ does not approve of a life-style which shows disrespect for God and other people. Christ's way is that words and deed equally show Him alive and active in the life of believers. In the end you can be sure the father in Jesus' story was as displeased with the words of his first son as with the actions of the second.

Strong Words and Strong Actions

The Third Son

Some Bible teachers suggest that there is a third Son in the story. This third Son takes the *words* of obedience spoken from the second, and the *action* of obedience from the first. He is the Son who pleases the Father in word *and* deed.

The third Son is the one who told the story. He is Jesus Christ, the Son of the Father, who was completely obedient to the Father's will in word and deed. Paul speaks of this obedience in Phil. 2:8, "And being found in appearance as a man, he humbled himself and became obedient to death—even death on a cross!"

His words and actions were consistent from the beginning to the end of His life. His will was to do the will of His Father in heaven. His actions backed up and underscored His words from His birth of the Virgin Mary to His death on Calvary's cross.

His work, given to Him by the Father, was to suffer and die on the cross for us and all people. His work was to bring us the forgiveness of sins and life with God.

God continues to love even the likes of us who often show ourselves to be disobedient sons and daughters. In the cross of Christ we see the love of God for us and all people. By faith in the obedient Son of God the Holy Spirit enables us to confess our disobedience and turn to Christ in faith for help to live for Christ in word and deed. To live a life not only in proper God-exalting words, but in proper God-reflecting deeds, too.

We hear His Word, and the Holy Spirit causes repentance to begin. The Word calls us to examine our words in the light of our deeds. Where words and deeds do not follow deeds and words, we resolve through the power of the Spirit to make both words and deeds give a single testimony of faith in Jesus Christ.

Christ and Christ alone gives the power to say to our Father in heaven, "I will, sir," and then to go. To say and to do the will of God in life pleases Him and shows our gratitude for the forgiveness of sins and eternal life we have through faith in Jesus Christ.

Enabled by Christ

When the journey of obedient faith to the Father gets rough, His Son provides us with the refreshment and renewed motivation we need along the way. He calls us to remember our Baptism which made us God's sons and daughters. In the water and word of Baptism, God has established a covenant relationship with us. He is our Father; we are His children. We have been bought with the price of the Savior's blood shed on the cross. We are not our own; we belong to Him.

In God's Word, the Scriptures, we are instructed on the kind of living which witnesses day by day to Christian faith. His presence and power are with us even as we struggle with sin, the world, and the devil.

His Holy Supper nourishes and supports us when the pull becomes strong to throw in the towel and give up the struggle with self-centered nature. We eat the bread and drink from the cup and receive Christ's true body and blood. Faith and courage are increased as we eat and drink, and we are renewed in our resolve to speak strong words of commitment to the Savior and to do strong deeds for the Lord who loved us so much.

"Actions speak louder than words," indeed, but stronger still are strong words coupled with strong actions, particularly when words and deeds come from a Christian. By the power of the Holy Spirit, resolve with me that with the help of Christ our words and actions will be strong in faith and love.

How Much of God's Grace Can You Carry?

TWENTIETH SUNDAY AFTER PENTECOST
MATTHEW 21:33-43

Hubert Beck

Once upon a time when things were very bad on the earth, two beggars roamed the countryside seeking food. Both were, in fact, quite successful at their "trade," if you wish to call it that. But a significant difference separated them.

The one found many open hands and stored up his food in a sack he carried over his back. Times were bad, he reasoned, but they could get much worse. Better to keep what he had, live as frugally as possible, and save against a worse day yet to come. As he thus gathered his food, the bread hardened and the vegetables rotted into an awful stench, but the man would not stop his gathering. The more he gathered, of course, the heavier his sack became, and the harder it became for him to travel from village to village and from house to house. But he continued as a man obsessed until one day the proverbial "straw that broke the camel's back" went into his sack. The sheer weight of the sack with all its hoarded, but by now virtually useless, contents broke the man's back in a deserted place, and there he died with a broken body munching on stale bread.

The other also found remarkable success, as has been noted, in his gathering. For him, though, the sack never grew heavy nor did the bread grow stale or the vegetables rotten. In his wanderings he regularly came across beggars less successful than he who were badly in need. To each of them he opened his sack and the bread was consumed before it grew hard, the vegetables made into soup before they grew old. Far and wide he traveled, but he always traveled lightly, for those people of need seemed to sense his very nearness, and he was never stingy in his sharing. Thus, for many years he wandered the countryside as far more than merely a beggar. He was also the provider for many in greater need than he. And with his sack carried so lightly on his shoulder he never felt the burden that ultimately became the first beggar's doom.

The Richness of God's Grace

The story is a backdoor way to gain entry to the parable that forms the heart of the Gospel for today.

The men in the vineyard were neither the owners of nor even the builders of the vineyard in which they toiled. They were beggars, as it were, men who lived by the grace of a good master who had himself toiled long and hard to plant the vineyard, to set a hedge around it, to dig a wine press in it, to build a tower for its protection, and to provide all that was necessary to sustain the workers. They were merely those who were available when the master went into another country and needed people to care for his vineyard.

The vineyard keepers, of course, are clearly the people of Israel to whom God entrusted the care of a part of the earth that had come from his hand. They were, in fact, a particular and chosen people, as the Scriptures make plain. They were to be models to the earth of what it meant to be the people of God. Through them the light of God's grace was to be seen by all those who had commerce with them. The land was a gift; their place in the world was made especially by God for them; they were beggars who had been richly graced.

Nor is our position any different. We must be careful not to scold Israel through this parable without also seeing ourselves as the new Israel created in Christ for the very same purpose. To us, also, is given a special place in life—renewal through the forgiveness of our sins—a place from which the light of God's grace is to be seen by all around us. We, too, are beggars who cannot live off the land but must depend on God's merciful hand filling the sack of our need with his rich gifts.

The Arrogance of Humanity

How strange a twist, then, to hear the story of the men in the vineyard (which, remember, is our story, also!) when they actually take the servants sent by the owner to get his share of the harvest and beat one, kill another, and stone still another. As if that were not strange enough the first time, they do it the second time and finally kill even the son of the vineyard owner when he is sent in a last desperate effort to collect what was rightfully due the master.

"Could such a thing have ever happened?" one must ask. If commentators are correct, it evidently *did* happen on occasion in the Israel of Jesus' day, for there were many absentee landowners distant enough away that workers of the soil actually felt that they could get by with such acts of malice without serious fear of retribution. There were, in fact, a few loopholes in the laws that made it work on a few occasions if those who study the times are correct. So Jesus is very likely drawing off a real life situation of sorts to tell his story.

The story is more real to life than that, however, when one digs still deeper. The parable borders on allegory as it is told here (it is told in slightly different forms in Mark and Luke where it is more directly a parable than an allegory). It "tells the story of Jesus" in rather straightforward fashion when one compares its imagery with the Biblical narratives.

The beginning of the story, as you may have noticed, is taken almost word for word, and certainly entirely in its basic structure, from the Old Testament parable found in Isaiah 5, read as our First Lesson today. That puts Israel squarely into the vineyard as the people who receive the messengers and servants of God so cruelly. Those sent are without question the prophets and messengers God gave to Israel through the ages, none of whom were greeted well and many of whom were indeed martyred for their efforts.

Finally the son, himself, comes. And the way the story develops clearly points to the account of the crucifixion, for he is taken prisoner, thrown outside the walls of the vineyard, and there killed. The Gospel accounts focus attention on how Jesus is led outside the city walls to be crucified. The arrogance of the vineyard workers who refuse to give the owner his due is now the arrogance of a people who refuse to accept God's own Son, but treat Him cruelly and put Him to death. Not only have the ancient people of Israel abused their position as children of God, but these contemporaries of Jesus follow in their fathers' and mothers' footsteps. They are as arrogant as the generations before. All of God's grace showered so richly on them in their designation as God's people is gladly received. But that gift does not result in a sharing of God's grace. It results in pride. It is as though one could receive from God, hoard His gifts, and keep them for oneself. They do not recognize God's grace in Christ as a treasure to be received, used in behalf of their nation and the world, and thus become the very stuff of life in all that they do.

"Could such a thing have ever happened?" we question. And it is a hard blow to realize that the answer is not only, "Yes, it did happen," but also, "Yes, and it happens among us every day!" It is much easier to see these stories related to the people of Jesus' time or directed to the scoundrels and knaves of the world. This parable must strike *our* lives, though, if we are to be honest with God and ourselves. For it is our own lives that we claim for ourselves. We guard the vineyard of our own existence carefully lest the rent on it be collected. We develop many ways to lay claim to our own little corner of life. We do not concentrate on what has been given to us as a gift, but rather on how much we can carve out for ourselves and claim as our own possession. We thereby reject not only the word of the Owner who claims His own, but we also keep our brothers and sisters at arm's length lest they claim our vineyard.

It is all justified, of course, in our minds. After all, one never knows for sure whether the messengers are legitimate or not. They may be wolves in sheep's clothing, coming in the name of the Master to obtain for themselves what is due the Master. Better to guard the rent carefully, we tell ourselves, so that we will have it for the Master should He personally come to claim it. Of course, it is all a subterfuge, a way of keeping it for ourselves, for even the Son is thrown out and killed when He comes. We just do not want to give up the corner of existence we call our "life" to the Master. We claim to act "out of love for the Master" in ways that keep what is his for ourselves and will not let it go. Each of us is named in the parable!

Thus we turn into a shambles the blessings of God's grace so richly given. The blessings become hard crusts of hoarded bread and rotting vegetables. We carry them about as though they were meant for nothing other than our own existence. We shut out all who, in the name of the Father, come to "collect the rent" of our faithful response to His grace. And "the rent" becomes heavier and heavier in the sacks on our backs.

The Humility of Christ

It is this that throws Jesus into such bold relief in the latter part of the Gospel. He who comes as the Son is rejected, but He will not reject. Even in His dying He cries, "Father, forgive them, for they do not know what they are doing." He who owns all things, even the vineyard of our lives, gave up all that He owned and became one of us, possessing nothing—not even his life. He it is to whom we must look if we would know how a true Son of the Father lives—and how a true Son of the Father dies! Having given up all things for us—even His life—he is laid in another man's grave. In life and in death He has no place to lay His head. The King of all has become the Beggar Supreme who goes about the wastelands of the earth receiving richly from the Father and giving it to His brothers and sisters for their sustenance. He dies with His bag empty, not from a broken back burdened with hard bread and rotting vegetables, but from the wounds inflicted by those who could not and would not understand Him. He who revealed the Father's heart pierced the bags of those who were storing all things up for themselves and their "possessions" went tumbling every which way, and they killed him.

"The stone the builders rejected has become the capstone; the Lord has done this, and it is marvelous in our eyes" (Ps. 118:22-23).

These words speak of the vindication of the Son. God affirmed His way of life and thereby crushed all alternative views and understandings. Those who would have life must find in the Christ that rich gift that comes only from the Father's hand. To look elsewhere is only to find disappointment. It is the cross of Christ, affirmed in His resurrection, that is the pathway to life. It cannot be found by hoarding the wealth of this world nor even by trying to store up God's grace. It is to be found only by going with Jesus to the cross so that His cross becomes our life and our life becomes the way of the cross, the way of poverty in which we claim nothing and give freely of that which is given us.

Two Beggars on the Road with Bags on Their Back

There were two men on the road with bags on their back, both living only as beggars. One looks for, longs for, and gladly accepts all of God's gifts. He carefully hoards them in a bag already filled to bursting. One day the bag of God's grace becomes so great that it actually crushes his back. He falls broken to the ground under, of all things, the weight of grace selfishly hoarded. "Therefore I tell you that the kingdom of God will be taken away from you and given to a people who will produce its fruit."

Your bag is filled to the point of breaking, Jesus is saying. You are called to use it in behalf of the world or it will be lost to you. One can only hoard so much of God's grace without response before it becomes a deadly burden.

For God's grace is to be passed on, given away, channeled to others. It is never merely our own possession. The other man, beggar though he was, kept his bag light. All that was given to him became a gift for others. His life knew all the hardships of a beggar, but it also knew the riches of God who always gives more than one can ever give away. Even in his dying moment he was a beggar, but what a gift still lay before him at the very point when all was taken away from him! He died empty-handed, but infinitely wealthier than the man whose full sack of riches broke his back.

For the stone rejected by the builders had become the capstone of his life.

Two beggars are on the way with bags on their back. One of them is you.

Which one?

The Invitation

TWENTY-FIRST SUNDAY AFTER PENTECOST
MATTHEW 22:1-10(11-14)

Hubert Beck

A disturbing sign of our time is the frequent complaint about how hard it is to get a family together, even for meal time. Something about eating together establishes a bond among the participants, and when families no longer eat together some of the glue that binds them together dries up and weakens.

This is not merely a longing for the good old days. Eating together has been a way of creating a bond through the ages. Although it can be found in all cultures, one finds with considerable frequency in the Bible the idea that promises, covenants, and friendships are sealed around a table. Celebrations of special events also require such eating together as the First Lesson for today indicates. Rejoicing is a community project and requires food and fellowship.

It is not surprising, then, to find that the last great gathering of God's people is pictured as a wedding feast—a meal observing the end of an old way of life and the beginning of a whole new life when bride and bridegroom are joined into an indissoluble unity. That is where we encounter "the kingdom of heaven" in today's text: "The kingdom of heaven is like a king who prepared a wedding banquet for his son."

Elements Common to Parables and Stories of Meals and Feasts

Since this is but one of several such parables and allusions throughout the Bible to God's gathering of His people around a meal (and is not Holy Communion but an extension of all such stories?), we can learn important things from elements that are almost universal in the stories. We do little more than list them at this point:

The meal itself speaks about the joy and reunion of God's people. Whether the prodigal returns home or a king celebrates his son's wedding, a meal must be prepared and people gathered at a common table.

A second universal is to note that the master, the king, the father is always the one to host the meal.

A third thing to note is that virtually always there are servants—intermediaries of some sort—who are almost hidden characters in the story.

One frequently finds guests who either refuse to come and eat or are at best reluctant to the point of refusing to do so.

Lastly, there occurs with considerable regularity in these parables, as in today's text, a scouring of the countryside for people to fill the seats of those who refuse to come. The seats are inevitably filled, but not with the people expected to fill them.

Elements Never Found in These Parables

For a contrast, note what is not found in these parables of the Kingdom.

The meals are not merely casual gatherings in which the king is chatting with his subjects or the father is simply having a heart to heart talk with his son sharing good advice. "The kingdom of heaven is like . . ." ordinary things such as seeds growing and sowers sowing, but the kingdom of heaven also intrudes into this ordinariness so that it becomes a lost thing that is found and treasured or a precious thing for which one sells less important things. The wedding meal suggests something special is happening. Human enterprises are turned from their usual course because divine initiative has interrupted the normal course of human affairs.

Again, one never finds servants honoring masters, children honoring parents, subjects honoring kings. No matter how good he may be, the king or parent or master is never the one being honored. He is the one doing the honoring.

A third thing to note is that there are never volunteers. Servants are no more volunteers than are children. All do their job at the request of the king. The feast is not attended by volunteers, but by invited guests. Guests never solicit their invitations. The way to the banquet is by royal invitation, and that must originate with the king.

Lastly, the seats at the banquet table are never filled with people you would expect to find at royal tables. In today's Gospel, the servants "gathered all the people they could find, both good and bad." They are seated side by side. Ideal guests never seem to end up at the table, at least not alone.

What Do We Learn from This?

From such observations we can note some particular points about the parable before us today.

Above all we see God's initiating grace. The banquet table is consistently accessible only to those who are invited, and the invitation comes from the King Himself. We are not volunteers at His table. We are recipients of grace.

Although this parable does not quite as directly depict the story of Jesus as did the Gospel last week, the statement that some of the invited guests "seized his servants, mistreated them, and killed them" seems to hint at the long history of mistreatment of the prophets and messengers of God. Without pressing this image upon the parable, one can see in a very broad form a suggestion of the vision of His own death that lay before Him. And it is in His death that we see God's grace most directly revealed. His death is the climactic moment of God's gracious activity in behalf of mankind. John describes Christ's mission poignantly: ". . . though the world was made through him, the world did not recognize him" (John 1:10). He by whom the world was made became subject to the curse of death. He opened to us a window to the Father's heart of gracious lovingkindness.

The Holy Spirit extends the invitation to us in our baptism, naming us with the name of Christ. He takes our poor bread and wine brought to the table by our hands and makes of it food for our spirit as the body and blood of Christ nourishes us through the gift returned to us in our eating and drinking. Water, bread, wine, and words that have no significance whatever on our lips and in our hands are touched by the Spirit of God. They become the invitations into fellowship with God and each other, the "foretaste of the feast to come" as some of our liturgies put it. "A king prepared a wedding banquet for his son," and the invitation goes out to *us*!

In the similarities and mutual voids found in these parables, however, we also note the hardness of the human heart. The gracious invitation falls on deaf ears. Well, not quite deaf ears. Perhaps it would be better if at least one could plead that. But they are ears unprepared and unwilling to heed the invitation. It is not that they necessarily dislike the king and his prepared feast. Not all of them are opposed to it. It is just not as important as their farms and businesses. Those things are good enough in themselves. The problem is in how they are prioritized. These good things have suddenly become the most important, taking precedence over the king's invitation.

If only it were extraordinary situations that made it impossible to attend—a terminal illness or an alien master who had bound them and would not let them go. It is precisely the opposite, though, and that is the pathos of the parable. It is the simple little everyday things that hold their highest attention. Their farms will still be there after the feast, and the business can wait. Even the loss of a few dollars due to untended business and farm during the time of the feast is not great catastrophe. That can be made up later. The invitation, though, is a once in a lifetime kind of thing.

Here we see how deeply rooted our own self-serving and self-seeking is perceived to be by Jesus. He is not a psychologist suggesting some flaws in our personality or a pessimist who simply looks at the bad side of things. He is the One through whom the invitation is extended as well as the Son who is honored by the feast. He it is who tells us that the basic human problem is not a minor flaw, but a deep-seatedly false prioritization of life. It is a reminder of the first commandment's warning us about the dangers of idolizing our business, farm, or daily routine, refusing to let it be interrupted or changed in any way—not even by a royal invitation. Our life is our own. Even kings cannot have claim on it! Although some make a violent response, most tragic are the words "They paid no attention and went off."

A last thing we learn is what might be called the unpredictability of the kingdom of heaven. The Kingdom, of course, is highly predictable in many ways, but what is meant by this term here is reflected in the way the servants scoured the streets and "gathered all the people they could find, both good and bad."

Such a statement, found regularly in these parables, destroys many of our mental images of the Kingdom. The absence of the very guests one would expect to find at this feast is itself a great warning against taking the grace of which we have been speaking for granted. One dare never presume upon the invitation of the King as though another invitation will come next week or as though this is a less important engagement than others that may come in the future. *Any* invitation from the King is already a vital invitation, for through this invitation the very doors of the kingdom of heaven are opened to us.

And we are drawn into a Kingdom where brothers and sisters of all sorts must be recognized and acknowledged. The household of faith has people in it we would hardly consider candidates from our perspective. The question is not whether the candidates are good, but whether the invitation is heard and heeded. All depends on the invitation!

The Uniqueness of This Text

The end of the parable causes it to stand out from the others in a particular way. It seems a bit odd at first to hear of the man thrown out of the banquet hall because he has no wedding garment. After all, if he has just been drawn off the street without a chance to go home and change, how could he have a wedding garment? Since others apparently *do* have such a garment even though they, too, have just come off the street, it seems that the King Himself has provided them with festal garments. The grace of the King provides not only the invitation but also the wedding garments!

Is this not what forgiveness of sins is—a garment of God's grace covering the stains of our life? "Blessed is he whose transgressions are forgiven, whose sins are covered," the psalmist says (Ps. 32:1).

Our renewed life is also spoken of as something to put on. We "have put on the new self, which is being renewed in knowledge in the image of its Creator. . . . Therefore . . . clothe yourselves with compassion, kindness, humility, gentleness and patience. . . . and over all these virtues put on love" (Col. 3:10,12,14). A way of life is "put on" with the "covering" of the forgiveness of sins.

What arrogance, then, to enter the wedding hall on our own terms! The King who issues the invitation can set the terms of entering the hall since all that is necessary for entering is available from and through Him. When a person attempts to enter it on terms other than the invitation, as though the outsider establishes the criteria for entrance, it becomes apparent that, rather than being honored, such a person is asserting himself, flaunting himself before the King as entrance is sought on terms other than the invitation. "Then the king told the attendants, 'Tie him hand and foot, and throw him outside, into the darkness, where there will be weeping and gnashing of teeth.'"

The stress on grace in the early part of the parable becomes a warning in the latter part against accepting this free gift as though through it we become free to do as we please. The gift enables us to do as *God* pleases!

"For many are invited, but few are chosen." The hard-heartedness of mankind makes even God's grace work overtime to achieve the ends which He seeks. God's ways are always gracious, but they are indeed *His* ways and not ours! We walk by faith, not by sight; we live by grace, not by works; we live by trust in God and not merely by assenting to an idea that God is good. His invitation is our only hope!

The way of God, then, calls for obedience and righteousness, which is far more than mere good will to God and an outwardly decent life. It calls for our full attention to the King in every way, for when we give Him such attention, we soon discover that even the farms and businesses we were afraid to leave are not really ours anyway. They, too, belong to the King and are gifts from Him to us that we might care for them in His name!

So we are not even asked to leave *our* farm or *our* business when the invitation comes! He knows very well what He is doing, and His invitation is extended to discover among us whether we know who really possesses not only the wedding hall but all other things as well. All that counts is that He extends the invitation!

The invitation is the ultimate Word of the Lord. And the feast is nothing less than life itself. The invitation has gone out! Come, let us gather at the table!

When Religion Is Empty

THIRD-LAST SUNDAY IN THE CHURCH YEAR
MATTHEW 23:1-12

David S. Belasic

With less than 50 percent of the people of America going to worship on a given Sunday, it is probably safe to say that many people find religion stifling, deadening, oppressive, or at least boring. Obviously, when that happens, many people in our community miss the meaning of the Gospel and the life our Lord offers.

Today's Gospel shows what happens when religion is empty—when ceremony outweighs service, when burdens overpower blessings, when love for position replaces love for people, when hypocrisy covers humility. It also points us to the One who fills the emptiness!

I. Ceremony Outweighs Service

Jesus was speaking both to disciples, his close, dearly loved followers, and to the crowds of onlookers, the curious. Today He speaks to us—the "insiders" in His church—and to the "seeker," the questioner, the wonderer and would-be-disciple. He says, "The teachers of the law and the Pharisees sit in Moses' seat. So you must obey them and do everything they tell you. But do not do what they do, for they do not practice what they preach" (v. 2-3).

We are all familiar with the old story of the father saying to his young son, "Don't do as I do, but do as I say." When that is the character of a so-called life with God, it is empty. Going through the motions, merely putting in our time, saying the right words, or doing the right thing, whether on the job, in a marriage, in school, on an athletic team, in piano practice, in preaching, or in any area of life, has never really stood up. It never endures.

In Jesus' day ceremonies abounded. Civic and religious holidays marked the calendar, and the distinction between them often blurred, just as in our own day. The heart of God's will for His creatures—*service* to one another as reflectors of the Creator and Redeemer in whose image we are made and remade—was overlooked in favor of ceremonies that made a person look good. But it didn't add to the substance of life.

Going to the temple or to church, being circumcised or baptized, observing the Passover or communing with our Lord, calling upon God in prayer—these activities were never intended by God to be mere ceremony. They are God's ways of filling our lives with Himself and equipping us for service. But when going through the ceremony loses the goal of service to God and men that He calls for, then surely our religion is empty. It happens if we send our children to Sunday school or a private Christian school just so we as parents look respectable and appear to be religiously concerned. If we say the right words in our favorite liturgy or serve as godparents at a child's baptism, come to the special holiday services because "it's the thing to do" or get involved in projects and groups in the congregation or community only because we want the publicity and recognition of people, then we ultimately serve only ourselves. We fake sincerity and perform a less than honorable service. It is self-exalting deception, and when it is done in the name of God, it is sin! We are all subject to that danger.

II. A Burden Instead of a Blessing

Jesus says of those in positions of authority in His day, "They tie up heavy loads and put them on men's shoulders, but they themselves are not willing to lift a finger to move them. The average person in our community and congregation has plenty of burdens. Hardly anyone among us is untouched by fears about the future, illnesses of various kinds, unemployment, concerns for aging parents or rebellious children. Families come apart; parents don't listen; children don't seem to care. Many face financial fears, the loss of a loved one, or the need for a true friend. "Each day has enough trouble of its own," our Lord says in the Sermon on the Mount. He speaks the truth!

When the blessings of God-given faith; the privileges of worship, church membership, and participation in the Holy Sacrament; and the study of the Word are twisted and distorted by man-made regulations or an inordinate concern for order—or when those things are presented in ways that make us feel inferior and burdened—then, surely, the blessings of God are turned into burdens impossible to bear. It happened in our Lord's time. It can happen in our church too! It happens when we look down on those who don't worship with us anymore and label them "delinquent" without knowing their need in life. It happens when we put stumbling blocks and restrictions in front of needy sinners who ask for the Sacrament, but don't meet our regulations or human practices. It happens when we give the impression that only certain people are welcome in our fellowship and we neglect those who look different from us. Those practices are burdens to God's people and rob them of the grace and strength of our Lord. We live in danger of adding burdens to people in our homes, families, neighborhoods, and congregation.

III. Love for Position Replaces Compassion

In today's Gospel Jesus says of the Pharisees, "Everything they do is done for men to see." They flaunt their special clothes. They love the places of honor at feasts, the best seats at worship, and greetings in the marketplaces. That is also a picture of religion grown empty. It has the form but not the substance of religion. Our Lord warns all of us. He condemns presumptuous behavior. It reminds us of His warning in the Sermon on the Mount about praying so as to be seen by others. He says that's the only reward that will ever come from that kind of prayer!

This text gets close to home for all of us. It's not the kind of Bible reading that we can easily gloss over or quickly dismiss by pointing to our fellow member three rows back!

Jesus admonishes you and me as disciples to beware of losing our love for people in our quest for piety and our show of being religious. It takes prayer to put our discipleship into practice, but it takes more. The Pharisees were not known for their compassion for the poor, the dispossessed, the downtrodden. Our Lord was. And in so far as His Spirit lives in us, we are called to put the emphasis on *people*—all God's people! We are not called to attainment of position, prominence, or influence, personally or corporately.

At a congregational meeting in which officers were being elected, a man came to vote. He watched and waited, and when the three major positions were filled by the electors, he got up and left. The pastor went after the man to see if something was wrong. The sharp reply was "There's nothing else worth doing around here. I may as well leave." The man did. Later the pastor called together a few elders and some of the man's acquaintances. They prayed and planned a strategy to help the proud man know that positions in the church are not more important than serving God's people—no matter what form that service may take.

We are all subject to making our religion empty when we make positions take priority over people. St. Paul says, "Your attitude should be the same as that of Christ Jesus: Who being in very nature God, did not consider equality with God something to be grasped, but made himself nothing, taking the very nature of a servant, being made in human likeness. And being found in appearance as a man, he humbled himself and became obedient to death—even death on the cross!" (Phil. 2:5-8).

IV. Hypocrisy Displaces Humility

To do our deeds only to receive a pat on the back from others or to love the titles of "teacher" or "master" more than the role of servant of Christ, is to miss the whole point of our Savior's love for us and our following of Him as disciples. In our generation, as in the past, the charge of hypocrisy is continually brought against the church of Jesus Christ. It is one thing to be charged; it is another thing to continue in our guilt!

Christ came to redeem, to change, to forgive hypocrites—all of us, inside and outside the church. The good thing about belonging to Jesus Christ in the fellowship of the church is that He is our Master. He is the one Servant of the living God who allows and encourages us to remove our masks and with humble hearts accept His pardon, His forgiveness, His reconciling and freeing love. By His death on the cross and His rising to life again, Jesus Christ has set us free from having to impress others or to hide behind a show of rightness or religiosity. He forgives and accepts us. He is the One who fills the void of empty religion and removes the fearsome burdens of having to always be "right" or "proper" and of having to impress others. He is the one who fills our ceremonies with meaning and positions each of us for loving and accepting service to one another.

Our Lord incarnated His own advice: "The greatest among you will be your servant." We become great in His greatness for us. He lifts the lowly, exalts the oppressed, forgives us sinners. He does it for you and me and all people today. He is our Master. He fills our emptiness with His Spirit, His presence, His love, and His power for living.

Today our Lord calls us to repentance and renewed faith, to change the old ways and be filled with the new. What He began in Holy Baptism; what He heard us witness in confirmation; what He offers, renews, and seals in Holy Communion He calls forth in our lives so that our character and inner life are transformed by the power of His Gospel and His Spirit. As that happens, empty religion is replaced by dynamic discipleship. Living with confidence in His love for us is more blessing than burden. His love leads us to be more concerned with real service to others than with merely going through the motions of religion. The love of Christ for us helps us focus our lives on people who can be loved, rather than on positions we may desire or attain.

May God grant each of us that fullness of life with Him and one another every day—always! For Jesus' sake!

Jesus Is Coming Again

SECOND-LAST SUNDAY IN THE CHURCH YEAR
MATTHEW 24:1-14

David S. Belasic

Ever since the Ascension of our Lord the church has lived in expectation of His return. He is coming again. That's sure! He said so. What we don't know is when. As we near the close of this church year, it is well that we consider the implications of our faith in the return of our Lord, especially since, as we confess in the Apostle's Creed, we believe He "will come to judge the living and the dead." Today's Gospel helps us live as disciples who believe that Jesus is coming again. We'll consider three points in today's message:

1. Jesus *is* coming again, false witnesses not withstanding.
2. Jesus is coming again in spite of current attitudes of fatalism.
3. Jesus is coming again—and because He is, we are called to be faithful witnesses.

I. False Witnesses

Hardly a week goes by without some newspaper, magazine, tract, or new book being published about the signs of Christ's second coming. Newspapers, TV talk shows, and especially religious radio stations spill out thousands of words about the signs people see or look for to predict His return. There is a growing fascination with the millenium—the supposed thousand-year reign of our Lord—either just before we Christians are violently persecuted for our faith or just after that happens, depending on how one takes a few verses in Rev. 20.

For centuries there have been those who believe they have special revelations from God or special insights into the interpretation of Scripture and therefore know more than Jesus Himself who said, "No one knows about that day or hour, not even the angels in heaven, nor the Son, but only the Father" (Matt. 24:36).

Back in 1833 William Miller, a man who began the Seventh-day Adventist movement, set the date of Oct. 10, 1843, for Christ's return. That year he and his friends did not plant crops, and the children did not go to school. Why plant seeds and study if the world will end in a few months? When the day came and our Lord did not, Mr. Miller said he was off by one year. The next year he admitted he was wrong, and was dismissed by his white-robed followers.

Jesus says, "Watch out that no one deceives you. For many will come in my name, claiming 'I am the Christ,' and will deceive many." One problem we Christians face today is that we can get so caught up in speculations about the return of our Lord that we focus our minds and energy on an unknowable plan, a plan our heavenly Father has purposely not revealed to us. He wants us to live in faith and trust in His good and gracious will, not in an unbelief that seeks times and places for our Lord's return. Jesus is coming again! In the time until He does, we get on with living for Him.

Jesus says, "Watch out!" Be watchful, alert, discerning! That does not mean be afraid, or live in fear. We must remember that the stage has been set for the return of our Lord ever since the first Pentecost. St. Peter reminds us (2 Peter 3:9) that the only reason He delays His return is to give more people a chance to repent and believe in Him. For people of faith in the Savior who once came to share our human life, even to die on the cross to forgive our sins, His physical return is not a fearsome thing; it is rather the time for our final, complete redemption (Luke 21:28)!

Back on March 10, 1982, the planets of our solar system were all aligned in a unique pattern called "the Jupiter effect." Many well-meaning but wrong Biblical interpreters jumped on a few comments made by a scientist and predicted that was the day the world would end. All it did was scare the insecure and bring mocking hoots and howls from the scoffers.

Make no mistake about it, Jesus *is* coming again—at the time our heavenly Father has determined. Our call is to be alert to that continuing reality and get on with living—living for Him!

II. Fatalism

That's easier said than done in our age, isn't it? Many in our generation have given up on a meaningful future. Many of the young and old alike seem consumed by meaninglessness. Many think that the future is now and that only the pursuit of momentary pleasure is meaningful. It is a sign of the despair and unbelief in our divine Creator into which many have fallen.

The threat of nuclear war heightens the tension, and the reports of troubles, strife, war, and unrest in nation after nation around the globe add to the gloom. Even Christians, who at one time confessed the creed with deep sincerity, have resorted to "survivalist" movements, stockpiling mountain hideaways and suburban home basements with a combination of dried foods and assorted armaments to ward off the hungry survivors of a nuclear attack. Such is the result of fear and hatred that replaces faith and confidence in the living Lord!

My Christian friends, Jesus is coming again! Count on it! But He will decide the time and place. While He waits and gives us time for change of heart and attitude toward God and one another, and also time to mature in the fruits of faith, He does not expect us to be consumed with fatalism or survivalism. Christ did not ask any of us who believe in Him to be survivors. He calls us to be followers. He went to the cross, not as a survivor, but as our Suffering Servant! He laid down His life to redeem us from sin, fear, death—even nuclear holocaust—so that we could be His servants to people all around us. For this He has called and empowered us with his eternal grace and love. He sustains us in spite of the problems, hatred, false prophets, and other forms of wickedness that arise when love for God and men grows cold.

III. Faithful Witnesses

Into this very time our Lord has placed us. By the assurance of His divine pardon He has blessed us to be a blessing to others. Jesus says, ". . . he who stands firm to the end will be saved. And this gospel of the kingdom will be preached in the whole world as a testimony to all nations, and then the end will come." Jesus *is* coming again, and because He is, He looks for us to be His faithful witnesses to the Good News that gives people power to live and even lifts us over the chasm of death itself. In 2 Peter 3:11–12 the apostle writes concerning the Day of the Lord, "Since everything will be destroyed in this way, what kind of people ought you to be? You ought to live holy and godly lives as you look forward to the day of God and speed its coming."

We are people of faith in the promises of the mighty God who created us and in Jesus Christ who redeemed us from a life of fear, anger, and selfishness. He has called and appointed us to be a people of hope and confidence in Him as we testify to the meaning of His forgiveness for sin, His victory over death, and His Spirit at work in the lives of all who will believe.

In an age where love grows cold, where cynicism needs to be challenged and disillusionment met with steadfast, humble, Christ-like service to people all around us—we are sent by our Lord. In our families, community, and country we need to be servants, faithful witnesses by word and deed, so we can let people know that life with Jesus Christ *does* have meaning. The future belongs to God, and therefore we can live—today, tomorrow and always!

St. Paul says, "No eye has seen, no ear has heard, no mind has conceived what God has prepared for those who love him." (1 Cor. 2:9). Jesus *is* coming again, and as we wait for Him to call us to Himself, we go on our way living, working, serving, seeking justice, practicing God's compassion, and rejoicing because He is with us and for us. Nothing will ever separate us from His love! False prophets can't. Fatalism won't. As witnesses full of faith in our Lord we can get on with living confidently because Jesus *is* coming again!

Judgment

LAST SUNDAY IN THE CHURCH YEAR
SUNDAY OF FULFILLMENT
MATTHEW 25:31-46

Ronald G. Folle

Some people are more courageous than others. That's an evaluation to which one may come through the simple act of observation. And pastors as a group are no different. For example, there is a story about one preacher of the Word who challenged his congregation from the pulpit one Sunday morning to begin critiquing his sermons. Speaking personally from a pastoral point of view, this is being courageous. Most pastors, I think, would feel, "Brother, you are asking for it when you issue an invitation like that!" Nevertheless, he issued the challenge, and at least one of his parishoners took him up on it. The next Sunday in the suggestion box was a note to the pastor. It said simply and pointedly, "Pastor, we would see more of Jesus."

We would see more of Jesus! That was the desire of the parishioner, and, according to the Gospel today, that is a desire that will be fulfilled for every believer, for the Word says that we shall see more of Him because He is coming in judgment.

I. It's Going to Take Place

When the prophets of the Old Testament looked into the future and prophesied regarding the things that would come to pass, they saw the future of the world being dominated by the figure of One who would come from God with mighty power to put all things right and bring in that great final triumph of God. They looked for a glorious Messiah. When Jesus looked into the future, He did not say "a Messiah will come." Rather, He saw the fulfillment of all of the Old Testament prophecies in Himself, and He said in effect, "I will come again."

There are two comings of Jesus Christ spoken of in Scripture. When we celebrate Christmas, we celebrate His first coming. At that point we rejoice that the Messiah clothed in our flesh and blood. We rejoice that our Redeemer, the Son of God, came in lowliness, in the form of a human being like ourselves. He could suffer want and pain and thirst and sorrow and temptation. He could be plotted against, spit upon, mistreated, despised, and killed. We rejoice that He came and loved us. He did not run in the other direction or crawl away. He figuratively and literally opened His heart and His hands to us as He looked straight ahead to the cross. This is how He came the first time in all lowliness. This is what we confess with gladness of heart in the first part of the second article of the Apostles' Creed: "And [I believe] in Jesus Christ, his only Son, our Lord, who was conceived by the Holy Spirit, born of the Virgin Mary, suffered under Pontius Pilate, was crucified, died, and was buried." He came—the first time, and we love what we see!

But we would also like to see more of Jesus, and we shall! For He is going to come again in fulfillment of the Scriptures. And this second coming, more sudden than the first, will also be much more wonderful. "He ascended into heaven," continues the Creed. "and sits at the right hand of God the Father Almighty. From thence he will come to judge the living and the dead."

His second coming will be a coming in glory for the purpose of judgment. His first coming was for the purpose of saving mankind —for befriending, for lovingly providing a sin offering for the world by means of His blood. That is why Jesus took such a lowly, appealing form—the form of a carpenter, an approachable teacher, a king riding on a donkey, One with whom people can make friends. Had He first come in His full glory, majesty, and manifest divinity, we could not have made friends with Him. Rather, like Adam and Eve in the garden after they had fallen into sin, we would have run from His approach in an attempt to hide. But He did not come "in the form of God." For our sakes He concealed His glory and came in "the form of a servant." In other words, our Lord's first coming was a preparation for His second coming, which will be in order to judge. And on that day He will not come disguised. On that day He will not come incognito. He will not come in the form of an ordinary man. On that day He will come as the true and righteous Judge and King over all creation, and with "all the angels with him, he will sit on His throne in heavenly glory." Would you and I like to see more of Jesus? We shall on the day of judgment!

II. And It Is Going to Take Place on the Basis of Faith

Now as Jesus gives us a picture of that Day of Judgment, Lutheran Christians are immediately not just a little bit upset over the scene with which we are confronted. The expression of our religious faith has pretty well been given form by the "hammer blows" of the Reformation, namely, *sola gratia, sola fidei, sola Scriptura,* and *solus Christus*—grace alone, faith alone, Scripture alone, and Jesus Christ alone. Suddenly we are carried to that last great Day, that Day of Fulfillment of our hope, of Jesus' promise, and of all the Scriptural prophecies, and we seem to be viewing a judgment scene based on good works. Jesus says to those on His right, "I was hungry and thirsty and a stranger and naked and sick and imprisoned and you ministered to Me as you ministered to those in need. Therefore, come!" And to those on His left He says in effect, "You had your chance to minister to Me by ministering to those in need, and you did not. Therefore, away with you!" And with that we are ready to go into shock, are we not, asking, "What happened to 'by grace through faith'?"

This certainly does seem to be a dilemma. How does one solve it? Well, the Lord Himself solves it as His Spirit simply points us to the Word. And the Word which reassures us that it is by grace through faith is the Word which introduces this scene of judgment. *Before* Jesus begins to enumerate their works, He has already separated the sheep from the goats. And on what basis has He separated them? On the basis of their faith in Him as their Savior from sin—a gift which has been given to them by grace. Then, and only then, does He mention works as physical, objective evidence of faith, or their absence as proof of the lack of it.

Please notice, also, that the sheep have not been cognizant of their works as if they were trusting them for salvation or finding eternal comfort and consolation in them. For when Jesus enumerates their works and calls their attention to them, they respond by asking "When? When did we see You in need and minister to You?" On the surface this judgment scene may appear to be works-oriented. Nevertheless, the message comes through loud and clear: "Nothing in my hands I bring, simply to Thy cross I cling."

The sheep are unaware of their good works. And this is as it should be. When Christ lives in us, we do them naturally without focusing our attention on them. In Matt. 6:3 Jesus says, "When you give to the needy, do not let your left hand know what the right hand is doing." Both hands should be busy, but through this hyperbole Jesus is warning us against making a show of our goodness.

The book of Exodus also contains a very instructive comment regarding consciousness of good works. Regarding Moses at the time of his second descent from Mount Sinai, the writer indicates that as he drew near to the people who were waiting for him at the base of the mountain with the two tables of stone in his hand they noticed something strange and majestic about him. He had been in the company of God, and his face showed it. But, and here is the insight, "he was not aware that his face was radiant because he had spoken with the Lord" (Ex. 34:29). In other words, Moses was unaware of his spiritual radiance.

And on the Day of Judgment so it will be for those at the Lord's right hand. The righteous do not keep a running record of their life of service, thereby making God indebted to them. Rather, they love and serve, not for selfish reasons, but simply because they love Jesus and have faith in Him. On the Day of Judgment they are unaware of the good works they have done, their attention being on their blessed Lord. There is an old saying that angels have wings because they take themselves so lightly. Sheep, too, look beyond themselves to the Shepherd and His grace.

Would you like to see more of Jesus? Then look for Him today as He wanders about the earth as one of the countless naked and poor and hungry. Because Jesus has so wonderfully loved you and because you love Jesus, minister to Him by ministering to the least of these. And in faith look forward to His coming in judgment. A man was once arrested on a criminal charge, and he sought the help of a friend who was a distinguished lawyer. He asked him to plead his case in court. But on that very day his lawyer friend had been raised to the bench. "Yesterday," he said, "I might have been your advocate. But today I can only be your judge." That sounds fearful. But Jesus, our Judge, is One who loves us enough to die for us.

Would you like to see more of Jesus? Then serve Him today, "lightly," like the angels. And when He comes in judgment and sits in glory on His throne, by His grace you may have the joy and experience the thrill of the fulfillment of all your hopes as you hear Him say, "Come, you who are blessed by my Father; take your inheritance, the kingdom prepared for you."

INDEX OF SCRIPTURE TEXTS